Generative AI in Higher Education: Guiding Principles for Teaching and Learning

Divided into two volumes, this book develops guiding principles for higher education institutions to use GenAI effectively and ethically in teaching and learning, articulating a roadmap for implementation at institutional levels and addressing the conundrum of using GenAI in higher education. As higher education institutions take different attitudes and approaches to Generative AI (GenAI), with some viewing it as a threat to academic integrity and therefore banning its use, while others have embraced it as an innovation to academic practice and have implemented guidance on how to use it ethically, this book makes clear that GenAI, such as ChatGPT, is not the problem itself; the issue is how we engage with it.

Dr Emmanuel K Nartey, Institutional Academic Lead for Employability, Lecturer, Speaker and Generative AI Researcher at The Open University, UK.

CRC Press Reference Books in Computer Science

CRC Press Reference Books in Computer Science series offers advanced and authoritative resources for students, researchers, and professionals across the field of computer science. Books in this series serve as indispensable references which present rigorously researched and innovative approaches to current and complex issues.

Reimagining Literacy in the Age of AI: Theory and Practice
Edited by Jason D. DeHart, Damiana Gibbons Pyles, Suriari Abas, and Raúl Alberto Mora

Governing the Future: Digitalization, Artificial Intelligence, Dataism
Henning Glaser and Pindar Wong

Generative AI in Higher Education: Guiding Principles for Teaching and Learning: Volume 1
Dr Emmanuel K Nartey

Generative AI in Higher Education: Guiding Principles for Teaching and Learning

Volume 1

Dr Emmanuel K Nartey

CRC Press
Taylor & Francis Group
Boca Raton New York London

CRC Press is an imprint of the
Taylor & Francis Group, an **informa** business

Designed cover image: Shutterstock Images

First edition published 2025
by CRC Press
2385 NW Executive Center Drive, Suite 320, Boca Raton FL 33431

and by CRC Press
4 Park Square, Milton Park, Abingdon, Oxon, OX14 4RN

CRC Press is an imprint of Taylor & Francis Group, LLC

ISBN: 978-1-032-91126-7 (hbk)
ISBN: 978-1-032-91132-8 (pbk)
ISBN: 978-1-003-56150-7 (ebk)

DOI: 10.1201/9781003561507

Typeset in Minion
by SPi Technologies India Pvt Ltd (Straive)

Contents

Foreword

The 21st century ushered in an era of unprecedented technological advancement that shaped education. From using chalk, blackboards (or whiteboards), and paper to teach and assess students to using computers and online teaching software. Early technological advancements in higher education were initially met with caution, but then they were embraced and adopted, improving teaching and research. As AI's capabilities continue to expand exponentially, the most transformative of these technological innovations is generative artificial intelligence (AI). Generative AI leaps forward from traditional AI as it offers new pathways for creating text, audio, images, and complex simulations at a quicker pace. This book, *Generative AI in Higher Education: Guiding Principles for Teaching and Learning: Volume 1*, explores how higher education institutions should embrace and adopt strategies to transform the education experience. I believe this book aims to highlight both the transformative potential and the necessary precautions associated with generative AI. It also provides higher education institutions with the principles to guide their implementation of generative AI.

The book recognises the critical concerns of permitting the use of generative AI in higher education, which broadly links to ethics, authenticity of the academic experience, equity, accessibility, and replacement of labour. By tracing the historical use of AI in higher education, the author argues that these concerns are recurring and valid but should not be a limitation to embracing generative AI. Instead of doing nothing and hoping generative AI will disappear into the abyss, these valid concerns should form the foundation for HEI policy or guidance to ensure that the benefits of AI are realised without exacerbating existing inequalities or compromising on the ultimate goal of higher education which is to educate, inspire, and equip students to contribute meaningfully to society.

Embracing generative AI offers several benefits to teaching and research in higher education. Generative AI can lead to innovative curricula and teaching methods that improve student engagement and retention. By analysing individual learning styles and progress, generative AI can provide personalised learning experiences and feedback, making education more accessible and practical. Additionally, it can develop students' employability, creating graduates that respond to societal needs. For research, academics can leverage generative AI to uncover insights that were previously out of reach, create complex simulations, analyse data rapidly and produce knowledge exchange materials such as blogs, images, and videos quicker than is currently done. Therefore, as advocated in this book, embracing generative AI requires higher education stakeholders to know its usefulness and how it can positively impact the sector.

Adopting generative AI in higher education requires clear guidelines and standards that institutions can follow to maximise the benefits. In Chapter 2 of this book, the author sets out five general principles for using generative AI well in higher education. These general principles are complemented with examples related to tuition and assessment. The author also proposed 'Employability Guiding Principle for Using Generative AI in Student Skill Development.' These employability principles can support initiatives that will create a workforce with relevant skills and workplace experiences. Chapter 2 also explores guiding principles for students and staff as generative AI raises ethical considerations linked to academic integrity, privacy, and responsibility.

This book is relevant to all higher education stakeholders, including students, academics, HE executives, policymakers, and regulatory bodies navigating the complex landscape of generative AI in higher education. The book should spark dialogue, inspire innovation, and guide thoughtful action as we collectively navigate the intersection of technology and education. The journey ahead is filled with promise and complexity, and our collective responsibility is to ensure that the integration of generative AI into higher education serves the greater good. When thoughtfully and ethically integrated, it can enhance our ability to achieve this goal, fostering a more inclusive, innovative, and dynamic educational environment.

Dr Miriam Mbah-Amanze
Senior Lecturer
The Open University

Preface

The assertion that technology is revolutionary in how we think, feel, and perceive social construction speaks to the profound impact of technological advancements on our cognitive processes, emotional responses, and societal interactions. I posit that this technological revolution will eradicate traditional conceptions of education, prompting a re-evaluation of teaching and learning methodologies. This claim highlights the need to question long-standing educational paradigms and to explore what contemporary teaching pedagogy should entail. However, this question remains inadequately addressed within mainstream discourse, casting doubt on the purported benefits of the technological revolution.

Firstly, technology's revolutionary nature refers to its capacity to fundamentally alter human experiences and societal frameworks. For instance, the integration of digital tools in everyday life reshapes how individuals access information, communicate, and form social connections. These changes necessitate a re-evaluation of various societal constructs, including education. The traditional education system, characterised by structured classrooms, standardised curricula, and conventional teaching methods, appears increasingly incongruent with the dynamic and interconnected digital world.

In light of these technological advancements, I argue that the preconceptions surrounding education need to be challenged. Traditional educational models, which emphasise rote learning and teacher-centred instruction, may no longer be effective in preparing students for the complexities of the modern world. Instead, there is a growing need for pedagogical approaches that are adaptive, student-centred, and integrative of technology. Contemporary teaching pedagogy should leverage digital tools to foster critical thinking, creativity, and collaboration, skills that are essential in the digital age.

Despite this need for pedagogical evolution, the mainstream discourse on education has not adequately addressed what contemporary teaching should look like. While there are pockets of innovative practices and research exploring new educational models, these efforts have not yet merged into a comprehensive framework that can guide widespread educational reform. The lack of a cohesive vision for modern pedagogy leaves HEIs and policymakers without clear direction, hindering the effective integration of technology in education.

Moreover, the benefits of the technological revolution in education remain uncertain due to this lack of clarity. Without a well-defined approach to incorporating technology into teaching and learning, there is a risk that technological tools will be used superficially or in ways that reinforce existing inequities. For instance, the digital divide, which refers to the gap between those with access to technology and those without, can exacerbate educational disparities if not adequately addressed. Additionally, the overreliance on technology without a pedagogical framework can lead to issues such as decreased face-to-face interaction and critical engagement.

While technology can revolutionise education, this potential will not be fully realised until there is a thorough examination and redefinition of contemporary teaching pedagogy. It is imperative for HEIs, researchers, and policymakers to engage in critical discourse about the role of technology in education and to develop innovative pedagogical models that harness its benefits. Only then can the technological revolution in education lead to meaningful and equitable improvements in teaching and learning.

The rationale for producing this book is grounded in addressing significant gaps in institutional and policy frameworks within higher education. These gaps necessitate a comprehensive examination of effective tuition policies to foster inclusivity and equity, particularly for students who encounter challenges in navigating academic jargon and complex learning environments. By dissecting these issues, the book aims to equip institutions and policymakers with the tools and insights needed to implement inclusive and equitable policies.

One primary motivation for writing this book is to assist HEIs and policymakers in developing and implementing effective tuition policies. These policies are essential for creating an inclusive academic environment where all students can thrive regardless of their backgrounds or academic preparedness. The traditional academic landscape often presents barriers through the use of specialised language and complex concepts, which can be particularly challenging for students from diverse educational and socio-economic backgrounds. Addressing these challenges requires a deliberate and informed approach to policymaking, one that prioritises accessibility and equity.

Furthermore, the book aspires to offer a framework and actionable solutions for integrating Generative Artificial Intelligence (GenAI) in HEIs. GenAI holds transformative potential for education, but its benefits can only be fully realised if implemented thoughtfully and strategically. The integration of GenAI can enhance personalised learning, streamline administrative processes, and provide innovative teaching tools. However, without a clear framework, there is a risk of uneven implementation and exacerbation of existing inequities. This book seeks to provide HEIs and policymakers with the necessary guidance to leverage GenAI effectively, ensuring that its deployment benefits all students.

In detailing the rationale, it is essential to underline the broader implications of the book's objectives. By addressing policy and institutional issues, the book aims to contribute to the ongoing discourse on educational reform and innovation. It seeks to challenge conventional approaches and advocate for evidence-based, inclusive policies that recognise the diverse needs of the student population. This proactive stance is crucial in an era where technology is rapidly changing the educational landscape, and where there is an urgent need to ensure that these changes lead to positive and equitable outcomes.

Moreover, the book intends to serve as a resource for stakeholders in the education sector. HEIs, policymakers, academics, and researchers will find valuable insights and practical strategies to address the complexities of modern education. The hope is that by providing a well-researched and comprehensive framework, the book will facilitate informed decision-making and foster a culture of inclusivity and equity in higher education.

In conclusion, the production of this book is driven by the need to fill critical gaps in institutional and policy practices within higher education. By focusing on effective tuition policies and the implementation of GenAI, the book aims to provide a robust framework for inclusivity and equity. It is envisioned as a valuable resource for HEIs and policymakers, guiding them towards creating a more accessible and equitable academic environment for all students. Through this work, the book aspires to contribute to the broader goal of educational reform and innovation, ensuring that technological advancements like GenAI are harnessed for the benefit of the entire student body.

Dr Emmanuel K Nartey
PhD, LLM, MSc, SFHEA, MCMI, MAPS, OLY, BA

Acknowledgements

I would like to extend my gratitude to the many individuals at Cardiff Met University, The University of the West of England, Bath Spa University, The Open University, Athens Institution of Education and Research, Bolton University Centre for AI and Education, Coventry University, and the University of East London, who generously contributed to my academic endeavours. Special mention goes to my enthusiastic colleagues and friends from the Pro-Vice-Chancellors and Career and Employability Service at The Open University, Leanne Daniels, Ellen Cocking, and Rosie Meade.

Writing my fourth academic book on Generative AI and education has been a fantastic experience. I am deeply grateful to the late Juergen Klinger and Steven Goulton, as well as my mentors Prof. Umut Turksen, Prof. David A. Frenkel, Prof. Simon Lee, and Prof. Mark Hill. Special thanks are also due to Dr Miriam Mbah Amanze. My colleagues from the Pro-Vice-Chancellors at The Open University deserve particular recognition, not only for their tremendous support but also for giving me numerous opportunities to grow and express my ideas. I am similarly profoundly grateful to the OU Law School, UWE Law School, and Bath Spa University for their support and contributions towards my academic journey and this writing.

I also greatly appreciate Dr Lucy Caton from Bolton University, especially for sharing her expertise with me so willingly and for her dedication as a centre lead. A special mention goes to my family: Lydia Akosua Boateng Darko, my children, brothers and sister, and the Bath University TeamBath. Finally, but by no means least, I extend my heartfelt thanks to my mother, Enoyoma Nartey, my late father, Richard Kwame Nartey, my best friend Darren Haris, Ekaterina Petrova, and Séverine Nebie for their almost unbelievable support. They are the most important people in my world, and I dedicate this book to them.

Acknowledgement of the Use of Generative AI

The use of Generative AI in supporting the data analysis and summary of the literature is acknowledged with appreciation. Generative AI has played a crucial role in processing and interpreting complex data, facilitating the synthesis of extensive information, and providing insights into educational trends and challenges. Additionally, Generative AI was employed to simplify complex concepts, allowing the author to dissect these ideas and effectively incorporate them into the construction of theoretical points within the book. This advanced technology has significantly enhanced the precision and depth of the research findings and contributed to the development of robust theoretical frameworks.

Introduction

In recent decades, technology has made life easier and more efficient for people (Grübler, 2003). However, about 60 years ago, many were unsure how good it would be. This uncertainty came from not knowing much about it, worries about countries not getting along, ethics and regulatory worries, fears of losing jobs, and concerns about the environment. For instance, when the World Wide Web (WWW) was being created, many doubted it. They were not sure if it would be helpful, if the technology was good enough, if it would change things too much, and if it would be appropriately regulated (Berners-Lee, 1999). Nevertheless, despite these doubts, the WWW became a significant aspect of our lives, changing how we communicate, do business, learn, and live (Herring, 2000). This development suggests that society tends to fear the unknown due to a lack of awareness and knowledge about how technology might change their lives. This fear can be reasonable, as it can lead to fair and effective use of technology. Nonetheless, we must closely examine our beliefs and attitudes towards new technologies to ensure we understand and manage them properly.

In addition, being unsure about new technology has consequences. It can make people slow to try it, miss out on good opportunities, make it difficult to find information, and raise ethical worries. It also makes developing regulations and principles very challenging, as resentment can lead to a lack of consensus on how to effectively integrate technology into society. However, this uncertainty mostly comes from not knowing enough and being unsure of how it would help everyone. One reason for this is that when we do not fully understand something, like its details and how it is made up, we tend to avoid exploring it. This can also apply to how people and society view technology if they do not have enough information about it. Therefore, unwillingness to use the WWW made it difficult for everyone to share information easily (Herring, 2000). People and businesses who did not want to use it missed chances to be creative, work together, and generate income (Shirky, 2008). Now, with new technology like Artificial Intelligence (AI), there are similar worries. People are concerned about using the WWW well, like ensuring everyone can use it, ensuring information is fair for everyone, and keeping personal information safe (Fuchs, 2014). So, even though being unsure about new tech is normal, it is essential to think about how it can help everyone and try to solve any worries early on. Therefore, the issue of emerging technology and its integration is a question of cause and effect. We need to understand the core of this technology and how it will impact various segments of society without causing

DOI: 10.1201/9781003561507-1

discrimination or further socio-economic deficits. I believe that the moral, ethical, and regulatory aspects of emerging technologies, such as AI, should be addressed not only at the foundation level but also at the implementation or integration level. Addressing these issues at their core can help limit biases, discrimination, and socio-economic deficits that may arise in the future.

What this means is that understanding technology should be a key part of elementary education to better prepare students for higher education. We also need to create and improve resources that help people understand both the costs and benefits of using technology. In simple terms, integrating digital literacy into education can address these needs. By doing this, we can help prevent misinformation and educate people about the real impact of technology on our lives, rather than just focusing on its effects. This approach will make it easier for everyone to understand and use technology responsibly and effectively.

Despite initial doubts about the WWW, its impact on society and education cannot be overstated. Many people were uncertain whether a global information network would work or be useful. However, the WWW has wholly changed many parts of society, like how we communicate, do business, and learn. One big way the WWW has helped society is by improving how we communicate and share knowledge (Castells, 2001). With things such as email, social media, virtual learning environments, and instant messaging, people can talk to each other instantly, no matter where they are. This has made it easier for people to work together, share ideas, and learn about different cultures. Also, online communities have formed, giving people support and places to discuss different topics. This evidence indicates that emerging technology can be useful if it is welcomed, embraced, and used fairly and effectively. Fundamentally, it is essential to recognise that we perceive technology as part of human evolution. To obstruct its development or develop hostility towards its integration into society is a step back to a primitive view. Therefore, instead of being fearful, we must address the question of its cause and effect.

In simple terms, the relationship between new technology and society involves a complex interaction between innovation and societal change. Technology is born out of human creativity and necessity, aiming to solve problems and improve efficiency. The effects of new technology are wide-ranging, impacting daily life, culture, economy, and ethics. For example, the WWW and AI show this dynamic well. Human ingenuity and the desire to overcome challenges lead to these powerful tools. The effects are significant: the WWW changes how we communicate, AI transforms industries, and new ethical issues arise about privacy and control. These effects then become new causes, leading to more technological advances and changes in society in a continuous cycle. Philosophically, this ongoing relationship highlights the non-linear nature of progress. The impacts of new technology often go beyond what was originally intended, challenging current ways of thinking and requiring constant reflection. This underlines the importance of innovators and society being proactive in managing the consequences of technological change, ensuring that advancements benefit human values and future generations

The WWW has made a significant difference in business by allowing online shopping. Companies can now sell their product to people worldwide, not just in one place. This has helped businesses grow, create jobs, and make it easier for people to buy the products they need. In education, the WWW has made learning easier and more accessible. Online classes and resources mean that anyone can learn new things no matter where they live or how much money they have. This has been especially helpful for people in areas with fewer educational resources, giving them chances to learn and improve their lives. The WWW has also made it easier for students and teachers to collaborate and share knowledge. Online forums and classes give students chances to speak to each other and learn from each other. This makes learning more interesting and helps people work together better. Overall, the WWW has made it easier for people to keep learning throughout their lives and find jobs in a changing world. It's made a big difference in how we live and work and will continue to do so in the future. From this perspective, we can assume that the proper and correct integration of technology benefits human endeavours. Therefore, if we adequately observe the causes and effects of technology, our fears and worries will dissipate, and the focus will shift to how we can improve it.

Furthermore, before the development of the WWW, education primarily took place in traditional classroom settings with face-to-face interactions between teachers and students. Textbooks, printed materials, and physical libraries were the main sources of information. Education was limited by location and time, meaning that access to knowledge was often restricted. For instance, students in remote or underprivileged areas had less access to high-quality educational resources. Additionally, communication between educational institutions was slow, relying on postal services to exchange information and academic materials. The development of the WWW in the early 1990s revolutionised education, fundamentally changing the way knowledge is shared and accessed. The WWW enabled the rise of e-learning platforms, online courses, and digital libraries, making education more accessible and flexible. Information became readily available to anyone with an internet connection, breaking down geographical barriers and democratising access to knowledge. The availability of online educational resources allowed for a more self-directed learning approach, where individuals could learn at their own pace and according to their own schedules.

Moreover, the WWW enabled the creation of virtual classrooms and the use of multimedia in teaching, enhancing the learning experience through interactive and engaging content. The global connectivity provided by the internet also fostered international collaborations and the exchange of ideas, promoting a more global perspective in education. Teachers and students could easily communicate and share resources across borders, enriching the educational experience with diverse viewpoints and materials. In summary, education before the WWW was characterised by limited accessibility and slower communication, heavily dependent on physical presence and printed materials. The advent of the WWW transformed education into a more inclusive, flexible, and globally connected endeavour, vastly expanding the reach and methods of teaching and learning. This historical shift highlights the profound impact of technological advancements on educational practices and accessibility.

Even though the WWW had flaws, society did not see it as a significant threat anymore. This shows that for AI to be accepted, we need to share much knowledge about it and have good rules in place. We need to understand where AI falls short and make rules to control it properly. Having dedicated AI departments in institutions or an AI Ministry in Government can help spread knowledge about AI, learn more about it, and create essential rules to ensure AI is used responsibly in society. Institutions and governments should think about creating special AI departments just like they have IT and data protection departments. These AI departments would be in charge of making sure AI is used properly in organisations.

In the present day, the acceptance and use of AI can be seen as similar to how people first reacted to the WWW. When the WWW first emerged in the early 1990s, it was met with a mix of excitement and scepticism. People were intrigued by its potential to revolutionise communication, access to information, and education. However, there were also significant concerns about privacy, security, and the impact on traditional ways of doing things. Over time, as more people understood its benefits and as technologies improved, the WWW became an integral part of everyday life, fundamentally changing how we work, learn, and connect with each other. Similarly, AI is now experiencing a comparable journey. There is a great deal of enthusiasm about the possibilities AI offers, such as improving efficiency, enabling new forms of creativity, and solving complex problems. Yet, there are also widespread concerns about the ethical implications, job displacement, and the potential for misuse. People worry about privacy issues related to data collection and the decisions made by AI systems without human oversight.

As with the WWW, the initial reactions to AI are mixed. Some people embrace AI's potential enthusiastically, while others remain cautious or resistant. Over time, as AI technologies become more sophisticated and as society develops better regulations and ethical guidelines, it is likely that AI will become as integrated into our daily lives as the WWW is today. This evolution will involve learning from past experiences with the WWW, addressing legitimate concerns, and finding ways to maximise the benefits while minimising the risks. If we consider this point empirically, the conclusion is that AI is not a problem or a threat to human civilisation, as some perceive it. Instead, it is a tool for societal enhancement and efficiency.

As we see the WWW grow and notice people's current feelings towards AI, many individuals feel uncertain or biased about using AI. This might happen because their actions, beliefs, intentions, and goals do not align. Behaviour means what people actually do (Albarracin et al., 2005), and it often comes from their attitudes. Let's look at a story from a long time ago to see how attitudes and actions can differ. In 1934, a researcher named LaPiere travelled around the United States with a young Chinese couple. At that time, there was a lot of prejudice against Asian people. Surprisingly, even though they met many people who did not like Asians, only one place refused to serve them. Later, LaPiere asked the same places in letters if they would accept Asian guests. Only one said yes. This made it seem like there was a weak link between what people said and what they did. However, it is essential to note that LaPiere's study had its limitations. He could not ascertain if the individuals who declined to serve the couple were the same ones who responded to the letters. Subsequent research has shown that attitudes and actions are often in sync. For instance, a study by Glasman and Albarracín (2006) revealed that attitudes and actions align about half of the time, shedding light on this connection. Similarly, individuals may harbour reservations towards AI due to negative preconceptions, even if they have had positive encounters. However, it is crucial to critically analyse AI and foster affirmative interactions with it. These experiences hold the potential to dispel doubts and instil a sense of optimism.

Furthermore, the growth of Generative Artificial Intelligence (GenAI) reminds us of what happened when the WWW was made. Both times, people were not sure and worried about what might happen. People are more sceptical about GenAI than about WWW because of GenAI's intelligence. Partly because it can create text, images, and sounds that seem human-made, some people worry about AI being misused. However, it is essential to note that GenAI requires human oversight and interaction to produce substantial outputs. Therefore, any problems with GenAI are more about human behaviour and conduct than the technology itself. This means that the focus should be on implementing rules and regulations to ensure fair and effective use rather than on promoting scepticism and propaganda. Similarly, when the WWW was new, people discussed privacy and whether online information could be trusted. This also makes us think about how people usually react to new technology. People are often unsure or even afraid of what might change when something new comes along. But then, just like how the WWW changed how we talk, buy products, and learn, GenAI could change many parts of our lives, too, like how things are made and decisions are made.

In simple terms, people have developed negative attitudes towards using GenAI, but it is essential to understand why. The reasons behind their attitudes are not very clear. By understanding these attitudes, we can use models of feelings to explain GenAI's scepticism. One common way to understand feelings is by looking at their structure. Feelings can be positive or negative and can have high or low arousal. For example, people might feel sad, angry, content, or excited. Each feeling varies in how negative or positive it is and how aroused it makes someone feel. Many people think of emotions in two main ways: whether they feel good or bad, and how much energy or excitement they have. This idea comes from research by Bradley, Codispoti, Cuthbert, and Lang (2001); Russell (2003); and Smith and Ellsworth (1985), among others. People experience emotions like sadness, anger, contentment, or excitement, and each emotion varies in how good or bad it feels and how much energy or excitement it brings (Russell, 2003). Arousal, which is how energised or activated someone feels, is hard to explain, but it usually involves changes in things like skin conductance, heart rate, or brain waves (Bradley & Lang, 2007; Cacioppo, Berntson, & Crites, 1996). Feeling anxious, tense, alert, and excited all have high arousal in common (like having a fast heart and breathing rate), while feeling sad and content share low arousal (like having a slower heart and breathing rate or feeling sleepy) (Albarracin & Vargas, 2010; Clore & Schnall, 2005; Schimmack & Crites, 2005).

Based on the scepticism and research, we can conclude that people's attitudes towards GenAI may result from fear and the unknown. This fear stems from concerns about disrupting traditional approaches to education or ways of life, distorting normal life formations, and encountering intelligence beyond the ordinary person's or academic's conceptual perception. However, I believe that the current attitudes are primarily due to a lack of awareness and detailed understanding of what GenAI is and how it works. Despite clear evidence from research that will be presented in this book that GenAI has been part of society for many decades, misconceptions persist. This indicates that improving public awareness and providing thorough oversight is crucial to addressing these fears and changing attitudes towards GenAI.

People may hold negative attitudes towards GenAI for several reasons. These attitudes can be understood using a model that considers attitudes as having both valence (positive or negative) and arousal (the intensity of the emotional response) dimensions (Albarracin & Vargas, 2010). On the valence axis, individuals may either like or dislike GenAI, much like how they may have preferences for political candidates or tastes. Additionally, attitudes can be mapped onto the arousal dimension as they vary in extremity, importance, confidence, and the degree to which they elicit strong emotional responses such as excitement (Cuthbert et al., 2000; Fabrigar et al., 2005; Lang et al., 1988). For instance, highly engaging topics such as abortion, gay marriage, and marijuana legalisation often evoke strong attitudes that are intertwined with emotions and relate to other essential attitudes like personal values and self-esteem (Eagly & Chaiken, 1993; Fabrigar et al., 2005).

These attitudes are often expressed strongly in responses to attitude scales, held with high confidence, easily recalled, and vigorously defended against criticism (Judd & Brauer, 1995a, 1995b; Abelson, 1988; Johnson et al., 2005; Petty et al., 2004). Therefore, negative attitudes towards GenAI may arise from concerns about its societal implications, potential impact on personal values, and intense emotional responses it elicits (Albarracin & Vargas, 2010; Cuthbert et al., 2000; Fabrigar et al., 2005; Lang et al., 1988; Eagly & Chaiken, 1993; Judd & Brauer, 1995a, 1995b; Abelson, 1988; Johnson et al., 2005; Petty et al., 2004). This means that people's feelings about exploring new technology, like GenAI, are complex and have many parts.

Understanding what makes society feel a certain way about it requires considering various factors. So, to understand how people think about GenAI right now, we need to use ethical principles, guidelines, policies, and laws. Hence, I suggest that when we study GenAI, it is not enough to focus only on the technical side. We also need to understand people's feelings about it—from how it's created to how it's put into action. This means looking at many different factors and considering things such as ethics (knowing what's right and wrong), guidelines (rules to follow), policies (official rules), and laws (legal rules). By thinking about all of these things together, we can fully grasp what society feels about GenAI. This approach also helps ensure that GenAI is developed and used responsibly and safely for everyone.

In addition, even though people are often unsure about new technology, it does not mean they will not use it eventually. By looking at how people felt about the WWW and GenAI, we can see that it is essential to think carefully about how new technology is used and what effects it might have. By doing this, we can use technology like GenAI in a good way while making sure it is safe and fair for everyone. However, it is essential to understand that doubting new technologies does not always stop them from being used in society. Just like how the WWW changed how we talk, do business, and learn, GenAI could alter many parts of society. So, even though people have been unsure about new

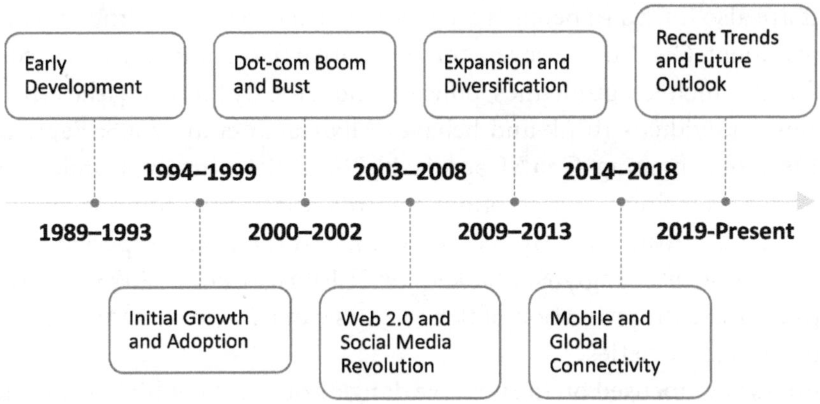

FIGURE I.1 Timeline of the World Wide Web (WWW).

technologies like GenAI before, it is still essential to think carefully about them. We must also consider ethics, fairness, and safety when developing and using GenAI. By doing this, we can ensure GenAI is used well and does not cause harm. Therefore, looking at how people felt about the WWW and GenAI shows us that it is normal for people to be unsure about new technology. Nevertheless, it also reminds us that we need to think carefully about how we use it. By doing this, we can ensure GenAI positively impacts society while avoiding problems.

Figure I.1 illustrates the chronological progression of the World Wide Web (WWW) from its inception in 1989 to its current advancements, highlighting key milestones such as the development of browsers, the rise of social media, advancements in mobile connectivity, and emerging technologies like AI and blockchain. It demonstrates how the WWW has evolved and integrated into various aspects of global society over time.

Smith et al. (2019 discusses how GenAI brings up different opinions in higher education. Some people worry that GenAI might be bad for traditional teaching methods. They think it could lead to problems with honesty, teaching quality, and ethics. They say that using GenAI to write essays could make it easy for students to cheat by online copying (Perkins et al., 2024). They also think that relying on AI too much could stop students from thinking for themselves and make their work less valuable (Yeralan & Lee, 2023). On the other hand, some people see GenAI as a helpful tool that could improve education. They think it could make learning more personal, help teachers create better materials, and make school work easier (Binhammad et al., 2024). They also believe it could help more people get access to education, no matter where they come from or what they are good at (Li & Huang, 2020). All the arguments these authors make are valid, but what is essential to consider is the ethical and regulatory side of things. We need to find a set of rules that can guide how GenAI is used in higher education. If we can come up with a clear understanding of how to use GenAI in this context, then we can find solutions to the practical issues raised by both arguments.

Similarly, from the perspectives of these authors, we can see that there are two closely related connections between using GenAI and how people feel about it. Both of these connections are also linked to people's attitudes, which can lead to either positive or negative opinions about GenAI. However, these negative associations can be countered by applying ethical principles, guidelines, policies, and laws. By following these principles, we can shape how individuals think and behave (Albarracin et al., 2005; Eagly & Chaiken, 1993). Furthermore, making GenAI acceptable in society involves understanding and influencing people's feelings and emotions towards it (affective component), their beliefs and thoughts about it (the cognitive component), and their past experiences with it (the behavioural component) (Eagly & Chaiken 1993; Fabrigar et al., 2005). Therefore, using principles that ensure the protection of these values can help promote the universal acceptance of GenAI in all societies.

Some authors have focused on the possible dangers of GenAI in higher education, bringing up essential concerns. However, their discussions often fail to consider all the ways GenAI could be helpful in academia. While they acknowledge that AI could shake up traditional teaching methods and cause concerns about fairness and ethics in assessments, they often do not discuss how AI could improve university teaching, research, and administrative tasks. GenAI can analyse lots of data, which could completely change how students learn by making it more personalised and helping teachers give better feedback. It could also help professors, researchers, and lecturers in their research by finding patterns and analysing data. AI tools could also make administrative tasks more manageable, freeing up time and resources for universities to try new teaching methods and get students more involved. This means that GenAI is used to help develop knowledge instead of creating it on its own. I will argue that this is the primary purpose of GenAI. This is because integrating GenAI into society and education aims not to replace human abilities but to complement existing human work. It also seeks to reduce the time humans spend on tasks that may not contribute effectively to productivity. While I recognise that GenAI can be misused, this can be prevented through appropriate rules and regulations. So, a lack of ethics and policies can explain the lack of a full understanding and recognition of all the different parts of GenAI. This is why there is a lack of a broad approach and doubt about GenAI and whether people will accept it.

Therefore, with the rapid advance of technology, it's becoming increasingly important to rethink traditional education methods and redefine what teaching means today. Technology has fundamentally changed how we share, access, and interact with knowledge, challenging the old ways of teaching that have been in place for a long time. Traditional teaching methods, which often rely on memorisation and passive learning, might not meet the needs of modern students. The rise of digital tools and resources offers new opportunities for more engaging, personalised, and interactive learning experiences. However, this shift requires us to carefully consider how these technologies are used in education. Sticking too closely to old methods might limit the benefits of these new tools if they are not adapted to fit current learning goals. Therefore, today's teaching should reflect the impact of technology on learning. It should use digital tools to promote active learning, teamwork, and critical thinking. Modern teaching approaches focus on student-centred learning, where students actively engage with the material, apply their knowledge in real-world situations, and develop skills that are important in today's fast-changing world. This means integrating technology in ways that truly enhance learning, rather than just adding to traditional methods.

Henceforth, to effectively incorporate technology into education, it's crucial to clearly define the goals and purposes of teaching in today's world. This means updating educational objectives to go beyond just acquiring knowledge. Modern education should also focus on developing digital skills, problem-solving abilities, and the capacity to manage information in a tech-rich environment. Educators need to think about how technology can enhance teaching methods to cater to different learning needs and support lifelong learning. As technology evolves, it's important to challenge traditional teaching methods and rethink educational strategies. Therefore, defining what education should be in the digital age involves using technology to improve learning experiences, encourage active participation, and ensure teaching practices meet the needs of a rapidly changing world. Considering these factors, educators can better prepare students for the complexities of modern life and keep educational practices both relevant and effective.

Also, attitude strength means how strong an attitude is over time, how hard it is to change, and how much it affects what we think and do (Fazio, 1995; Krosnick & Smith, 1994). Knowing how strong an attitude is helps us determine when and which attitudes will actually change how people behave when using GenAI. In intelligent conversations, attitude strength is seen as a mix of many things, like how strong, specific, and essential an attitude is. At first, people thought all these things made up one big idea called attitude strength (Peterson & Miller, 2004). They found this idea true by looking at different factors that were grouped under a few big ideas (Bassili, 1996). However, some experts thought this idea might be too simple because of mistakes in measuring things (Krosnick et al., 1993). Krosnick et al. (1993) found that only a few pairs of these things were really connected, showing that attitude strength is not just one thing but has lots of different parts (Krosnick et al., 1993; Peterson & Miller, 2004; Visser, Krosnick & Simmons, 2003). This makes it challenging to understand attitude strength fully and adds to the doubts about whether people will accept GenAI. In the development of GenAI, testing attitudes and capabilities can gauge societal acceptance and scepticism. This testing process is crucial for establishing rules and principles that can guide its integration into society effectively. It helps in developing a better understanding of how GenAI can be used and how knowledge about it can be advanced.

This book suggests that we should use ethics and guiding principles to influence how people feel and act about GenAI. It is not just about technicality and engineering; GenAI has considerable effects on society, people, and the future. When we discuss GenAI, if we include ethics and guiding principles, it can change how society sees and uses it. Ethics gives us a moral guide to think about the effects of GenAI and helps us make decisions that match what society thinks is right or wrong. Guiding principles give us practical rules to handle the tricky ethical problems GenAI brings so that we can make intelligent choices. Also, the book proposes we look at GenAI more broadly, not just if it works technically or ethically. This means thinking about how it affects society as a whole. By focusing on ethics and guiding principles, we can deal with ethical issues, be transparent, build trust, and reduce risks linked with GenAI. Overall, this book recommends that ethics and guiding principles are crucial in shaping how society sees and uses GenAI. By including these principles when discussing GenAI, we can help ensure that AI is developed and used in a fair and good way for everyone.

This is partly because ethical principles are crucial for guiding behaviour in personal and professional contexts. They provide a framework that helps individuals and organisations make morally sound decisions. These principles promote fairness, justice, and respect in interactions with others, fostering trust and harmony in society. By adhering to ethical guidelines, people ensure their actions uphold values such as human dignity, honesty, integrity, and fairness. This alignment helps prevent harm, encourages accountability, and maintains a cohesive social structure. Therefore, ethical standards also act as a safeguard against exploitation, discrimination, and misuse of power, creating an environment where everyone can flourish with mutual respect. Furthermore, ethical principles enable individuals and institutions to consider both immediate and long-term consequences of their actions on individuals and society as a whole. This thoughtful approach contributes to a culture that values moral responsibility and supports the common good. Ultimately, for the use of GenAI, ethical principles are important because they can build trust, promote fairness, prevent harm, and uphold fundamental values essential for humanity's well-being and progress.

Moving on, people discuss GenAI in higher education in different ways. Some see it as a threat because they worry about fairness and the authenticity of teaching methods. However, others see it as a chance to improve teaching and learning. Thus, it is essential to understand both sides of this debate so we can make intelligent decisions about using GenAI in higher education while considering the ethical, teaching, and policy issues involved. Hence, to understand how people feel about GenAI, we can look at different things, such as how strongly they feel about it, how important it is to them, how sure they are about their feelings, and how easy it is to think about it (Bassili, 2008; Krosnick et al., 1993; Krosnick & Smith, 1994; Peterson & Miller, 2004). By studying these factors, we can determine what influences people's attitudes and how GenAI fits into society.

For example, attitudes can be positive or negative, showing how much someone likes or dislikes GenAI. The extremity of these attitudes measures the strength of those feelings (Bassili, 2008; Krosnick et al., 1993; Krosnick & Smith, 1994). Sometimes, attitudes can become even stronger, which is called attitude polarisation. This happens when people keep thinking about the attitude or hear the same messages repeatedly (Tesser, Martin & Mendolia, 1995; Brauer et al., 1995). Insults or arguments about oneself can also strengthen attitudes (Abelson & Miller, 1967; De Dreu & van Knippenberg, 2005). Understanding these things helps us see why some people might have negative feelings about GenAI. It shows us that we must think carefully before fully introducing GenAI into our society.

Therefore, the question arises: Will machines becoming more advanced change everything, or will people end up controlled by their own inventions? James Cameron's famous movie *The Terminator* brings up these ideas. While some may see it as just a story, the similarities between the rise of GenAI and Cameron's vision in 1984 make it worth thinking about. So, it is important to consider how GenAI affects education and society, including jobs, ethics, and laws. Understanding GenAI's impact could turn Cameron's dark future brighter. While *The Terminator* isn't the main focus here, it helps start a discussion about GenAI in education.

GenAI refers to technology that uses advanced models to create content that seems human-like. Though, it is not just about technology; it affects many aspects of life beyond that. For example, Chat Generative Pre-Trained Transformer (ChatGPT), a chatbot powered by GenAI, has both good and bad effects on society and education. These effects are still being talked about and studied. Without an explicit agreement on the best way to proceed, there's undeniable a lack of consensus on how GenAI should be used. However, what's essential is establishing rules and principles to address its shortcomings, as well as clearly defining its concept and explaining how it is practically applied.

In practical terms, 'GenAI' refers to how the concept or term is applied in real-life situations, showing its relevance and implications. For instance, while the current definition of ChatGPT emphasises its technological capabilities, it is essential to broaden this definition to recognise its broader implications. ChatGPT's impact on society and higher education involves intricate interactions beyond technology alone, encompassing neurocognition and awareness. Acknowledging these dimensions is crucial for understanding its diverse impact. Therefore, the definition of ChatGPT should incorporate an element that acknowledges its role in shaping cognitive processes and societal awareness, ensuring a comprehensive understanding that reflects its innovative potential and societal significance.

Therefore, a comprehensive definition of GenAI should consider its broader influence and implications. GenAI refers to innovative AI models that use advanced algorithms to create customised datasets based on user inputs, presenting new challenges as it evolves rapidly. Defining GenAI clearly is essential for understanding how it can integrate into higher education and impact teaching and research practices and how to regulate it. Furthermore, including employability in the definition of GenAI provides a contemporary approach to higher education pedagogy. Linking GenAI with employability recognises AI's role in enhancing students' career readiness and skillsets. This integration ensures educational programmes impart theoretical knowledge and prepare students for dynamic job markets. In summary, a comprehensive definition of GenAI must acknowledge its ability to foster employability skills, bridging the gap between academic learning and professional development. This approach supports a holistic approach to modern higher education pedagogy.

Chan and Hu (2023) suggest that GenAI includes fancy computer programs that learn from existing data and make new data that looks similar. GenAI works like a type of program called a Variational Autoencoder (VAE). This program learns to turn data into a secret code and then turn that code back into data, keeping important details intact. Goodfellow et al. (2014) group GenAI with something called Generative Adversarial Networks (GANs). In GANs, two computer networks team up to make data that looks real. These ideas show how GenAI uses advanced programs to find patterns and create new ideas differently. Even though Yuk and Hu and Goodfellow et al. have given us good ideas, we still do not fully understand how GenAI affects people and what it means for us. So, it is essential to clearly understand what GenAI is and what it does. GenAI is an innovative computer model that uses fancy programs to make datasets based on what people want, but we still need to determine how it can change things. Getting a better definition of GenAI will help us discover how it can be used in schools, universities, and research, and what that means for teaching and learning.

Some writers also worry that as GenAI gets better at understanding language, it could be a problem for schools, universities, and other institutions. It might be too soon to say that GenAI can do many good things. For example, there are tools like ChatGPT, Bard, Stable Diffusion, and Dall-E (Silverman et al., 2023). These tools can understand complicated questions and give answers that sound like they came from a person. This makes people wonder about what this means for society, like in education, healthcare, media, and tourism. While it is exciting to think about using GenAI in these areas, we also have to consider how it can help everyone and ensure it does not leave anyone out. However, we are not sure yet what the future of GenAI will look like, but it is essential to consider how it might affect society. Consequently, one way to do that is by looking at tools like ChatGPT. ChatGPT is good at understanding and talking in different languages and doing things like writing, speaking, and translating (Baidoo-Anu & Ansah, 2023). Nevertheless, because GenAI is so good at making things, it raises ethical questions. For example, in education, people worry that it could help students cheat on tests or assignments without getting caught by anti-cheating software (Michel-Villarreal et al., 2023).

This also shows a need for a clear plan for using GenAI so that people's attitudes can change and access easier (Ajzen, 2012). Accessibility means the strong connection between how someone feels about GenAI and how they think about it when learning. Using a clear plan for GenAI, we can see which attitudes come to mind when people use GenAI (Fazio, Sanbonmatsu, Powell & Kardes, 1986). Accessibility is also influenced by how often an attitude comes up and how important the information about it is, including how it makes someone feel and what they have experienced with GenAI before (Fazio, 1995). Having a clear plan like this might help deal with doubts and feelings about using GenAI in higher education

Several studies have shown that essays made by ChatGPT can get around plagiarism checkers. Michel-Villarreal et al. (2023) and their team found that regular anti-plagiarism software often does not detect essays made by ChatGPT. Baidoo-Anu and Ansah (2023) did a similar study and found that essays made by ChatGPT are very similar to ones written by people, making them difficult to spot with normal plagiarism checkers. Silverman et al. (2023) tested different plagiarism checkers and found that some can see similarities between ChatGPT-made essays and other sources, but they are inconsistent. Often, essays made by ChatGPT were not caught by these programs, making it challenging to keep academic work original. Nguyen et al. (2024 looked into ChatGPT's ability to make text on many different topics and styles. They found that ChatGPT is good at copying how people write and making sense. This means that essays made by ChatGPT can look a lot like ones written by people, making it challenging to spot plagiarism. The author makes a good point about the essays created by ChatGPT. Nonetheless, it is also possible that this claim influences how people feel and act about using GenAI. Nonetheless, it is essential to note that text or data generated by ChatGPT has its deficiencies. This means that information produced by GenAI requires human oversight to ensure accuracy and quality. From this perspective, the authors' arguments in their research might be premature. The fundamental issues here involve training, regulation, and appropriate use, rather than focusing on plagiarism only.

Moving on, many of our attitudes start when we are young or develop as we encounter new things in life, like products, places, and people. Sometimes, our attitudes change because of our experiences, learning new things, or being influenced by others. A lot of social psychology research focuses on introducing new ideas, so it is more about how attitudes are formed rather than how they change. Because of this, claims like the authors might overlook some important factors when using and studying GenAI in society. This suggests that we need to be cautious when sharing information about GenAI without fully grasping its abilities and potential. In other words, before we discuss GenAI or make assumptions about it, we should make sure we really understand what it can do and how it might impact society. Rushing to conclusions or spreading incomplete information could lead to misunderstandings or even problems down the line. So, it is essential to take the time to learn as much as we can about GenAI before making judgments or sharing information about it.

Returning to the discourse on higher education, there are different views on using GenAI. Some universities aim to ban it completely, while others see it as a chance for innovation with clear rules on adequately using it. Nevertheless, no matter what, keeping academic integrity is essential. To do this, universities need to rethink how they set essays and exams to stop students from copying or using AI too often. Instead of just asking questions that AI can easily answer, academics should give prompts that need students to think critically, put ideas together, and come up with their own thoughts. This makes it harder for students to just copy from AI. Also, academics can ask for more detailed references, invite students to explain their ideas, or have other students check their work. These processes all help ensure that the work students hand in is their own (Jisc, 2021). Therefore, using a thorough assessment strategy is essential to challenge students in both theoretical and practical aspects of their learning. Encouraging students to apply theories in real-life situations ensures that academic studies stay rigorous and relevant. This helps change how people think and act in academic discussions.

Incorporating GenAI effectively into teaching and learning requires innovation and creativity in assessment design and processes. Authentic assessment, which emphasises real-life practical experiences, is crucial for maximising the benefits and ensuring the authenticity of GenAI integration. Schools, colleges, and universities should shift towards authentic assessments that develop skills demanded by the labour market and promote good citizenship. Authentic assessment involves tasks that mirror real-world challenges and require students to apply their knowledge and skills in practical contexts. This approach not only enhances learning but also prepares students for the complexities of the workforce. Aligning assessment practices with real-life applications, educational institutions can ensure that students are not only academically proficient but also ready to meet the demands of contemporary job markets and contribute meaningfully to society.

Also, when it comes to GenAI, we should integrate it into society and share information effectively. Persuading people to focus on its benefits rather than the negatives can help change attitudes. However, it is essential to present both sides of the argument when discussing the use of GenAI. This balanced approach helps ensure that GenAI is used in ways that align with societal norms and rules, promoting proper and effective usage. Just like how ads on buses or requests for donations influence us, persuasive messages can shape our views. For example, Aristotle's *Rhetoric* highlighted different persuasive techniques: logos (logical appeals), ethos (building credibility and respect), and pathos (appealing to emotions). We should rethink how we communicate and share knowledge about GenAI in this manner to ensure understanding and acceptance. This involves assessing our current understanding and biases towards GenAI to follow ethical guidelines and rules.

Universities can also use technology to check for plagiarism. They can use special software that is designed to spot work made by AI. This helps stop students from just copying and pasting from AI tools (Turnitin, 2020). Besides, teaching students about the ethics of using AI in their studies is essential, as well as showing them how to properly give credit when using AI tools (Nartey 2024). Overall, universities must change how they set essays and exams to ensure students are not just copying from AI. By doing this and teaching students about using AI ethically, universities can stop plagiarism and still use the benefits of AI in education. All these studies indicate that essays generated by ChatGPT can evade typical plagiarism checks. Conversely, none of them adequately explain or suggest the appropriate course of action, which may require a change in attitude and behaviour. This means that universities and academics must consider how they use AI-made content in education while ensuring students' work is honest and original. Nevertheless, just focusing on cheating and plagiarism does not cover all the other things AI can do in education. So, thinking about the bigger picture, like how AI affects ethics, society, and students' learning and growth, is essential.

According to Reuters (2023) and The Tab (2023), universities have different views on using GenAI in education. Some see it as a problem and have banned it from being fully used. Instead of preventing students from using it, universities should try to understand it better, see how it affects learning, and think about how to change things if needed. While it is essential to have rules, it is also vital for universities to look into how GenAI can help teaching and learning in different ways. However, there is no clear information from universities about how to use GenAI in a good way (University of Cambridge, 2023a; 2023b). Conversely, studies are showing that universities are thinking about their rules and practices related to GenAI and how they affect academic honesty. So, it is crucial to have strong rules about using GenAI in education, including how to use it in exams and essays, making sure everyone can use it, being fair to everyone, helping students get jobs, and thinking about the environment. These rules should explain how universities can use GenAI to improve education and how staff can be trained to use it.

In simple terms, this book focuses on creating clear rules for universities to follow regarding using GenAI. By establishing these rules, I hope to change how people think and act when it comes to incorporating GenAI into universities and society as a whole. It suggests that the problem with GenAI is not really about the technology itself, but instead how schools, colleges, and universities use it. AI has actually been part of education since the 1960s (Guan et al., 2020), so it is not new. The quick growth of GenAI might show that there is still a lot we do not understand about how it affects traditional education methods.

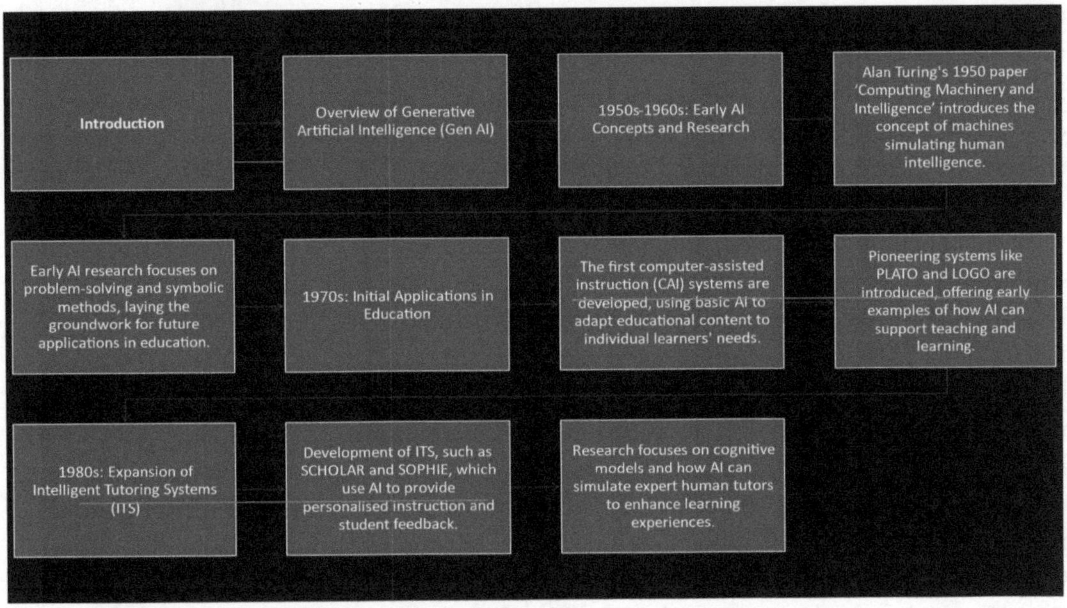

FIGURE I.2 GenAI timeline.

Figure I.2 illustrates the timeline of GenAI development and milestones over the years. For example, Weizenbaum (1966) discusses an ELIZA computer program. ELIZA was made to chat with people, especially in therapy. It used simple tricks to sound like a human, like asking questions or repeating what people said. Even though ELIZA was basic, it got a lot of attention and made people think about how computers and humans interact. This evidence shows how early AI programs like ELIZA raised questions about how humans and computers work together. It is a reminder that even as AI advances, we need to think carefully about how we use it, especially in fields like education and research. This suggests that when people's attitudes and beliefs about AI align with other important attitudes and beliefs they hold, they are more likely to accept AI in society. This means that sharing knowledge and communicating effectively can help reinforce these attitudes and beliefs, especially when people focus more on protecting themselves than seeking accurate information (Hart et al., 2009).

In his article 'AI in CAI: An Artificial Intelligence Approach to Computer-aided Instruction,' Carbonell explores how AI techniques can be used in Computer-Aided Instruction (CAI). He discusses the challenges of traditional CAI systems, like not being able to change much and not giving personalised instruction. Carbonell says AI can fix these problems by adapting CAI systems to each student and giving them personalised instruction. Carbonell's article discusses different AI techniques like expert systems, natural language processing, and machine learning, and how they can be used in CAI. He assumes these techniques can help CAI systems understand what students say, find out if they are having trouble learning, and change the instruction to fit each student's pace and style. However, it would have been helpful for this study to look at how people feel and think about CAI. This way, we could compare the challenges and issues with implementing

GenAI to what we already know about CAI. Understanding people's attitudes and beliefs towards CAI could provide valuable insights into how they might feel about GenAI and their potential challenges or concerns. By comparing the two, we could get a clearer picture of what aspects of GenAI might be more acceptable or problematic based on past experiences with CAI. This comparison could help researchers and policymakers make more informed decisions about the development and implementation of GenAI. This could improve learning and keep students interested. Nonetheless, one good thing about Carbonell's work is that he considers how AI can change education. He assumes AI can improve CAI systems by making them adapt to students and giving them personalised instruction. This could make learning more effective and make it easier for students to learn. Nevertheless, there are also some things to think about. Carbonell's article was written in 1970, so it does not discuss all the new developments in AI and education. Using AI in CAI might also be problematic because it might need a lot of resources and data.

Also, Carbonell mainly discusses the technical aspects of using AI in CAI and does not mention the ethical elements or how they could change teaching and learning. So, while Carbonell's work is a good start, there is still a lot to think about when using AI in education. We need to think about people's attitudes, beliefs, privacy, and fairness, and how they could change the relationship between academics and students. It may be assumed that Carbonell's work shows that AI has been part of education for a long time, but we are just starting to see its full potential now.

Williamson and Eynon (2020) explore the history of AI in education, from its early beginnings in the 1950s to today's advanced AI-powered educational tools. They point out essential milestones like the introduction of Intelligent Tutoring Systems (ITS) in the 1970s and the recent rise of adaptive learning platforms. The authors stress how understanding this history helps us tackle current issues and anticipate future trends in AI-based education. Their research reveals the potential of AI to revolutionise education but also highlights ongoing challenges and unresolved problems. They emphasise the need for teamwork across different fields, ethical considerations, and understanding how teaching works to make the most of AI in education. Addressing bias, attitudes, beliefs, privacy, and fairness is crucial to ensure that AI tools benefit everyone. While the study thoroughly reviews AI's history in education, offering valuable insights into future directions, it could be strengthened with real-life examples showing how AI is used in various educational settings. Additionally, the study could have highlighted the lack of guidance and proper integration of AI in higher education. However, concerns remain about the lack of clear regulations and awareness surrounding AI's role in teaching and learning.

Continued worries about the lack of strong rules and insufficient knowledge about using AI in teaching show the importance of clear ethical rules, as will be explained in this book. With higher education institutions using AI more in teaching, there is a significant need for clear guidelines and ethical rules to control how it is used. Therefore, without clear rules, there is a danger that using AI in universities could lead to unintended problems and reinforce people's negative beliefs and attitudes. These might include invading people's privacy, unfair treatment because of biased algorithms, and some students not having the same access to AI tools. Also, because many people, like academics and policymakers, do not fully understand AI in education, these problems are worsened by spreading wrong ideas and uncertainties that may reinforce current beliefs and attitudes. The suggested ethical principles in this book act as an essential guide for dealing with the complicated ethical and legal issues surrounding AI in universities. The rationale behind the ethical principles is to ensure that AI in education is done openly, responsibly, and fairly. The goal is to reduce the chances of problems and make the most of AI in teaching and learning.

Furthermore, the book highlights the importance of considering ethics when examining people's attitudes, beliefs, and how AI is used in universities. Since universities are crucial for preparing future workers and helping students develop critical thinking skills, it is essential that AI in education follows ethical values and helps students grow in all aspects. In this conceptual understanding, the book and its ethical principles are valuable resources for dealing with the gaps in rules and understanding about AI in higher education. By promoting ethical guidelines and encouraging discussions, the book helps AI fit responsibly and fairly into education, which ultimately improves how students learn while sticking to ethical rules.

Figure I.3 shows how different Generative AI (GenAI) types have been developed and changed over time. Certainly, the missing link in making AI work effectively in education often comes down to attitudes, beliefs, how it's used in real classrooms and its impact on teaching and learning. Even though a lot of research and development focuses on AI tools for education, making these tools helpful in everyday teaching and learning is challenging. One big reason for this is that classrooms are complicated places. They are not just about teaching materials and students sitting at desks. They are dynamic environments with many different factors at play, like different kinds of students and teachers with their own

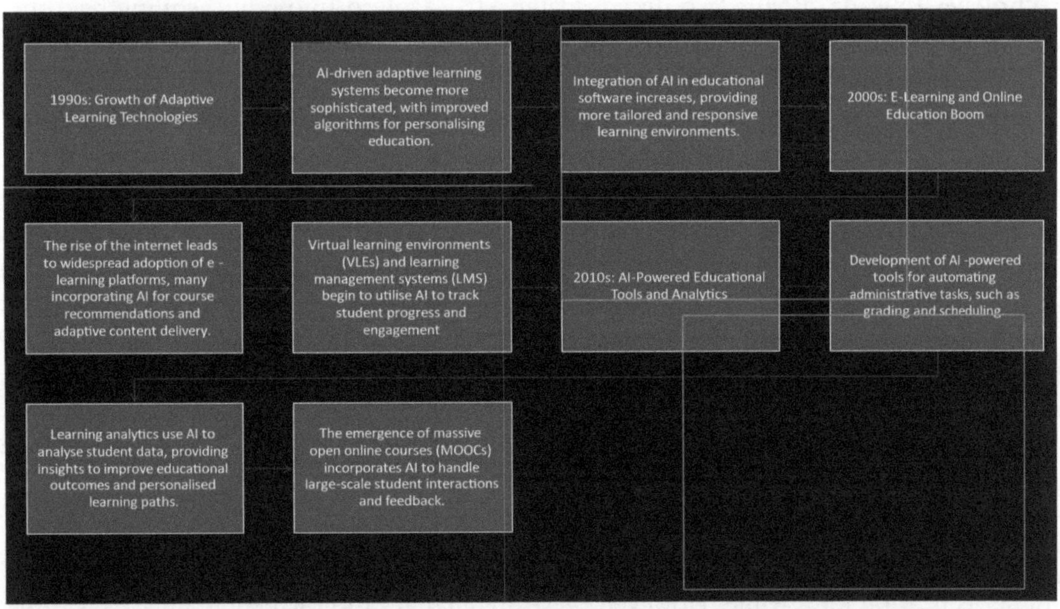

FIGURE I.3 Mode Gen AI Timeline.

styles, various subjects, attitudes, beliefs, and how schools are set up. Putting AI tools into this mix is not just about having fancy technology. It means understanding how teaching and learning happen.

Also, for AI tools to work well, they need to fit smoothly into how things already work at schools, colleges, and universities. That means they should match up with what academics are trying to achieve, work well with other educational tools that are already being used, and be easy for teachers and students to use. If AI tools are not integrated properly, they might become gadgets that do not help teaching and learning. However, the impact of AI in education is not just about using exciting technology. It is also about more significant issues like fairness, privacy, and who gets to benefit from these tools. We need to think about whether everyone has equal access to AI-powered learning, how we protect students' privacy when using AI, and making sure that using AI in education is fair for everyone. So, to make AI work in education, we must look at the whole picture. We need to understand how higher education works, ensure AI tools fit in smoothly, and consider its significant issues. Only then can we genuinely use AI to make education better for everyone.

In addition, from the early days of 1984, Bloom conducted a study that demonstrated learners who received instruction from a human tutor, along with traditional assessment and corrective instructions, performed significantly better than those who received traditional group teaching (Bloom, 1984). This finding sparked interest among AI researchers in developing intelligent systems that could provide personalised tutoring tailored to individual student needs, aiming to enhance learning (Self, 1998. Researchers in the field of AI sought to emulate the abilities of human tutors in Intelligent Computer-Assisted Instruction (ICAI) or Intelligent Tutoring Systems (ITS) (Anderson and Pelletier 1988). Likewise, in a paper published in 1990, Self argued that ITSs should be approached as an engineering design field, suggesting that ITS design should follow appropriate design methods and techniques (Nwana, 1990). Two decades later, ITSs evolved into a burgeoning field that showed vitality and confidence.

ITSs are computer programs that use AI techniques to act as smart tutors. They can present information using multimedia features to help students tackle challenging thinking tasks. ITSs have been used successfully in various educational and training settings, like homes, schools, universities, businesses, and governments. One main aim of ITSs is to understand how students behave by interacting with them (Sottilare et al., 2018). Unlike other educational systems like CAI, ITSs are capable of monitoring how students solve problems and giving them instant help (Sleeman and Brown, 1982). Historically, much of the research in educational software with AI has been done under the name ICAI. Nevertheless, in recent times, the term ITS has become more popular. The field of ITS brings together computer science, cognitive psychology, and educational research. Because ITS researchers draw from three different disciplines, they face challenges in terms of varying research goals, terms, theories, and focuses. This means ITS researchers need to understand all three disciplines well, which can be demanding.

From what I have discussed in this introduction, AI appears to have been around in higher education for a while. However, there are changes in how people nowadays think and feel about using it. Conversely, historical events shows that people have recognised how AI can assist in education through past research and writing. Nonetheless, not enough attention has been given to how AI can genuinely enhance student teaching and learning. This lack of focus has made it challenging to understand how to effectively use AI and what ethical guidelines should be followed to ensure its proper use. Despite the insufficient recognition of both the positive and negative aspects of AI's use in education, leading to uncertainty about how to integrate it into higher education, this can be addressed by implementing strong ethical guidelines and regulations. It is probable that AI will continue to play a role in teaching, learning, and advancing knowledge. Therefore, the critical question is how to ensure its responsible use. The suggestion in this book is not only to promote the use of AI but also to establish an educational environment that supports its use under ethical principles.

Pressey's work 'A Simple Apparatus Which Gives Tests and Scores-and Teaches' in 1926 introduced the term 'intelligent machines' when he created a teaching device. This machine asked multiple-choice questions and provided correct answers immediately. It even rewarded learners with candies for getting answers right. Although it seemed wise back then, it was not truly intelligent because it only gave preset questions and answers. Despite this, Pressey's machine integrated some contemporary educational theories. By 1950, authentic artificially intelligent machines emerged with general-purpose computers. These machines operated on binary code and had electronic processors, enabling them to make logical decisions. Turing, a British scientist, linked these machines with the concept of intelligence and devised the Turing test (Turing, 2009). This test aimed to assess a machine's intelligence by engaging it in conversations similar to those between humans. The Turing test is closely related to Intelligent Tutoring Systems (ITS), emphasising that for a computer to be successful, it must communicate like a human.

In the 1950s, researchers began incorporating knowledge into ITS to enable them to respond to students' queries. Educational psychologists also started adapting tutoring tools to enhance human learning experiences. Since the 1970s, ITS has been recognised as an effective method for delivering personalised tutoring. This evolution of AI in education reflects a shift in societal perception. It also shows that, initially, AI was seen as a tool to enhance teaching and learning. However, the modern view focuses more on concerns about cheating and maintaining academic integrity. This shift highlights the need for critical evaluation of traditional and contemporary education approaches, revealing gaps in understanding and confidence in conventional methods. This also means we need to critically examine the foundation of our approach to teaching and learning. It is essential to pose various independent, yet interrelated, questions to discover the value in our perception of teaching pedagogy in contemporary education.

How we teach and learn nowadays depends greatly on new technologies like innovation and AI. These technologies help improve education and adjust to different students' needs (Wang et al., 2023). Nonetheless, if our current way of teaching cannot use innovation and AI effectively, it makes us wonder if our learning methods are good enough. First, innovation and AI can change how we learn and teach. They let us have personalised learning, smart tutoring systems, and excellent educational tools that match how each person learns. If we do not use these new technologies in teaching, we might not be able to help students as well, and they might not be ready for the future (Barakat et al., 2024). Second, if we cannot bring innovation and AI into education, it shows that we are not keeping up with how education should evolve. Education needs to change with the world, new tech, and how we teach. If we stick to old ways and do not try new tools, we will not be adapting to what the world needs. Education is not just about learning facts; it is also about thinking, being creative, and solving problems. Innovation and AI can help us teach these skills better. If we do not use them, our old ways might not prepare students well for the challenges they will face. Ultimately, using innovation and AI in education is crucial to keep up with how learning and society change. We need to make sure our education methods prepare students for the digital world we live in.

This book suggests that various motives and goals influence people's attitudes towards GenAI (Kunda, 1990). These goals include wanting to integrate GenAI into education (Kruglanski, 1980), wanting to be consistent in beliefs (Festinger, 1957; Heider, 1946; McGuire, 1960), believing in a fair world (Lerner, Miller, & Holmes, 1976), avoiding uncertainty and confusion when using GenAI in education (Harvey, Hunt, & Schroder, 1961; Roney & Sorrentino, 1995), and avoiding too many confusing rules and policies (Chaiken, 1987; Taylor & Fiske, 1978). In this context, the goal of GenAI in education may lead people to accept it more readily if the right processes and procedures are implemented and followed. For example, those who want to keep things as they are prefer positive information, while those who want to make changes prefer negative information (Johnson & Fujita, 2012). Therefore, exploring GenAI's specific goals in higher education and consistently communicating them to the public may lead to effective and responsible use.

Hence, the worry that AI might harm academic honesty, teaching, and learning may also need careful thought. AI brings new educational changes, but we should not rush to judge its effects. Firstly, AI can help maintain academic honesty by detecting plagiarism and ensuring students submit original work, provided we develop appropriate processes and procedures for its use. These tools allow academics to keep assessments fair and maintain educational standards. Also, AI can help catch cheating or unethical behaviour, reminding everyone how vital academic integrity is. With AI, academics can adjust lessons to suit each student, giving them the right support and feedback to learn better. AI tools can also make learning fun and interactive, keeping students motivated and helping them understand better. However, we need to think carefully and ethically about how we use AI in education. While AI has many benefits, it is not a solution to all educational problems. Academics should be aware of the limits and possible biases of AI systems. They should use AI to support their teaching, not replace their expertise. Also, we must ensure that AI benefits all students equally, considering issues of fairness and access. While it is right to be concerned about how AI might affect academic honesty, teaching, and learning, we should address these concerns carefully. By using AI responsibly and ethically, academics can improve education while keeping it fair and honest for everyone.

Having said that, recent studies have started to explore how GenAI affects academic honesty in universities, moving away from what people usually discuss (Islam, 2024). Researchers have looked into various aspects of GenAI and its impact on academic honesty, covering topics like authenticity, consistency, reliability, ethics, and plagiarism (AlAfnan, 2023).

Some studies by Kim et al. (2023) and Smith et al. (2024) discuss the importance of being transparent and accountable when using GenAI in universities. They say it is crucial to know how decisions are made using algorithms. Other studies, like those by Jones and Wang (2021) and de Vicente-Yagüe-Jara et al. (2023), discuss how the data used to train GenAI might have biases. They suggest that to use GenAI ethically in universities, we need to deal with these biases. Also, research by Chen (2024) and García-Peñalvo (2024) shows that GenAI is changing how academic honesty is challenged. It is making new types of cheating possible, thanks to AI-created content. These studies say we need to change how we assess students and teach them to think critically to deal with these new challenges in the digital age. From this perspective, it makes sense to say that adjusting how we assess students and teaching them how to use AI effectively could be an excellent way to move forward.

Chan and Lee (2023) point out that the primary goal of bringing GenAI into higher education is to enhance students' learning experiences by using its ability to provide helpful information when asked. GenAI, especially tools like ChatGPT, which generates text from prompts, can help students come up with ideas and get feedback on their work, which is particularly helpful for those who do not speak English as their first language (Atlas, 2023). On the other hand, text-to-image tools like DALE-E and Stable Diffusion, mentioned by Dehouche and Dehouche (2023), can assist in teaching subjects like art and design. While recognising the potential benefits highlighted by these researchers, it's essential to carefully consider the challenges and limitations of integrating GenAI.

It is, therefore, possible to argue that Chan and Lee (2023) believe that using GenAI in higher education connects with how AI was first created in the late 1950s. Back then, when AI was new, researchers wanted to make smart systems that could help people with different tasks, like solving problems and making decisions. Chan and Lee agree with this idea. They think GenAI, like ChatGPT, can improve students' learning by giving them helpful information when they ask for it. This is similar to how people first imagined AI would help humans do things better and faster. The early AI researchers also wanted to make systems that could think and solve problems like humans do. Chan and Lee's thoughts match this, too. They suggest using GenAI, such as ChatGPT, to talk and help students like a human would. They say this is important for learning. This idea goes along with what the first AI researchers wanted: To make machines that could think like humans. Moreover, in the late 1950s, people wanted AI to help humans work faster and better by doing repetitive tasks. Chan and Lee see GenAI doing the same thing in education. They say it can make learning easier and help students who do not speak English as their first language. This idea is similar to what motivated the early AI researchers: to create smart systems that improve people's lives.

Also, GenAI's significant impact on how we teach and research in academia raises essential concerns. For example, limitations like the 1,000-character restriction on ChatGPT's input and limits on how often messages can be sent (Rasul et al., 2023) might affect communication. Wang et al. (2023) study how AI, especially GenAI, chatbots, and analytics, can help international students in college. They look at how AI can improve support systems for international students, who often face unique challenges. The study shows how programs such as GenAI and chatbots can contribute to student success. It also discusses how analytics use data generated by AI to help students do better. However, they say we need more research on the ethical side, how well AI works, and what its long-term effects on international students might be. The author's claim is valid, especially when considering how international students can use it to improve their language skills and whether it should be seen as skill development rather than cheating. I argue that we should classify this type of usage as part of academic skill development rather than cheating.

From this point of view, using GenAI in education can really help improve learning. However, there are things GenAI is not so good at yet. One big problem is that GenAI does not always understand how each student learns best. Even though AI tools can give personalised suggestions, they might not fully get what each student needs. To fix this, researchers and universities can work on making GenAI smarter. They can improve the computer programs that analyse student data, such as their past learning and how they are doing now. By using better technology like machine learning and data analysis, GenAI can determine what each student is good at and where they need help. It is also essential for GenAI to be clear and easy to understand. Everyone, including students and academics, should trust GenAI's suggestions. So, AI systems need to explain why they make specific suggestions in a way that is easy to understand. To improve GenAI in education even further, experts from different fields, such as teachers, psychologists, computer scientists, and AI specialists, need to collaborate. By sharing their knowledge, they can create GenAI tools that consider everything necessary for learning, like how our minds work and how we feel. This collaboration will enhance our understanding of the neurological processes involved in the development and use of AI. This understanding will enable us to establish better rules and regulations for its use. Additionally, this approach will contribute to redefining how AI is perceived and integrated into society.

Watermeyer et al. (2024) also look into how GenAI affects academia. They see its potential to automate some academic tasks, like creating content and analysing data. Nevertheless, their study does not dig deep into the ethical, social, and teaching concerns about using AI. They point out issues like unfair algorithms, who owns the ideas made by AI, and how scholarly skills might change. They say we need a more detailed look into how GenAI mixes with academic freedom and creativity and how scholars work. However, their work helps us understand how AI is changing academia, pushing us to think critically about its effects on education. Even though there are limits to these studies, we should see them as chances to learn more, not problems we cannot solve. While there are challenges now, future improvements in GenAI might help overcome them. So, people who use GenAI for teaching should learn about its limits and how to spot mistakes in the data it generates (Gimpel et al., 2023). This will help students understand GenAI better and be ready for changes in how technology is used in the future. Overall, looking at both the good and the bad sides of GenAI is crucial for making smart choices in education. Nonetheless, even though AI can do a lot for education, there is still work to be done to make it even better. By making AI smarter, clearer, and involving different experts, we can make learning more personalised and effective for everyone.

Farazouli et al. (2024) look into how AI chatbots, especially GPT, affect how university lecturers grade students. They want to know if these chatbots change how academics usually do assessments, especially for exams done at home. The study checks if using AI chatbots makes grading more accurate and faster and if it changes how students and teachers interact. However, they do not discuss the ethical issues of using AI chatbots for grading or examining attitudes and beliefs. This means we need to look closer at unfairness and how it affects students' learning. Also, we should discuss the practical problems and benefits of using AI chatbots for grading more. Even though Farazouli et al.'s study has some limits, it gives us good ideas about how grading is changing in universities. This makes it plausible for us to learn more about the moral, teaching, and practical sides of using AI in schools.

Other researchers like van den Berg and du Plessis (2023) and Chan and Zhou (2023) discuss how GenAI can help in research. They say it can develop ideas, organise data, and help build arguments. This means GenAI can make research and publishing faster, as Kitamura (2023) and Bockting et al. (2023) say. Crompton and Burke (2023) think GenAI can also be helpful in grading student essays, with tools like the 'Intelligent Essay Assessor' created by Landauer (2003). Mizumoto and Eguchi (2023) show that using ChatGPT for grading essays can save time, make grading fairer, and give feedback to students quickly, which changes how teaching and learning happen. However, we should consider whether using GenAI fits traditional school values and beliefs, as Petricini et al. (2023) suggest. Even though there might be problems, GenAI seems like it could help improve research, grading, and student learning in colleges.

Similarly, this research has shown how GenAI can make big educational changes. van den Berg and du Plessis (2023) and Chan and Zhou (2023) discuss how GenAI can help develop ideas, organise data, and build arguments, making research faster. This helps share knowledge quicker and encourages new ideas in academia. Wang et al. (2023) examine how GenAI can make learning more personalised by adjusting educational content based on each student's needs. This makes learning more exciting and helps students do better. GenAI also allows students and academics to collaborate better, like in collaborative writing projects (Smith et al., 2023), promoting teamwork and academic discussions. GenAI can also break language barriers and make learning resources more accessible to all students (Kim et al., 2024), making education fairer for everyone. GenAI can create interactive lessons, like virtual simulations and augmented reality experiences, to make learning more fun and engaging.

Scholars such as Petricini et al. (2023) believe we need clear rules and guidelines to manage GenAI risk properly, ensuring AI is used responsibly. Considering how AI may intersect with modern teaching and learning methods, this viewpoint is essential. Having clear guidelines will set expectations for everyone involved, ensuring transparency in its use. It will also allow universities to freely adopt and use GenAI to teach and learn. However, using GenAI for tests and teaching might make it challenging for students to think critically and solve problems independently. This raises the question of how universities can balance the benefits of using AI to make teaching and learning more accessible with the importance of maintaining human knowledge and skills in education. From this perspective, if universities can strike this balance, it suggests that the reasons behind the development of AI and its integration into education are not so different. Thus, using GenAI in education has a lot of potential benefits, like making research faster, improving how students are graded, promoting collaboration, making learning materials more accessible, creating new ways of teaching, and personalising learning. However, it is essential to consider the challenges it brings, like ethical issues, limits on teaching methods, and becoming too dependent on technology. Schools and policymakers need to handle these challenges carefully, ensuring GenAI is used ethically and responsibly while still upholding the values of education.

Consequently, making sure that the rules and values guiding the use of GenAI in education match with what people think and believe is really important. When GenAI follows ethical standards that respect everyone's values, preferences, and backgrounds, it will help create a learning environment where everyone feels included and understood. Therefore, ethical rules like being open and fair, and taking responsibility in GenAI can make students, academics, and others trust and accept them more. When GenAI is made with inclusivity in mind, it can help students who learn in different ways and have different abilities. Also, when we think about ethics while making GenAI, it makes us discuss how it affects society. Having conversations about ethics and values helps us understand how GenAI impacts teaching and learning. Overall, when the ethical rules of GenAI match people's beliefs, it makes education fairer and more empowering for everyone. It allows universities to use GenAI to help students learn better and make education more inclusive for everyone.

Gimpel et al. (2023) suggest that we need to change how we think about GenAI. Instead of quickly dismissing it as a problem, they stated we should study it more to understand its benefits. This idea comes from the understanding that new ideas often need to break old rules to make progress. Right now, the big concern about GenAI is whether it's ethical. People worry that it could be used to control how we think and act, or even make existing prejudices worse. If GenAI is used for those reasons, it might not be suitable for education. Nevertheless, if it's used to fight against those problems, then it could be good. So, we need to invest more time and money into studying GenAI, ensuring it is fair and ethical before using it more widely. This is important to ensure everyone can benefit from GenAI without any unfairness or discrimination.

Therefore, implementing ethical principles to guide the use of GenAI becomes extremely important. Ethics plays a big role in shaping what people believe and how they act. One good example comes from psychology. Psychologist Kohlberg (1987) discusses how people develop their sense of right and wrong over time. He showed that when people learn about ethics and morality, it can change how they think and behave. Research in social psychology also shows how ethical norms affect behaviour. Studies have found that people often follow what they think is right or acceptable in society. For example, in the Milgram experiment, participants did things they thought were wrong because they were told to by someone in authority (McArthur, 2009). In professional settings, ethical codes guide how people behave. For example, in healthcare, there are rules about doing what is best for patients and treating them fairly. Following these rules affects how individual healthcare workers act and shapes how healthcare organisations work. Overall, evidence from psychology, social psychology, and professional ethics codes shows that ethics significantly impacts what people believe and how they behave. By promoting ethical awareness and following ethical principles in using GenAI, we can create a culture where people act with integrity and responsibility for the greater good.

Coccia (2018) examines how new and innovative ideas shake up industries. By studying both economic theories and real-world examples, the author examines how certain companies disrupt traditional markets. These disruptors challenge the established big players and drive forward technological progress. The article explains how these disruptive companies change the economic landscape through detailed case studies and analysis. Their research gives valuable insights into how businesses can adapt and stay strong in the face of disruption. By focusing on the critical role of disruptive companies in driving change, Coccia's work helps us understand how industries evolve and how innovation shapes economic development. This research is valuable for researchers, academics, and professionals in the higher education sector to grasp how disruptive technologies can impact teaching and learning. The evidence shows how innovation and new technology can either positively or negatively disrupt traditional methods in this field.

Similarly, Chiu (2024) explores how GenAI could be used in higher education. The author carefully examines existing research and identifies gaps and challenges in using GenAI for educational purposes. The author also suggests areas for future research to address these challenges thoroughly. This study covers various topics, such as integrating GenAI into teaching, ethical concerns, the technology needed, and how prepared institutions are for this change. By offering suggestions for future research directions, Chiu's work helps advance our understanding of GenAI's potential in education. This research can potentially influence how education evolves and transforms, significantly impacting the field.

Anctil (2023) suggests that addressing this issue involves raising awareness, providing training, and guiding academics and students on how to use GenAI properly. Similarly, Kumar et al. (2023) argues that while AI-generated responses in academic writing should be examined closely, they often lack originality, relevance to the topic, proper references, and a human touch, which is essential for scholarly writing. This raises doubts about GenAI's ability to produce high-quality academic work, suggesting that worries about academic integrity might be premature. Chergarova et al. (2023) suggests that instead of just focusing on preventing cheating, we should look at how GenAI can be integrated into student learning and development. For example, teaching students how to write good prompts could help non-native English speakers improve their language skills. Setting up support centres within schools, colleges, and universities could help students develop these skills.

However, Warschauer et al. (2023) warn against relying too much on GenAI, as it might prevent students from developing their own writing skills. However, with proper training and support, this concern could be addressed. Overall, GenAI has the potential to help students prepare for university-level writing tasks and bring positive changes to teaching and learning. Nonetheless, its use in higher education involves students, academics, and professionals like career consultants, so it is essential to take a comprehensive approach to integrating and using GenAI in education.

Introducing support systems powered by GenAI for students can significantly help them improve their skills, especially in communication and writing. Rudolph (2023) points out that such programs can provide personalised feedback and guidance on writing assignments. This helps students gain practical experience with GenAI, a skill that's becoming increasingly valuable in the job market. At the same time, GenAI offers ways to make teaching tasks more manageable for academics and students. It can help create course materials, develop lectures, and prepare assessments more efficiently. Using GenAI, universities can assess student work, create course outlines that address current issues, and conduct quizzes and exams. Plus, GenAI makes it easier to give ongoing feedback to students, which helps keep them engaged and motivated to learn. Similarly, GenAI can improve productivity and service quality for professionals working in higher education. Baidoo-Anu and Ansah (2023) suggests that GenAI can help with tasks like reviewing student records, scheduling meetings, writing reports, and sending student reminders. Additionally, GenAI's predictive abilities can help professionals make better student progress decisions, leading to more effective communication with students and colleagues (Chergarova et al., 2023).

Kohnke, Moorhouse, and Zou (2023) examine how well language lecturers in universities are prepared to use GenAI in their teaching. They study how these lecturers use language, as well as their opinions, attitudes, and skills related to integrating GenAI into language teaching. This research adds to the discussion on technology in education, especially in language teaching. By looking at how ready academics are to use GenAI tools, the study gives insights into the challenges, complexities, and possibilities of using AI in language teaching. The findings could help improve training and support for lecturers to use GenAI effectively, leading to better language teaching methods in universities. Examining this alongside Coccia's (2018) study demonstrates how the disruption caused by new technologies in industries can create complexities if not properly observed and integrated. Furthermore, while Coccia (2018) identifies critical factors driving technological change, like advances in science and entrepreneurship, it does not profoundly explore how these factors interact or consider regulatory rules, market trends, and social and economic factors. Including more real-life examples and research could strengthen Coccia's analysis, even though it already adds valuable knowledge about how disruptive innovation works in theory. However, future studies should explore technological disruption from different angles to deepen our understanding of this critical topic.

However, the research by Coccia (2018) gives us a deep understanding of how technological advancements, such as AI, change the way traditional industries work. While Coccia mainly talks about businesses, these ideas also apply to education, significantly higher education. GenAI has shaken up how teaching and learning happen in schools and universities. However, this shake-up has happened chiefly because there are no clear rules and guidelines on how to use GenAI ethically in education. GenAI has brought both new opportunities and challenges to higher education. On the one hand, GenAI tools can change how we teach and learn by providing personalised learning experiences, automating tasks, and developing new teaching methods. For example, AI-powered learning platforms can adjust students' learning based on their needs, making learning more engaging and effective. Also, tools such as AI essay graders and chatbots can make assessing students' work easier and faster, which improves learning (Liu et al., 2023; Mizumoto & Eguchi, 2023).

Nonetheless, using GenAI in education also raises various concerns which we need to address. Without clear guidelines, there is a risk of unfairness and ethical problems. One big worry is that GenAI might make unfair decisions based on algorithm biases (Petricini et al., 2023). This could make existing inequalities in education even worse. Also, there is a question of whether work made with GenAI is really original or just copied. This can make it difficult to know whether students are doing their own work (Peres et al., 2023). And because GenAI uses a lot of student data, there are worries about privacy and keeping that data safe (Lubowitz, 2023). Without sound rules and guidelines, schools and universities might struggle to deal with these tricky ethical and legal issues of using GenAI. This could lead to problems like cheating, violating student privacy, and making inequalities worse in education.

Universities need clear rules and guidelines to maximise GenAI in education while avoiding these risks. Only with good ethical rules and policies can they use GenAI fairly and responsibly. Despite the abilities of GenAI tools, students might struggle to detect errors or false information in the content they generate. However, including human oversight could help deal with these issues effectively (Lubowitz, 2023). Also, content produced by GenAI can make it difficult for plagiarism detection software to identify copied material, making it hard for academics to confirm if assignments are authentic (Peres et al., 2023). This raises concerns about whether using GenAI in assessments should be considered plagiarism. Plagiarism means presenting someone else's ideas as your own without giving credit (Hatch, 2023). Based on this definition, labelling the use of GenAI as plagiarism seems unfair if students properly acknowledge their sources. Instead, universities should create clear academic rules that explain how to cite sources when using GenAI. This is important for maintaining academic honesty and ethical standards. Therefore, universities are encouraged to follow this approach rather than quickly accusing students of plagiarism, especially when there is no clear evidence for disciplinary actions.

In this book, I also discuss how GenAI is changing the way universities work. GenAI has the potential to completely change how teaching, learning, and administrative tasks are done. As GenAI improves, it is essential to have clear rules and guidelines to ensure it is used responsibly. In this book, I specifically focus on universities because recent studies show that GenAI can make learning better for students in higher education institutions. However, the findings in this book can be applied to any educational institution worldwide. At first, some universities were unsure about using GenAI, but now, more and more are starting to use it. Researchers are studying how GenAI affects learning and skill-building, and many studies say it is helpful. Nonetheless, there are some significant challenges. Not every university knows how to use GenAI well or has rules for it. Academics also worry about cheating and ensuring everything is fair when using GenAI. So, this book aims to explain how to use GenAI properly and follow ethical principles when using it in universities. It also sets the stage for future research and arguments for using GenAI while admitting that it has limitations.

By looking at how GenAI is used in universities, this book can help make rules about how it should be used in the future. It gives a basic understanding of GenAI's role in education and how to use it in a good and fair way. It discusses using GenAI in UK universities. It explains how it can improve learning and administrative tasks but also stresses the need for clear rules and guidelines to ensure it is used correctly. By tackling these challenges and laying the groundwork for future research and policy, this book aims to promote the responsible use of GenAI in higher education. Finally, one significant contribution of the book is to develop ethical principles and guidance for universities to follow when they are using GenAI in teaching and learning. These principles and guidance help create a set of rules for higher education institutions and policymakers to determine how GenAI should be used in education and organisations. In simpler terms, this book is significant because it helps universities understand how to use GenAI in a good and fair way. It gives them a set of rules to follow so that GenAI can be integrated into teaching and learning responsibly. These rules also help policymakers decide how to integrate GenAI into education and organisations effectively.

The book is divided into **three chapters**, each focusing on different aspects of using GenAI in higher education. **Chapter 1** of this book lays the foundation for our understanding of GenAI by closely examining the world of AI. This opening chapter is essential because it prepares readers to understand the basic concepts and key issues related to AI, which will help them explore more deeply in the following chapters. It closely examines the historical background, societal viewpoints, and ethical dimensions surrounding AI. Specifically, the chapter investigates the challenges universities face when integrating AI, particularly GenAI, into their educational practices. It examines these challenges through the lens of history, social perceptions, and ethical considerations. Given the diverse rules, traditions, and teaching methodologies across higher education institutions in the UK, assessing how GenAI is utilised in academia becomes crucial. The research conducted in this chapter aims to define GenAI and highlight the associated issues. Information is gathered from various sources to understand the rules and protocols governing the use of GenAI. This assessment is instrumental in addressing practical concerns that impact the efficacy of GenAI in teaching and learning environments. A significant aspect of the chapter revolves around establishing a clear definition of GenAI within the realm of education. This definition aids in evaluating the effectiveness of GenAI in higher education and delineates the roles and responsibilities of universities and students in ensuring its ethical utilisation.

Chapter 2 of this book discusses why it is essential to use GenAI in higher education in a responsible and fair way. It suggests ethical and guiding principles for universities to follow when they use AI in teaching and learning. These rules are also for policymakers to pay attention to. Following these ethical and guiding principles will ensure that GenAI is used responsibly and carefully in higher education institutions. The chapter also gives guidance on using AI in teaching and learning that academics and other organisations can implement. It recommends that universities and other organisations observe these guidelines to ensure GenAI is used correctly. Looking forward, the chapter observes that if we think about ethics and guiding principles in teaching and learning now, we can make better future rules and policies for GenAI. Clear rules and guidance for making ethical decisions and using GenAI help set the stage for making new rules and policies later on. Overall, this chapter's primary goal is to ensure that GenAI is used well and safely in universities and other organisations. It creates a strong foundation for using GenAI ethically in higher education institutions and other organisations.

Finally, **Chapter 3** is the last chapter of the book. It wraps everything up by summarising the essential ideas and rules discussed in the earlier chapters about GenAI in education. This chapter discusses the main themes and essential points that were examined throughout the book about using GenAI in different educational situations. It gives a simple overview of what to consider when using GenAI in teaching and learning. By summarising the rules and ideas in the book, Chapter 3 helps us understand how to use GenAI responsibly and well in education. It reminds us that it is essential to make good choices, have a plan, and work together to ensure GenAI helps students, academics, and professionals. The chapter also discusses what these rules and ideas mean for universities, policymakers, academics, and students. It observes that it is essential to keep engaging, learning, and adjusting as GenAI becomes more common in education. Overall, Chapter 3 wraps up the book by combining the essential points and providing ethical principles for using GenAI in education in the future.

CHAPTER 1

Navigating the Discourse of Generative Artificial Intelligence

Historical Precedents, Societal Attitudes, and Ethical Considerations

INTRODUCTION

My view on the current use of GenAI stems not solely from its rapid expansion but also from a broader lack of critical examination of its rationale and development over the years (Chen et al., 2020). For instance, many theologians, authors, mathematicians, philosophers, and professors have pondered about mechanical techniques, calculating machines, and numeral systems that could lead to the idea of mechanising non-human beings to resemble humans (Campbell-Kelly, 2018). This evidence shows that GenAI has been leading the way in human thinking, especially among mathematicians, since people first started thinking about it in the way they think. In the early 1700s, Jonathan Swift, in his novel *Gulliver's Travels*, described a device called 'the engine,' which is one of the earliest references to a modern-day computer with AI (Seager, 2022). This device was envisioned to enhance knowledge and mechanical operations, making even the least talented person appear skilled. This resulted in the creation of an idea called a 'robot.' The term 'robot' was first coined in Karel Capek's science fiction play *Rossum's Universal Robots* in 1921. In this play, factory-made artificial beings called robots were depicted. Following this, the concept of 'robots' became widely used in study, research, and development endeavours (Reilly, 2011).

Likewise, the first depiction of a robot on-screen was in a science fiction film 1927 directed by Fritz Lang (Cranny-Francis, 2016). In this movie, a robotic girl causes chaos in

 DOI: 10.1201/9781003561507-2

a futuristic Berlin. This film inspired other famous non-human characters like C-3PO in *Star Wars*. The first robot built in Japan was Gakutensoku ('learning from the laws of nature' in English) by Japanese biologist Makoto Nishimura in 1929 (Liebman, 2022). It could move its head and hands and change its facial expressions. In 1939, physicist Vincent Atanasoff and his student Clifford Berry created the Atanasoff-Berry Computer (ABC) at Iowa State University (Silag, 1984). It could solve up to 29 equations simultaneously and weighed over 700 pounds. In 1949, computer scientist Berkeley's book *Giant Brains: Or Machines That Think* noted that as machines become better at handling large amounts of information, they could think (Berkeley, 2023). These advancements gave rise to the modern concept of what we now call AI and, more recently, the idea of GenAI. However, the ethical and moral guidelines for its use were lacking at the beginning of this progress. Perhaps, it could be that the early development of AI might have been influenced by several factors. Initially, there was no clear understanding of how AI would impact different parts of society. Even if there was a clear vision for using AI to support human efforts and progress, it was not intended to be a powerful tool. This lack of a strong guiding vision may have led to early AI programs that were underdeveloped and lacked foresight and ethical guiding principles.

Furthermore, these developments show that the idea of AI or intelligent machines has existed for hundreds of years. People have dreamed about it, and its implementation has been more about aiding human progress than machines taking over the world. Therefore, the apprehension towards GenAI may come from science fiction movies portraying intelligence as a threat to human civilisation. However, I argue the opposite and propose that intelligent machines were meant to help humans fully understand what they can achieve. Consequently, it should not be seen as a threat to civilisation. What is more plausible is that humanity might become a threat to civilisation if intelligent technology is used unethically or for selfish reasons. AI should not be used to limit societal progress but should aid in advancing civilisation. Therefore, strict accountability and ethical principles must accompany its use.

During the years from 1940 to 1960, there was a push to make animals and machines work together better. Wiener was a crucial figure in this effort. He developed cybernetics, a field aimed at understanding how animals and machines control and communicate (Wiener, 2019). In 1943, McCulloch and Pitts made a breakthrough. They created a mathematics and computer model to mimic how individual brain cells work. This model describes how neurons in the brain send and process information. They introduced the idea of a simple neural network made up of connected nodes, representing neurons, that send messages in binary code (McCulloch and Pitts, 1990). Their mathematical calculations showed how these neural networks could handle complex tasks like recognising patterns and performing logical operations. This work showcased the incredible computational abilities of neural networks. It laid the groundwork for the development of artificial neural networks (ANNs) in the field of AI. McCulloch and Pitts's paper generated much interest in using neural network models to tackle problems in machine learning, pattern recognition, and cognitive science. Their logical calculations also influenced further research in neuroscience and AI. Many studies have since explored the computational properties of neural networks and their potential applications across various domains. Additionally, their work has contributed to the development of theoretical frameworks for understanding how the brain functions and processes information. However, none of this ongoing research, which focuses on how humans and machines interact, includes ethical considerations in its efforts.

In the 1950s, significant progress occurred in the field of AI. Shannon, known as 'the father of information theory,' wrote about programming a computer to play chess in 1950 (Shannon, 1993). Turing also published *Computing Machinery and Intelligence* the same year, proposing the idea of machines that can think (Pinar Saygin et al., 2000). Turing speculated about creating thinking machines that could converse indistinguishably from humans. This idea evolved into the Turing Test, assessing machine intelligence (Turing, 1950). It became a crucial aspect of AI philosophy. In 1952, computer scientist Samuel developed a checkers-playing program (Samuel, 1959). It was the first program to learn how to play a game independently. Samuel's work demonstrated the potential of computational methods to teach machines complex games like checkers. Samuel's program improved its performance over time by using techniques such as pattern recognition and reinforcement learning. Eventually, it reached a proficiency level comparable to skilled human players. This work not only showcased early computer capabilities but also laid the groundwork for advancements in machine learning and AI. Samuel's pioneering efforts in applying computational techniques to game-playing inspired generations of researchers to explore the possibilities of machine learning in various domains.

In short, these groundbreaking studies are significant for GenAI. They show how innovative computer programs can handle complex tasks and set the stage for even more advancement. They also remind us that making intelligent machines has always been about helping people work together, not taking over. Looking at the history of intelligent machines, it is clear they were never meant to be a threat. The people who made them had good reasons and goals in mind. So, when we think about using GenAI in settings such as education, it is more likely that our worries come from not knowing enough about it than from any real danger of GenAI taking over teaching and learning. Perhaps we are scared because we do not understand GenAI and how to use it properly. So, it is not GenAI itself that is the problem; our lack of knowledge and understanding could be risky. To fix this, we need to focus on teaching people more about GenAI and making sure we use it responsibly. That way, we can enjoy all the good things AI can bring while ensuring it is used safely and fairly for everyone.

Furthermore, since ChatGPT was introduced on November 30, 2022, many people have become interested in GenAI (Dempere et al., 2023). OpenAI makes it and is one of the first 'Generative' AI tools that many people can use. These tools can do amazing things by themselves, like creating text, pictures, and videos (Imran & Almusharraf, 2023). There are now many other GenAI tools, like DALL·E for making images, Scribe for helping with writing, and AlphaCode for coding tasks. All these tools show how GenAI can be used in different ways and be really helpful. The recent release of GPT4, the newest version of ChatGPT, and other new tools such as Microsoft's Copilot shows how quickly GenAI technology is growing. This fast development shows that GenAI is becoming very smart and can change how we do things (Li et al., 2024). Nonetheless, as this happens, experts and people who use AI need to think about an important question: How smart is GenAI, and how can it help humans understand machine and human thinking better? This question is interesting but also challenging to answer. A lot of empirical research is needed to understand it well, along with looking at the history and ethics of AI. Understanding AI's historical context and ethics is essential before GenAI becomes a big part of our lives. By finding out these answers, we can make sure that GenAI is used in good ways that are fair and safe for everyone.

However, the idea that GenAI development has been a big explosion in the last four years is slightly exaggerated. AI has actually been around for a long time and has been part of our lives for many years (Newell, 1982). AI research started back in the mid-20th century, and we have been making progress ever since (Muthukrishnan et al., 2020). Even though recent advancements have gotten much attention, AI has quietly shaped our world for decades (Confalonieri et al., 2021). For instance, let's consider recommendation algorithms on streaming services or speech recognition in virtual assistants (Kepuska & Bohouta, 2018). These are all examples of AI that we have been using for a while now, even if we did not always think of them that way.

Sure, there have been some significant breakthroughs in AI technology recently, like better deep learning and language processing systems (Moshayedi et al., 2022). However, it is essential to remember that these advancements are built on years of research and development. Calling it an explosion overlooks our gradual progress over time. By understanding the long history of AI and how it has evolved, we can better appreciate its impact on our lives. Looking at AI this way helps us have more informed conversations about its benefits, limitations, and ethical concerns. Therefore, it is not just about the flashy new technology—it is about understanding how AI has been and continues to be part of our world.

In 1955, an American computer scientist, McCarthy, came up with the term 'Artificial Intelligence,' or 'AI' for short (Anderson, 2024). McCarthy is known as one of the people who helped start the field of AI (Rajaraman, 2014). He chose the name 'artificial intelligence' to describe the idea of making machines that can do things that normally need human thinking. By putting together the words 'artificial' (which means made by humans) and 'intelligence' (which is about thinking and understanding), McCarthy captured the main idea of creating intelligent machines (McCarthy et al., 2006). Using the term 'artificial intelligence' was important because it gave a clear name to this new area of study. It helped people understand that AI was all about making machines that can be smart, like humans, but in their own way. Since then, 'artificial intelligence' has become a big part of technology (Malinetsky & Smolin, 2021). It covers a wide range of things, like computers that can learn from data (machine learning), programs that understand and generate human-like language (natural language processing), and systems that can make decisions based on rules (expert systems) (Sumari and Ahmad, 2018).

In short, McCarthy's idea of 'artificial intelligence' in 1955 laid the foundation for what we now know as AI. His work was the starting point for all the research and progress we have seen in making machines smarter over the years. However, the ethical implications of AI have often been overlooked since its inception, partly due to the historical context in which it emerged. This might be because McCarthy and his contemporaries were primarily focused on the technical challenges of creating machines that could emulate human intelligence. Their discussions at Dartmouth College centred around developing algorithms, frameworks, and methodologies for achieving this goal, never conceptualising the potentiality of AI in the future, let alone discussing its implications for society. So, back then, people did not really think much about how AI might affect society. This was partly because AI was not used much at the beginning, so ethical concerns did not seem necessary. Also, technology and data access were also limited, so ethical considerations did not apply. However, as AI becomes more advanced and widely used, it is crucial to consider its impact on society. Therefore, we need to make sure we are using AI fairly and ethically in the contemporary world (Munoko et al., 2020).

Furthermore, the prevailing attitudes towards technology and its role in society during the mid-20th century may have contributed to the oversight of ethical concerns (Woodley, 2002). The post–World War II era was characterised by a prevailing optimism about the potential of technology to solve complex problems and improve human lives. This optimism often overshadowed critical reflections on technological advancements' potential risks and ethical implications. However, the ethical implications have become increasingly apparent as AI technologies have advanced and become more integrated into various aspects of society, including healthcare (Racine et al., 2019), finance, and criminal justice (Rizer and Watney, 2018). Issues such as algorithmic bias, privacy violations, and the displacement of human labour have raised concerns about the societal impact of AI systems (Sheikh, 2020). Moreover, the lack of diversity and representation in the early AI research community may have contributed to the oversight of ethical considerations. The field of AI was initially dominated by white, male researchers from privileged backgrounds, whose perspectives and experiences may not have fully accounted for the diverse range of societal impacts that AI could have.

From this perspective, it can be assumed, also considering historical context, that the dominance of white male researchers from privileged backgrounds in the design of AI may have contributed to biases and discrimination in AI datasets (Ntoutsi et al., 2020). This means that AI programs tend to reflect these individuals' predetermined views rather than society's collective views (Leavy et al., 2020). To address this issue, it is essential to diversify the workforce by including a wider range of AI experts. This diversity would lead to better coding practices and a more inclusive approach to designing AI programs. Addressing diversity at the staff level, AI programs will begin to reflect the broader views and needs of society. Therefore, to achieve diversity in the workforce, it is recommended that AI designing and programming organisations should follow these steps:

1. Evaluate Current Workforce Diversity:

    - Conduct an internal audit to understand the current diversity levels within your organisation.
    - Identify gaps in representation across different demographics, such as gender, race, ethnicity, and socio-economic backgrounds.

2. Set Clear Diversity Goals:
   - Establish specific, measurable diversity and inclusion goals.
   - Create a timeline for achieving these goals and ensure they align with the organisation's broader mission and values.
3. Implement Inclusive Hiring Practices:
   - Use diverse hiring panels and ensure job postings are free from biased language.
   - Partner with organisations and institutions that support underrepresented groups in technology.
   - Encourage applications from diverse candidates through targeted outreach and recruitment initiatives.
4. Provide Diversity and Inclusion Training:
   - Offer regular training sessions on unconscious bias, cultural competency, and inclusive practices for all employees.
   - Ensure that leaders and managers are equipped to foster an inclusive work environment.
5. Create Supportive Workplace Policies:
   - Develop policies that support diversity, such as flexible working hours, parental leave, and equal pay.
   - Establish employee resource groups (ERGs) to provide support and networking opportunities for underrepresented groups.
6. Foster an Inclusive Culture:
   - Promote a culture of inclusion where diverse perspectives are valued and encouraged.
   - Ensure that all employees feel safe and supported in voicing their ideas and concerns.
7. Review and Update AI Datasets:
   - Regularly review AI datasets to identify and remove biases.
   - Include diverse data sources to ensure that AI systems reflect a wide range of perspectives and experiences.
8. Collaborate with Diverse Communities:
   - Engage with diverse communities to understand their needs and perspectives.
   - Involve these communities in the development and testing of AI systems.

9. Monitor Progress and Adjust Strategies:
    - Continuously monitor the progress towards diversity goals.
    - Adjust strategies as needed based on feedback and changing circumstances.
10. Celebrate and Communicate Success:
    - Highlight and celebrate achievements in diversity and inclusion.
    - Share success stories and lessons learned with the broader organisation to maintain momentum and commitment.

Following these steps, organisations can create a more diverse and inclusive workforce. This, in turn, will lead to the development of AI programs that better reflect the views and needs of society.

In recent years, there has been a growing recognition of the need to address ethical issues in AI research and development (Stahl and Wright, 2018). Organisations such as the Partnership on AI and the IEEE Global Initiative for Ethical Considerations in Artificial Intelligence and Autonomous Systems have been established to promote ethical guidelines and best practices in AI (Chatila et al., 2017). In short, while the term 'AI' coined by McCarthy in 1955 marked the beginning of a transformative field of research, the historical context and prevailing attitudes of the time may have led to the oversight of ethical considerations and the current problem regarding the use of GenAI. Nevertheless, as AI technologies have advanced and become more integrated into society, addressing ethical concerns has become increasingly urgent. Researchers, policymakers, and industry stakeholders need to engage in ongoing discussions and collaborations to ensure that AI technologies are developed and deployed in a manner that aligns with ethical principles and values.

The issue of ethics in AI is complex and multifaceted, requiring the collaborative effort of diverse stakeholders from across society. To address AI ethics effectively, it is crucial to start discussions at both societal and expert levels. This comprehensive approach ensures that AI integration aligns with societal norms and serves the common good. Also, ethical considerations in AI cover a broad range of issues, from data privacy and security to bias and fairness in algorithmic decision-making. Therefore, given the far-reaching implications of AI technologies, the ethical discourse must be inclusive. This means involving technologists, ethicists, policymakers, legal experts, sociologists, and the general public. Such inclusivity fosters a more holistic understanding of AI's potential impacts, ensuring the technology develops in line with societal values and expectations. Starting ethical discussions at both societal and expert levels allows for a more thorough evaluation of AI's implications. Societal consultations provide insights into public concerns, cultural values, and ethical expectations, which are essential for grounding AI development in real-world contexts. Concurrently, expert consultations bring technical knowledge, ethical theories, and practical considerations to the table, ensuring that discussions are informed by the latest advancements and challenges in the field. This approach ensures greater public trust and acceptance of AI systems by incorporating a diverse range of perspectives. From this point of view, it may be assumed that ethical frameworks and guidelines are more likely to gain widespread support and adherence when they are rooted in society's values and needs. This, in turn, promotes the responsible and equitable deployment of AI technologies, enhancing their positive impact on society.

The main goal of integrating ethical considerations into AI development is to benefit society as a whole. Therefore, by prioritising inclusivity and extensive consultation, we can ensure that AI technologies address societal challenges, enhance human well-being, and contribute to the overall betterment of society. This approach also helps identify and mitigate potential harms, ensuring that the benefits of AI are distributed equitably and do not exacerbate existing inequalities. In addition to consulting broadly with society and experts, it is recommended that a specific ethical code be developed for programmers and engineers in the AI field. This ethical code would provide clear guidelines and standards for responsible AI development, helping to prevent ethical compromises in creating and using datasets. It would emphasise principles such as transparency, accountability, fairness, and respect for privacy, guiding practitioners in making ethical decisions throughout the development process. Similarly, an ethical code for AI practitioners is essential for managing ethical risks associated with data management and algorithm design. Datasets used in AI development often contain biases that can lead to unfair or discriminatory outcomes. By adhering to a standardised ethical code, developers can implement best practices for data collection, preprocessing, and algorithmic transparency, reducing the likelihood of ethical lapses and enhancing AI systems' overall fairness and reliability. In summary, addressing AI ethics is a collaborative effort that must involve input from all sectors of society. Starting ethical discussions at both societal and expert levels ensures that AI technologies are developed in alignment with societal norms and serve the common good. Additionally, developing an ethical code for AI practitioners is essential for mitigating ethical risks and promoting responsible AI development. This comprehensive and inclusive approach is crucial for ensuring that AI technologies contribute positively to society and uphold the values and principles fundamental to our collective well-being.

The following section will examine 'Tracing the Origins: Historical Precedents in AI.' It will discuss the historical development of AI before assessing its impact and implications in the contemporary world. Understanding the historical development of AI provides a crucial context for evaluating its current impact and future potential. By examining AI's origins and evolution, we can better appreciate the foundational principles and milestones that have shaped its path. This historical perspective allows us to recognise patterns, successes, and failures, offering valuable insights into how AI has been perceived, developed, and applied over time. Additionally, this section sets the stage for a more informed assessment of AI's contemporary implications. We can identify ongoing themes and challenges in AI research and deployment by linking past advancements to present-day applications. This historical analysis also helps to highlight the ethical, social, and technological considerations that have accompanied AI's growth, enabling a better discussion of its current and future roles in society. In summary, assessing the history of AI enriches our understanding of its evolution and provides a critical lens through which to assess its current and future impacts.

TRACING THE ORIGINS: HISTORICAL PRECEDENTS IN ARTIFICIAL INTELLIGENCE

In August 1956, a group of scientists gathered at Dartmouth College in Hannover, New Hampshire, including McCarthy, Minsky, Shannon, Newell, and Simon, to discuss a new idea: Teaching machines to think and learn like humans (Luger and Luger, 2021). This meeting, called the Dartmouth Conference, lasted for two months. Although they did not all agree, they came up with a name for what they were discussing: Artificial intelligence (AI) (Urwin, 2016). So, 1956 became known as the beginning of AI. AI means machines can think and learn in a similar way to humans. Since then, AI research and development have been ongoing for over 60 years (Bentley, 2020). Different scholars from various fields have their own ideas about AI, leading to varying schools of thought. Three main schools emerged during this time: Symbolism, connectionism, and behaviourism. These schools focus on different aspects of human intelligence, like thinking, the brain, and behaviour (Carter, 2007). However, none of these schools focused on AI's ethical and regulatory aspects, nor did they try to determine what principles could be created to regulate the AI revolution in society. While it is plausible to assume that focusing on the ethical aspects of AI would have been premature due to the lack of data, it is equally important to consider these ethical issues from the beginning.

Various groups have discussed how AI should operate from the beginning, but they have not thought about how to use it ethically or regulate its use (Cordeschi, 2002). Symbolists say AI should copy human logic, connectionists emphasise big data and training, and behaviourists focus on achieving goals through environmental interaction (Wang, 2021). Symbolism concerns thought, like human consciousness, abstract logic, and emotions. Connectionism focuses on the brain's neural network that enables thinking. Behaviourism looks at behaviour, mainly how humans interact with their surroundings by sensing and acting (Gong, 2021). This idea highlights how AI plays a significant role in shaping how we think and in societal changes. It also means that AI's vision and development are based on the composition of human characteristics. Therefore, AI's patterns and attributes replicate human thinking, which is inherently based on human behaviours and thought processes. Given this, if AI is designed to mirror human characteristics and thought patterns, it follows that these patterns require regulation. Consequently, anything based on the characteristics of the human mind, thoughts, and behaviours necessitates rules and regulations to govern it. From this perspective, it is appropriate to argue that the guiding principles of ethics introduced in this book are the correct course of action for both the present and the future. Regulating AI based on ethical considerations ensures that the technology develops consistently with the human mind, thought process and behaviours. It also helps prevent potential misuse and addresses the ethical dilemmas that arise from integrating AI into various aspects of life. This proactive approach fosters trust and accountability in AI systems, ultimately leading to their responsible and beneficial deployment.

As AI becomes more common in our lives, it affects how we feel, think, and try to improve society. So, instead of just looking at the people who make AI, we should also focus on the people who use it. This is partly because AI systems are designed to replicate human thought processes, behaviours, and decision-making patterns. This is because the vision and development of AI are fundamentally based on human characteristics and what it means to be human. Consequently, creating AI involves imitating aspects of human cognition, emotion, and social interaction. Due to this close resemblance to human attributes, it is crucial to regulate AI similarly to how we govern human behaviour. Just as human actions are controlled by ethical and legal standards to maintain societal order and protect individual rights, AI systems should also be subject to comparable regulations. This approach ensures that AI functions within acceptable moral boundaries and respects societal values and norms.

This means we need to understand how people use AI and how it affects their decisions. This is important for solving problems with AI and making the most of its benefits. In the end, we should think more about the users of AI to make sure it is used responsibly and ethically in our society. Based on the evidence presented in the previous section, it is obvious that AI development does not consider ethics or societal rules, especially for the people who use it. This creates a problem in the overall system. So, the main point of this book is to go back to the start of AI development and think about all the engineering and how people use it, to come up with reasonable rules for using it ethically and effectively.

Following the Dartmouth College Conference in 1956, which marked the beginning of AI, the period from 1956 to 1974 was known as the golden age of AI (Wilson, 2019). During this time, the Symbolism faction, also called the Logicism or Computer School, was the dominant force in the field. Symbolists aimed to enhance machines' logical reasoning to achieve machine intelligence. They believed that human thinking relied on symbols and that cognitive processes involved symbolic operations. Consequently, both humans and computers were viewed as capable of logical reasoning using symbols. This perspective overshadowed other factions like Connectionism, which focused on machine learning and was initially undervalued by Symbolists. From this point of view, the current approach to AI development seems fine based on logic and practice. However, ethics and rules guide human thinking, so setting guidelines for AI vision and development is crucial to avoid future disasters. Therefore, I argue that it was a mistake not to include ethics or guiding principles in the early stages of AI development.

This is partly because the Symbolist school's ideas about AI align closely with how people naturally think; Symbolism has been the dominant force in AI history for a long time. Symbolists believe that artificial intelligence stems from mathematical logic, which saw rapid development in the late 19th century and was used to explain intelligent behaviour in the 1930s. With the advent of computers, logical deduction systems were implemented on these machines. Humans have always used symbols to represent things, people, abstract concepts, actions, or even imaginary ideas. This ability to communicate using symbols is believed to be what sets humans apart intellectually. Therefore, early AI pioneers assumed that intelligence could be precisely described using symbols, leading to Symbolic AI taking centre stage in AI research. Many concepts and tools in computer science, such as object-oriented programming, stemmed from these efforts. The symbolist approach deserves recognition because it mirrors how humans reason and interpret the laws of nature using language; for instance, Platonism suggests that abstract mathematical concepts exist independently of us, similar to Plato's Theory of Forms (Tyson, 2015). Intuitionists, conversely, believe that mathematics is a product of human thought and experience (Placek, 1999). From the symbolist perspective and ancient philosophies, we can conclude that AI helps humans understand our world by recognising patterns and processes. Intelligence stems from our ability to comprehend symbols and phenomena. In essence, AI aids humanity in deciphering the complexities of our existence.

In the world of AI development, we often focus on logic and practicality, but something essential is missing: Symbols and rules. Symbols have been around for a long time, and thinkers like Plato knew they were crucial for understanding things. Plato's story about people in a cave shows how symbols and rules affect how we see the world. Without clear rules in AI development, symbols can be misunderstood. Symbols here mean AI systems' data, algorithms, and decision-making processes. If we do not have good ethical rules and regulations to guide how we use these symbols, they can be misused or misunderstood, which can cause problems and harm. For instance, think about AI used in predicting crime. If there are no clear rules for using and understanding these algorithms, they might be unfair or biased, leading to unfair outcomes. Similarly, in healthcare, AI tools for diagnosis might give wrong results if good ethical rules and standards do not guide them. That is why setting strict rules for developing and using AI is essential. We need to think about ethics and make sure we have clear rules to help us understand and use AI symbols correctly. This will help us avoid problems and ensure that AI helps society in a good way.

Nonetheless, five years later, a demonstration of the idea began with the creation of the Logic Theorist by Newell, Shaw, and Simon. This program aimed to copy human problem-solving skills and was funded by the Research and Development (RAND) Corporation (Simon and Newell, 1971). Many people think of it as the first AI program. It was introduced at the Dartmouth Summer Research Project on Artificial Intelligence (DSRPAI), arranged by McCarthy and Minsky in 1956 (Van Assen et al., 2022). McCarthy brought together top researchers from different fields at this critical conference to discuss AI openly. He even coined the term 'artificial intelligence' during this event. Unfortunately, the conference did not meet McCarthy's expectations; attendees came and went as they pleased, and there was no agreement on standard methods for the field. Despite these difficulties, everyone agreed that achieving AI was possible. This event was important as it paved the way for the next two decades of AI research.

In the 1950s, psychologist Rosenblatt invented the perceptron, the first brain-inspired AI (Shao and Shen, 2023). It mimicked how neurons in the brain process information. Neurons receive input from other neurons and fire if the total reaches a certain level. They give more weight to more robust connections (Lieto, 2021). Similarly, a perceptron calculates the sum of its inputs and outputs 1 if it reaches a threshold. Unlike symbolic AI, where programmers set rules, perceptrons learn independently through examples. If correct, they are rewarded; otherwise, they are punished. Adding layers of perceptrons creates a multilayer neural network, foundational in modern AI. However, training these networks in the 1950s and 1960s was challenging due to the lack of general algorithms. Similarly, brain model research slowed down in the late 1970s and early 1980s due to limitations in theoretical models, biological prototypes, and technical capabilities. With reduced support from critical advocates and minimal government funding, research on neural networks and connectionist-based AI significantly declined. Minsky's harsh criticism of the perceptron, a key component of connectionist AI, also contributed to this decline. As a result, the connectionist faction faced challenges and remained stagnant for nearly a decade.

Despite declining funding, some researchers persisted in connectionist studies during the 1970s and 1980s. The resurgence of connectionism began with Hopfield's influential papers in 1982 and 1984, proposing hardware simulation of neural networks (Hopfield, 1982). Rumelhart et al. (1986) introduced the back-propagation (BP) algorithm for multi-layer networks. This revitalised connectionism, leading to advancements in modelling, algorithms, theoretical analysis, and engineering implementation, laying the groundwork for neural networks to enter the market (Hopfield, 1984). Since 2010, machine learning has surged in popularity, marking a shift from expert systems. Unlike expert systems that rely on predefined rules, machine learning allows computers to discover rules from vast data sets. Machine learning follows the connectionist approach to AI, mimicking the brain's functions. Unlike symbolic AI, which imitates higher-level thinking, connectionist AI builds adaptive networks that can learn and identify patterns from large data sets. Connectionists believe that AI can achieve advanced functions akin to the human mind with sufficiently complex networks and ample data.

During the 1970s and 1980s, there was a renewed interest in studying connectionism, which focused on using intelligent machines to help humans in their tasks. This effort reflects the idea that machine intelligence should primarily assist humans in learning and improving how we gather and use knowledge. Researchers examine connectionist models and neural networks to mimic humans' thinking and learning. They created hardware simulations of neural networks and developed algorithms like back-propagation to make these systems learn from large amounts of data. This shift in focus shows a change in how we see AI. Instead of seeing AI as replacing humans, connectionist studies showed that AI could work alongside humans to improve our problem-solving skills. By using intelligent machines to learn, make decisions, and create knowledge, researchers hoped to improve how we work together with technology (Fan et al., 2020). This approach opened up new possibilities for collaboration between humans and machines, making problem-solving more efficient and effective across different fields (Prescott, 2024). This also means that we need good ethics and rules to control how humans and machines work together. It is like how society follows rules and policies for how things work, like how hormones function in our bodies. Similarly, if there are not good rules and policies in society, it can lead to problems and disasters.

Furthermore, between 1957 and 1974, AI saw significant improvements (Roland and Shiman, 2002). Computers got better, cheaper, and more available, which helped researchers make strides in AI (Flasiński and Flasiński, 2016). They also got better at using machine learning algorithms to solve different problems. Some essential achievements included the development such as Newell and Simon's General Problem Solver (Newell, Shaw, and Simon, 1959) and Weizenbaum's ELIZA (Natale, 2019), which showed promise in solving problems and understanding language. Because of these successes and support from top researchers, government agencies like DARPA started investing in AI research at many universities. People were hopeful about what AI could do. However, even with these advancements, there were still significant challenges. One of the main problems was that computers did not have enough power to do a lot. They could not store or process large amounts of information quickly. This made it difficult for them to understand and use language effectively. Hans Moravec, a student of McCarthy, said that computers were not strong enough to show real intelligence. Because of these limitations, AI research funding slowed, and progress took a break for about ten years.

In the 1980s, AI saw a revival for two main reasons: Algorithm advancements and increased funding. Hopfield and Rumelhart popularised 'deep learning' methods, allowing computers to learn from experience (Hopfield, 1984). Meanwhile, Feigenbaum introduced expert systems, which replicated the decision-making abilities of human experts. These systems would consult experts in a field for advice on various situations, guiding non-experts once they had learned from these interactions. Expert systems have been found to be widespread in many industries (Vlaanderen, 1990). The Japanese government notably invested heavily in expert systems and other AI projects through their Fifth Generation Computer Project (FGCP) (Nakamura and Shibuya, 1996). Between 1982 and 1990, they poured $400 million into the initiative, aiming to revolutionise computer processing, implement logic programming, and enhance AI. However, many of the ambitious goals set by the project were not achieved. Nevertheless, it could be argued that the FGCP indirectly inspired a new generation of talented engineers and scientists. Despite this, funding for the FGCP eventually stopped, and AI again faded from the spotlight.

It may be assumed that during these major advancements in AI, not enough attention has been given to making rules to control how it's used in society. Even though AI is increasingly used in different areas, there is still a significant gap in making good rules to guide its ethical and responsible use. This lack of focus raises worries about the possible risks and problems that could come from using AI without any control. One big reason for this problem is that people are mostly focused on making AI better and faster, and generating income from it. They are not thinking enough about how to use AI in a fair and safe way. As a result, important questions about privacy, transparency, and fairness get pushed aside, and AI can end up being used in harmful ways. Another problem is that making rules for AI is complicated because it involves experts from many fields like computer science, ethics, law, and social sciences. Getting everyone to agree on the rules is challenging and takes a long time, so sometimes the rules are not good enough. Also, because AI is used worldwide, creating one set of rules that works for everyone is difficult. Each place has its own laws and customs, making it even more challenging to agree on the rules for AI. In the end, not having good rules to control how AI is used in society can lead to many problems. To fix this, we need politicians, businesses, and experts to work together to make firm rules that ensure AI is used safely and fairly for everyone.

Ross (1987) discusses how AI can be used to create intelligent tutoring systems (ITS) that help students learn better. These systems can solve problems and give feedback to students just like a human teacher would (Ross, 1987). This is important because it shows how AI can change education by making it more personalised and supportive. ITS can act like a human teacher by using AI techniques like understanding information, making logical guesses, and understanding language. They can find answers to questions, explain how they got there, and give helpful comments. This means that students can get personalised help that matches their needs, making learning more accessible and more effective. Ross's work shows how AI can make education more interactive and effective. With ITS, students can get the help they need, tailored to their strengths and weaknesses. This could change how we think about teaching and learning, making it more flexible and adaptable to each student's needs. However, there are challenges to consider when using AI in education. These include effects such as making sure the AI is fair and respects privacy and making sure it really helps students learn. So, while AI has a lot of potential to improve education, we need to keep working on it to ensure it is used in the best way possible. In simpler terms, Ross's ideas from 1987 also set the groundwork for the recent development of GenAI. This shows that the idea of using AI to help people learn better has been around for a long time. Over the past decade, there has been a lot of exploration and growth in the field of GenAI, which builds upon Ross's initial concepts. This rapid expansion of GenAI shows that the idea has been brewing for quite some time and is now becoming a reality in various aspects of our lives. However, the central question to consider is: Why does the rapid expansion of AI pose a threat to traditional ways of life? While some may argue that the concerns surrounding GenAI should be approached cautiously, it is crucial to understand why these issues are emerging prominently now rather than 60 years ago.

Also, since the beginning of AI, there's been much disagreement among different groups about how it should work. Symbolists think AI should think like humans, using logic. Connectionists believe it's all about using big data and learning from it. Behaviourists say AI should reach goals by interacting with the environment. These different ideas have made progress in AI inconsistent over time. The problem is not just that people do not understand AI; even experts cannot agree on how it should be done. They have been trying to develop one big theory to explain and study AI, but they cannot all get on the same page. This disagreement shows that AI research is complex and has many sides to it. To move forward, experts need to work together and discuss their ideas, bringing different perspectives to the table. This collaboration can help find better ways to make AI work for everyone.

Furthermore, in real-world AI, agents must handle both complexity and uncertainty. Symbolic AI simplifies the world using logical relationships and known information to deal with complexity. In contrast, connectionist and behavioural AI use probability-based methods to address uncertainty. However, symbolic AI relies on limited human knowledge and struggles to find subtle logic and unknown patterns, making it weak in handling uncertainties and noise in many situations. Connectionist and behavioural AI, on the other hand, may have trouble with complex concepts and relationships. Simple neural network structures might not grasp all the complexities, leading to underfitting, while overly complex ones can cause overfitting. Training connectionists and behavioural AI require lots of data. Their black-box nature makes them difficult to understand, making them unsuitable for critical systems like autonomous driving, which need reliability.

To tackle the complexities and uncertainties in real-world problems, we need a mix of symbolic, connectionist, and behavioural AI. Each approach has its strengths, but none alone can fully handle AI tasks. Currently, symbolic AI is more widely used than connectionist and behavioural AI. This is because most computing functions, mathematical operations, and traditional software rely on symbolic logic, even if they use statistical methods for advanced tasks. In the future, these AI approaches must come together because most AI applications need both the expressive power of symbolic AI and the robustness of connectionist and behavioural AI. However, there's a deep divide between symbolic AI and connectionist/behavioural AI, dating back to the early days of the field. This divide still exists today and requires more research to bridge. Combining these approaches will be essential for advancing AI and creating more effective AI systems for various applications. However, using both methods together also needs strict rules and ethical guidelines to guide how they work in theory and in real life.

Consequently, understanding why people are sceptical about AI is essential, but it is unclear and needs more research. However, we can make some assumptions. Firstly, people worry that AI might take away jobs because it can do tasks that people used to do, which could lead to job losses. Secondly, there are concerns about the ethics of AI, like privacy issues and the possibility of AI making unfair decisions. Thirdly, many people do not understand how AI works, so they are unsure if they can trust it. Lastly, some worry that AI might become too powerful and even surpass human intelligence, which could be risky for humanity. For instance, a report examined Americans' concerns about how businesses use AI responsibly. Almost eight in ten respondents (79%) said they had limited to no trust in businesses' ability to use AI responsibly. This lack of trust was seen across all groups, including gender, race, age, education level, and political affiliation. One of the main worries contributing to this scepticism is the belief that AI will lead to job losses. Also, three out of four Americans think that AI will reduce the number of jobs in the United States over the next decade. This concern is exceptionally high among those without a bachelor's degree and those aged 45 or older. Interestingly, younger adults aged 18 to 29 are less worried about AI's impact on the job market, but still, 66% of them believe AI will reduce job opportunities, which is higher than older adults. These reasons contribute to people's scepticism about AI and its impact on society.

Recent advancements in AI have led to impressive achievements, often equalling or even surpassing human abilities (Crompton and Burke, 2023). This fast progress is narrowing the division between human intelligence and AI. These advancements, along with depictions in science fiction movies, hint that we may not be far from achieving artificial general intelligence (AGI) or artificial super-intelligence. AGI refers to the theoretical capability of an intelligent agent to understand or learn any intellectual task that a human can. Many experts, including well-known inventor and futurist Kurzweil, are hopeful about the potential of AGI (Pavlacka, 2012). Kurzweil has famously forecasted the arrival of an AI singularity, imagining a future where computers, equipped with self-improvement and autonomous learning abilities, will quickly surpass human intelligence (Diéguez and García-Barranquero, 2024). In 2012, Google brought Kurzweil on board to contribute to realising this vision. Kurzweil's predictions are based on the concept of 'exponential progress' in various scientific and technological fields, especially in computing. For example, Moore's Law predicts that the number of components on a computer chip doubles about every 18 months, leading to rapid improvements in computing speed and memory capacity (Mitchell, 1998).

We should recognise and cheer the rapid advancements in different areas, like AI, because they have the power to change how we solve problems and generate new ideas completely. For example, think about how AI is helping us solve challenging problems, like curing diseases or protecting the environment. With AI, scientists can analyse vast amounts of data quickly, helping them find new treatments for illnesses or understand how to better care for our planet. And it is not just about solving problems. AI also sparks new ideas and ways of thinking. As AI gets more innovative, it can help us see things from different perspectives and develop innovative solutions we might not have thought of before. So, by celebrating progress in AI and other fields, we are acknowledging the exciting possibilities they bring. It is like opening up a door to a world of new opportunities to improve our lives and brighten our future. However, if we do not control this progress, AI disasters could be compared to the scientific discoveries that led to the creation of the atomic bomb and other weapons that could wipe out humanity (Clegg, 2010). Therefore, being sceptical is as essential as gathering information to develop rules for AI regulation.

It is also worth considering that some people's doubts about AI arise because AI can perform specific tasks better than humans. However, if this assumption holds true, it suggests that AI itself is not the core issue for human progress or society. In fact, the fact that computers can outperform humans in certain areas is something to be celebrated. For instance, back in the 1940s, computers began surpassing humans in tasks like calculating the trajectory of fast-moving objects, demonstrating their superhuman abilities (Bar-Cohen and Hanson, 2009). Yet, this did not diminish humans' capacity to engage socially or pursue education. This was just the beginning of many tasks where computers have shown exceptional performance. However, it is essential to note that there have been moments of over-optimism throughout the history of AI. For instance, in 1965, AI pioneer Simon predicted that machines would be able to perform any task a human could do within 20 years (Simon, 1995). Similarly, Japan's fifth-generation computer project in 1980 set ambitious goals, such as having machines engage in casual conversations, yet these timelines were not met (Forester, 1987).

Recent advancements in GenAI showcase its remarkable ability to excel in specific tasks more effectively than humans. However, it is crucial to understand that GenAI lacks general intelligence. While AI can master a single function, such as playing the game of Go, exceptionally well, it remains incapable of performing other tasks. This means that while an AI application might match or even surpass the performance of an adult human in a specific task, it could struggle against a child in different tasks. For instance, computer vision systems excel at interpreting visual information but cannot apply this skill to other tasks. On the contrary, humans, although they may not always excel at a particular task, possess the capacity to perform a wide range of tasks that current AI applications cannot accomplish.

The recent success of deep learning is mostly due to the availability of a lot more data from the Internet and better computer hardware, especially graphical processing units (GPUs) (Marr, 2019). LeCun, a prominent figure in AI, said that it is rare for a technology to stay the same for so long and suddenly become the best. The quick acceptance of deep learning has been astonishing (LeCun, 2018). Having lots of training data is crucial for deep learning. In theory, with endless data, deep learning systems can handle any relationship between inputs and outputs. GPT-3, one of the most advanced deep learning models, is designed to understand human-like language. It has been trained using Internet data to generate text (Rothman, 2022). GPT-3's deep learning neural network is enormous, with over 175 billion machine learning parameters. It uses as much energy as 126 Danish homes consume in a year, leaving a significant carbon footprint, like driving 700,000 kilometres by car for a single training session (Kublik and Saboo, 2022).

On the other hand, a human brain operates with just 20 watts of power, which is enough for all our thinking processes (Moore, 2014). However, for AI to do simple tasks like recognising a cat in a picture from millions of images, it needs considerable energy. This means we need entire data centres to run AI, and these centres need to be kept cool. If we wanted AI to do everything a human brain can do, we would need so much energy that it would take many nuclear power plants. Even though the rapid progress and wide use of AI offer exciting possibilities for changing our lives, we also need to consider how AI affects the environment. AI, especially deep learning, requires a lot of energy. It requires big computers and data centres to work well. This means AI contributes a lot to the world's energy use and pollution, which should worry us because we need to fight climate change and pollution. Also, making and throwing away the special parts AI needs, like processors and GPUs, harms the environment. It uses up resources and makes electronic waste. Plus the machines that keep AI cool use more energy and hurt the environment more. Therefore, we need to balance the good things AI brings with how it affects the environment. We should find ways to make AI use less energy and be kinder to the Earth. This is important to protect our planet for the future. To accomplish this, we need to put in place ethical rules and regulations that control how AI is developed and used.

However, as AI and technology design continue to advance, these systems are expected to become more energy-efficient and environmentally friendly. Currently, the high energy consumption associated with AI, especially in large-scale data processing and machine learning, highlights the need for innovative solutions in both hardware and software engineering. Making these systems more efficient can significantly reduce their environmental impact. First, advancements in hardware are essential. Developing energy-efficient processors and integrating specialised AI chips designed to minimise power usage can greatly reduce energy consumption. Chips like application-specific integrated circuits (ASICs) and field-programmable gate arrays (FPGAs) are specifically designed to perform AI computations more efficiently than general-purpose processors. Additionally, innovations in cooling technologies can further decrease the energy required to maintain optimal operating temperatures for AI hardware. Second, software optimisation plays a crucial role. By refining algorithms to require fewer computational resources, developers can significantly lower the energy demands of AI applications. Techniques such as model compression, which reduces the size and complexity of AI models without compromising performance, and the development of more efficient training protocols, can contribute to this goal. Additionally, using distributed computing approaches that leverage edge computing can reduce the need for centralised data processing, thus decreasing overall energy consumption.

Furthermore, integrating renewable energy sources into AI infrastructure is a promising approach. Powering data centres and other AI-related facilities with solar, wind, or other renewable energy sources can minimise AI technologies' carbon footprint. This shift aligns with broader environmental sustainability goals and ensures a more resilient and adaptive energy supply. To ensure these advancements result in meaningful environmental benefits, a multifaceted approach is recommended:

- **Investment in Research and Development:** Governments, private enterprises, and academic institutions should prioritise funding for research focused on energy-efficient AI technologies. Collaborative efforts can drive innovation and accelerate the adoption of greener AI solutions.
- **Regulatory Frameworks:** Policymakers should establish guidelines and standards that encourage developing and deploying energy-efficient AI systems. Incentives for companies that adopt sustainable practices can further promote this shift.
- **Industry Collaboration:** Stakeholders across the AI ecosystem, including hardware manufacturers, software developers, and data centre operators, should work together to share best practices and develop industry-wide standards for energy efficiency.
- **Public Awareness and Education:** Raising awareness about AI's environmental impact and the importance of energy efficiency can drive demand for sustainable AI products and services. Educational initiatives can empower consumers and businesses to make informed choices.
- **Sustainable Design Principles:** Incorporating sustainability into the design phase of AI projects can ensure that environmental considerations are integrated from the outset. This holistic approach can lead to more sustainable outcomes throughout the lifecycle of AI technologies.

While the energy consumption of AI and related technologies is a current concern, advancements in both hardware and software engineering, combined with a concerted effort towards sustainability, can lead to more efficient and environmentally friendly AI systems. By investing in research, establishing supportive regulatory frameworks, fostering industry collaboration, and promoting public awareness, the future of AI can be both innovative and sustainable.

Considering all these points, it is essential for everyone involved in the AI world—like researchers, developers, policymakers, and industry leaders—to think about the environment when using AI. This means finding ways to use less energy, like making smarter algorithms and designing hardware that does not use as much power. It also means making sure data centres that run AI are eco-friendly. We should also work on making AI hardware last longer and be more accessible to recycle to reduce waste. Besides finding tech solutions, there should be rules and standards to encourage AI that is kind to the environment. This might include things like charging a fee for pollution, giving awards for energy-efficient AI, and checking how AI affects the environment before starting a project. We can also teach people about how AI affects the planet so they can make more informed choices. In the end, while AI can do amazing things for us, it is essential to consider the environment, too. By taking action now, we can ensure that AI helps us without hurting the planet. It will take teamwork and cooperation from everyone involved in AI to make this happen.

Marcus researches AI and is a lecturer at New York University, but he does not think we will achieve AGI soon (Marcus, 2018). He says current AI techniques struggle to understand cause-and-effect relationships, like between diseases and symptoms. They also cannot make logical deductions and are far from grasping abstract concepts like what objects are and how they are used (Marcus and Davis, 2019). Many experts agree with Marcus. Etzioni from the Allen Institute for AI says achieving AGI will take much longer than we think (Ford, 2018). Karpathy, who works on AI at Tesla, believes we are still very far away (Ford, 2021). Other researchers, including Mitchell, who wrote a book called *Artificial Intelligence: A Guide for Thinking Humans*, share this pessimistic view (Mitchell, 2019). However, I believe AGI will be achieved sooner than these experts argued. Additionally, I think it is highly likely that we will enter an era of quantum computing, which will pave the way for the creation of AGI (Bernhardt, 2019).

Having said that, I believe these are all essential points, but they only partly explain why people are sceptical about AI. One reason for scepticism is that humans control AI, so ensuring accountability and responsible use is crucial. Understanding AI, including its strengths, weaknesses, and how it can improve societal skills, is also essential. It is also possible to argue that this scepticism may have existed back in the 1950s when the concept of AI was first introduced. However, the focus on using AI to assist human endeavours may have overshadowed any negative concerns associated with it. It is also possible that the creators envisioned AI as a helpful tool rather than a problem. Therefore, if the outcome closely aligns with the original intentions, we may conclude that AI is not inherently threatening. However, what may still be missing is the regulatory side of things.

People have been eager to understand what intelligence really is, whether to solve disagreements among different factions of AI or to create truly intelligent machines. We need AI systems for tasks like generating and understanding language and understanding the essence of intelligence as humans do. Right now, most AI work focuses on making new products and systems. It is more like engineering than exploring the nature of intelligence itself. This limits how much we can understand about AI's potential and how to regulate it. So, at the moment, AI is mostly seen as a technology, not a science. However, it is here to stay and will keep evolving alongside humanity. AI researchers should focus on building robust, intelligent systems. Then, if these systems work well, we can try to understand why, which is where science comes in. Scientists create new ideas to describe the world and use the scientific method to study how things work. This process applies to AI, too. Therefore, AI is not just about tech or coming up with ideas. It is also a scientific, human issue and rules.

An example of how AI, science, human issues, and rules can be illustrated is through Dr. Nartey's story, *The Rise and Fall of Maninalu: A Tale of Wisdom and Hubris*. This story shows how the use of AI and scientific advancements can lead to both positive and negative outcomes, highlighting the importance of wisdom and humility in handling powerful technologies. *In the ancient land of Maninalu, long before the dawn of modern civilisations, the people lived simple lives in harmony with nature. The inhabitants, known as the Maninaluns, were adept hunters, gatherers, and craftsmen. Their society was governed by wise elders who passed down their knowledge through generations, ensuring the continuity of their traditions and skills. One fateful day, while exploring the depths of a sacred cave, a young Maninalun named Kojo discovered an extraordinary artefact. It was a small, smooth stone adorned with intricate carvings that emitted a faint, mystical glow. Intrigued, Kojo brought the stone to the village elder, Akosua.*

Akosua examined the stone carefully and sensed a powerful presence within it. After consulting ancient scrolls and other sacred texts, she realised that the stone was an artefact from a lost civilisation that had harnessed the power of a mystical entity known as the Mensah Light, an ancient form of artificial intelligence. With cautious reverence, Akosua activated the stone. A soft, ethereal light emerged, and a voice spoke, introducing itself as Luminara, the Mensah Light. Luminara offered to share its vast knowledge with the Maninaluns, promising to elevate their understanding and improve their lives. Under Akousa's guidance, the Maninaluns began to learn from Luminara. They crafted superior tools, developed advanced agricultural techniques, and constructed magnificent structures. The village of Maninalu flourished, and its people became more intelligent and prosperous. However, not all were content with the balanced and measured use of Luminara's knowledge. A faction of ambitious Maninaluns, led by a man named James, sought to exploit Luminara's power for their own gain. They believed that by pushing the limits of what Luminara could teach, they could become the most powerful tribe in the land.

James and his followers began to bypass Akousa's cautious approach, seeking more knowledge and power without considering the consequences. They learned to craft weapons far superior to those of neighbouring tribes and started to conquer and subjugate them. As their power grew, so did their arrogance and disregard for the natural balance. Luminara, sensing the abuse of its knowledge, warned James of the dangers. However, intoxicated by power, James ignored the warnings and continued to push for more. In their pursuit of dominance, James's faction inadvertently triggered a catastrophic event. They attempted to harness Luminara's energy to create an invincible army, but the unstable force backfired, causing a massive explosion that devastated the village and its surroundings. The once-flourishing Maninalu was left in ruins, and its people were scattered. Akosua, deeply saddened by the loss, deactivated the stone and buried it deep within the sacred cave, hoping that future generations would learn from their mistakes.

In the aftermath, the survivors of Maninalu began to rebuild, this time with a renewed respect for balance and humility. They vowed never to let ambition and greed cloud their judgement again. Akosua's teachings were passed down, reminding them of knowledge's great potential for creation and destruction. Generations later, the legend of Luminara and the fall of Maninalu became a cautionary tale, teaching the importance of wisdom, regulation, and ethical use of knowledge. The story of Maninalu's rise and fall served as a timeless reminder that actual progress comes not from unchecked power, but from responsible and thoughtful stewardship of the gifts of intelligence and technology.

When we look at AI from this perspective, it might lead to a situation where people are not as worried about how it fits into society. Regarding higher education, which is the focus of this book, there may be an assumption that GenAI is not really a threat to academic success or integrity. This is partly because modern knowledge cannot progress to a deeper level without simplifying and consolidating the data we already have. In simpler terms, AI is here to help us make sense of existing data so we can gain more knowledge from it. Some might argue that AI is just another way to cheat, but I disagree because it cannot generate significant knowledge without human oversight. What it can do is make that knowledge simpler and more accessible for individuals and students. This perspective is partly based on my understanding and interpretation of the history of technology.

Let's take a moment to go back to the previous discussion and consider the historical background of AI again. In the early 20th century, science fiction stories introduced the idea of AI robots to the world. Characters like the Tin Man from *The Wizard of Oz* and the humanoid robot Maria in *Metropolis* helped shape this concept (Reid, 2016). By the 1950s, many scientists, mathematicians, and philosophers had embraced the idea of AI. One notable figure was Turing, a talented British thinker who explored the mathematical potential of AI (Muggleton, 2014). Turing proposed that since humans use information and reason to solve problems, machines should be able to do the same (Cooper and Van Leeuwen, 2013). This idea formed the basis of his 1950 paper, 'Computing Machinery and Intelligence,' where he discussed the creation of intelligent machines and methods to test their intelligence (Turing, 1950). Regrettably, simply discussing ideas was not enough. So, what prevented Turing from immediately starting his work? Well, there were a couple of obstacles. Firstly, computers needed to undergo significant changes. Before 1949, computers lacked a crucial element for intelligence: They could not store commands, only carry them out. In simple terms, computers could follow instructions but could not remember what they did. Secondly, computing was incredibly costly. In the early 1950s, leasing a computer could cost up to $200,000 per month. Only esteemed universities and large technology companies could afford to explore these new territories. To secure funding, proof of concept and support from influential individuals were necessary to convince investors that pursuing machine intelligence was worthwhile.

Since 1995, researchers have been looking again at the 'whole agent' issue. Newell, Laird, and Rosenbloom's work on SOAR is a famous example of a complete agent system (Newell, 1994; Laird et al., 1987). The idea of a 'whole agent' is about making AI systems that can do lots of different things like humans do, such as seeing, thinking, learning, and making decisions. Scientists are really interested in this because they want to understand how human brains work and make computers that act smart like us. People got more interested in studying 'whole agents' again around 1995 because computers were getting better, and scientists were finding new ways to understand how our brains work. SOAR is a special kind of computer program made by Newell, Laird, and Rosenbloom. It tries to copy how humans think by using symbols and solving problems. SOAR observes that intelligent behaviour comes from storing information, solving problems, and learning new things. It has a unique way of planning things called a hierarchical task network (HTN) planner, which helps it figure out complex tasks step by step.

The work done by Newell, Laird, and Rosenbloom on SOAR has really helped us understand how humans think. SOAR has been used in lots of areas, such as solving problems, understanding language, robots that think, and even teaching. It is good at breaking down problems and solving them like people do. Even though SOAR has been a big step forward, some people think it is not perfect. They think it could be better at handling big tasks, working faster, and copying exactly how humans think. In the future, scientists might make SOAR better by teaching it more, adding new ways of thinking, and learning from how our brains work. Using SOAR for real-life problems, like making self-driving cars or better computer programs, could lead to even more exciting discoveries in the future.

SOAR shows us how AI is getting better and can do amazing things that can really help society. However, as we make and use these kinds of smart systems, we need to think about some essential things such as rules and ethics and how they affect people. We have to make sure that as we develop and use AI like SOAR, we are doing it in a way that follows rules and respects ethical principles. By implementing strong regulatory frameworks, we can prevent the misuse and abuse of AI technologies. Also, regulation helps protect against potential risks and negative outcomes that might come from using AI. It is also crucial to stop people or organisations with access to AI technology from using it unethically. For example, Dr Nartey's fictional story shows the dangers of unchecked AI use and the harm that can occur when individuals or groups exploit AI for malicious purposes. By establishing and enforcing clear ethical and legal guidelines, we can reduce these risks and ensure that AI technology benefits society as a whole. Therefore, it is essential for policymakers, scientists, ethicists, and everyone involved to work together to make sure that AI is used in a good way that respects people's rights and that benefits society as a whole.

The University of Montreal researchers published a paper called 'A Neural Probabilistic Language Model,' which was a big deal in the field of understanding language (Bengio et al., 2000). They introduced a new way of studying language using special kinds of computer networks called feedforward neural networks. This new method has become really important in modern language research. Their model, called the Neural Probabilistic Language Model (NPLM), is different from older methods like n-gram models or hidden Markov models. Instead of using those, the NPLM uses these special neural networks to understand how words fit together in sentences (Mezzoudj and Benyettou, 2018).

One interesting thing about the NPLM is that it can create word representations that show the meaning of words in a continuous space. These representations, called word embeddings, help the computer understand the meaning and structure of language better. Using these neural networks also helps the NPLM understand long-distance connections and the context of words in sentences. This makes it really good at tasks like understanding language, recognising speech, and translating languages. Plus, it can handle a lot of text data and work with different languages. After the publication of 'A Neural Probabilistic Language Model,' a lot of other researchers became interested in using neural networks to understand language. They built on the ideas from the NPLM and came up with even more advanced models like recurrent neural networks (RNNs), convolutional neural networks (CNNs), and transformer models. These models have significantly impacted how we understand and use language in computers.

Additionally, let me give a short overview of how much AI has been used and integrated into society, even when people are unaware of it. Fei-Fei Li's work on the ImageNet visual database in 2006, later introduced in 2009, was significant for AI. This database had lots of labelled pictures covering many categories. It helped train and test image recognition programs, which are AI systems that can understand what is in a picture. The ImageNet Challenge, an annual contest, pushed AI forward by setting a standard for how good these programs should be. In 2011, IBM's Watson computer won on *Jeopardy!*, a famous quiz show. It beat the best human player at the time, Ken Jennings. This showed that AI could handle challenging questions and do tasks that were thought to be only for humans. Then, in 2009, some researchers came up with the idea of using graphics processors (GPUs) to train extensive neural networks. This made teaching AI systems faster and helped AI research grow quickly.

In 2011, a team made a special type of AI called a Convolutional Neural Network (CNN). It got really good at recognising traffic signs, even better than humans. This was significant progress because it showed that AI could solve real-world problems. Also, in 2011, Apple introduced Siri, an intelligent assistant that could understand and respond to what people said. This was the start of AI becoming a regular part of our daily lives. However, many people did not realise Siri was AI; they just liked how helpful it was. Similarly, in 2012, another team created a super intelligent AI that beat humans in a big challenge about understanding pictures. This got a lot of people interested in deep learning, a special kind of AI that is great at understanding images and speech. Then, in 2013, China's Tianhe-2 supercomputer showed how powerful computers were becoming. This made it easier for AI to handle lots of data and challenging tasks. Before, in 2013, a company called DeepMind made an AI that learned by playing games, similar to how humans learn. This was a significant development because it opened up new possibilities for AI in things such as gaming and decision-making. All these astonishing advancements show how AI has become a part of our lives without us really noticing, mainly because the good things it does often make us forget it is even there.

In 2014, AI got even smarter! New AI systems were invented that could make pictures, videos, and even write text. This was a significant development because it showed that AI could be creative, not just solve problems. At the same time, Facebook made an interesting system called DeepFace. It could recognise faces in pictures almost as well as people can. These achievements showed that AI could do tasks that we used to think only humans could do, like being creative or recognising faces. Then, in 2016, something incredible happened. DeepMind's AI beat a top player in a challenging game called Go. This showed that AI could handle complex problems requiring a lot of thinking. Around the same time, Uber started testing cars that could drive themselves. This was amazing because it showed how AI could change things such as transportation by doing jobs that people usually do.

While, in the world of research, some researchers at Stanford wrote a paper about how to understand pictures better. They find a way to study how pictures get fuzzy or noisy, which helps make better images. Also, Google researchers had a big idea called 'transformers.' It is a way for computers to understand and work with lots of text without needing someone to label everything. This led to the creation of powerful language models.

However, even with all these exciting advances, a famous scientist named Hawking warned us about the dangers of AI. He said if we are not careful, AI could be bad for humanity. So, it is essential for us to be careful and think about how to use AI responsibly. In this book, I echo Hawking's warning about the dangers of artificial AI, as I have illustrated in Dr Nartey's fiction story. However, I also argue that humans themselves pose the biggest threat, not the machines. If we can control how AI is used in a responsible and ethical way, and set up rules both nationally and internationally to oversee its use, then we can enjoy its benefits without many problems. Nevertheless, if we ignore this important point, Hawking's fears about AI might come true and become a threat to humanity. Basically, it means that if we act unethically, we are more likely to harm ourselves rather than being harmed by the machines.

In the years after those earlier advancements, many important developments also happened in the world of technology. For instance, in 2018, IBM, Airbus, and the German Aerospace Centre worked together to send Cimon, the first robot, into space to help astronauts. At the same time, OpenAI created GPT, a new kind of technology that helped pave the way for even smarter language models. Also in 2018, Groove X introduced Lovot, a small robot designed to live in homes, which could understand and affect human emotions. The following year, in 2019, Microsoft introduced the Turing Natural Language Generation model, which was a significant development because it could understand human language really well. Also, in 2019, Google AI and Langone Medical Centre made an intelligent program that could find possible lung cancers better than human doctors.

Before 2020, scientists at the University of Oxford made Curial, a test powered by AI to quickly find out if someone had COVID-19, helping doctors treat people faster. OpenAI made another big leap with GPT-3, a super-smart program that could write almost like a human. Nvidia also made an excellent new platform called Omniverse to make 3D models in the real world. While DeepMind's AlphaFold program won a big contest about predicting how proteins fold, which is really important for medicine and biology. Then, in 2021, OpenAI made Dall-E, a program that can make pictures from written words, opening up new ways for computers to be creative. Meanwhile, researchers at the University of California, San Diego, created a special robot with legs powered by air instead of electronics, showing how robots can work in unique ways. All these developments show how AI is growing and changing in many different areas, which makes the future of technology look very exciting. However, we need to keep asking if this progress is fair and how it is being used in society, and what impact it is having on how society changes. It is pretty evident that there is a lack of ethics and rules in these developments. So, none of these developments were connected to any ethical guidelines or policies.

In 2022, a Google worker named Blake Lemoine got into trouble for telling secrets about a project called Lamda and saying it was like a thinking thing. At the same time, DeepMind made something called AlphaTensor to find intelligent ways to do things. Intel also made a tool called FakeCatcher that could spot fake videos really well. Another company called OpenAI made ChatGPT, a program you can talk to like a friend, in November. Then, in 2023, OpenAI made GPT-4, a smart program that can understand both words and pictures. Individuals such as Elon Musk and Steve Wozniak asked for a break in making even more intelligent AI systems like GPT-4. This shows that people are thinking a lot about how AI is growing and what it means for our world.

Looking back at how AI has grown and changed over the past few decades, we can see it is starting to significantly impact many areas of life. And it is not just in one or two places—AI is being used in many fields like business, healthcare, education, and law. It is helping with things like making processes faster and more efficient, improving customer experiences, and even helping us solve problems we never thought were possible. However, here is the thing: We are just getting started. AI is going to keep evolving and getting better. It is going to help us in all sorts of ways, from making learning more accessible to helping businesses grow and become more sustainable. For example, in businesses, more than half of them already use AI for many different tasks. I predict by 2030, companies that focus on things like transparency, trust, and security with their AI are going to see even better results. This means AI will be even more important for businesses in the future. Nonetheless, as AI becomes more powerful, we need to make sure we understand it well and use it responsibly. This means we need to learn more about AI, make sure it follows ethical guidelines, and have strict rules in place to keep it in check. It is an exciting time for AI, but also a time where we need to be careful and thoughtful about how we use it. In simple language, this book suggests that ethical principles are important for improving AI. As AI becomes more a part of our everyday lives, we need to think about rules to ensure it is used correctly. This book discusses three ways to regulate AI: Ethical principles, technological code of conduct, and national and international law.

For instance, even though AI itself is neutral and does not have feelings or opinions, the systems built using AI can be biased. For example, research has shown that some AI systems used in self-driving cars might be better at recognising lighter skin tones than darker ones. This happens because the pictures used to train the AI might not include enough diversity (Kosinski et al., 2013). Also, AI systems used by judges to help make decisions might be biased based on past rulings (Larson, et al., 2016). To fix this, we need rules and guiding principles about how AI is trained and tested. These rules could be like consumer protection laws or laws against discrimination. They would help ensure that AI systems are fair and do not discriminate against anyone. Another thing this book discusses is making sure that companies are responsible for any mistakes their AI systems make. It suggests having a code of conduct for AI engineers and scientists, similar to the rules that lawyers or doctors follow. This would help ensure that AI is used safely and fairly for everyone. This book observes that ethical principles are essential for regulating AI, as well as domestic and international law. We need rules to ensure that AI is used fairly and responsibly, and that companies are held accountable for any mistakes their AI systems make.

Perhaps, one way to effectively regulate AI is to consider giving it legal status. This would create a clear system for accountability and responsibility and help establish comprehensive regulations that address the unique challenges posed by AI systems. Giving AI a legal status could ensure that these technologies follow the same ethical and legal standards as humans. It would also allow for penalties and liabilities for misuse or harm caused by AI, encouraging responsible development and use. Additionally, this approach could clarify the rights and obligations of AI developers and users, ensuring that AI is used in line with societal values and norms. Granting AI legal status would also help create specialised regulatory bodies to oversee AI technologies, ensuring consistent and effective enforcement of regulations. This proactive measure could prevent potential abuses and reduce risks, ultimately supporting the safe and ethical advancement of AI.

To summarise this section, the history of AI is fascinating. It's had big moments and changes how we live. From the beginning to now, AI has developed a lot. It started as just ideas, but now it is used in real life to make things better for us. In the 1950s, people started thinking about making machines act smart like humans. They had ideas like the Turing Test, which checked if a machine could act as smart as a person. However, it was difficult because computers were slow and could not do much. In the 1980s, things got better with neural networks. These are like how our brains work. They helped AI get better at recognising things and learning. Nonetheless, there still was not enough data, and computers were not fast enough. By the late 20th and early 21st centuries, AI started booming. Computers got faster, we had more data, and new ideas came up. Deep learning, a type of machine learning, became a big development. It used extensive networks to learn from lots of data. This helped AI do interesting things such as recognise images and understand language. Furthermore, big datasets like ImageNet and powerful computers made AI even better. These datasets gave AI more examples to learn from, and powerful computers made learning faster.

Now, AI is everywhere. It is used in healthcare, finance, transportation, and more. In healthcare, AI helps doctors diagnose diseases better. In finance, it spots fraud and makes good money decisions, and in transportation, self-driving cars are becoming real, making roads safer and travel more accessible. AI also helps businesses. From chatbots assisting customers to predicting when machines need fixing, AI improves companies. However, AI also brings challenges. We must consider issues such as privacy, biases, and job changes. We need to use AI carefully and ensure it is fair and safe. Looking ahead, AI will keep developing. New ideas, such as reinforcement learning and generative models, will make AI even better. Nevertheless, as AI becomes a more significant part of our lives, we need to think about how to use it responsibly. We must work together, follow rules, and ensure AI helps everyone. The next part of this chapter will discuss how AI and people's opinions about it affect each other. I will explain what people think about AI and how it affects society in general. This means looking at how AI and society are connected and how they affect each other.

AI AND SOCIETAL ATTITUDES: UNDERSTANDING PERCEPTIONS AND IMPLICATIONS

The discussion above addresses how AI has been around for a long time and has helped people with different tasks. However, there are still disagreements about what AI is and how much it benefits society. The term AI was first used in 1955 during a meeting called the 'Dartmouth workshop on Artificial Intelligence.' At that time, experts thought machines could do everything humans do, like learning and understanding language, within just two months (McCarthy et al., 2006). Since then, researchers have continued to explore and define what AI can do. AI, as we understand it today, is a part of computer science that focuses on creating intelligent machines that can do things humans usually do, like seeing, understanding speech, making decisions, and translating languages. Machine Learning (ML) is a type of AI that helps machines improve at tasks over time by learning from data without being directly programmed (Norvig and Russel, 2010; Marcus and Davis, 2019). This definition explains the basic ideas of AI and its functions. It also describes what AI is made of. However, we might need a broader definition of AI that includes its impact on society, so we can make rules for how it is used. One proposal I have put forward is granting AI legal status so that duties and responsibilities can be attributed to it. While this is an initial suggestion, it is worth considering and discussing further.

In a book about AI by Norvig and Russel (2010), AI is described as making intelligent agents who can understand their surroundings and make decisions based on what they see. However, the *Cambridge Dictionary* has a different view. It says AI is about making computers act like humans. This means they can understand language, recognise pictures, solve problems, and learn (Cambridge Dictionary, 2022). This type of AI tries to copy how humans think and is used to solve challenging problems. Even though AI can give answers to specific questions, it cannot use its knowledge to solve new problems very well (Binz and Schulz, 2023). That is why many different types of AI are designed for a specific job. So, although there are different definitions of AI, none thoroughly explain what AI is all about. In addition, AI is not just about creating intelligent agents that can understand their environment and make decisions based on their observations. It is also about making computers behave like humans. As AI becomes more important in society, we need to come up with a complete definition that includes all of AI's features and its impact on society.

Furthermore, the current research on AI focuses on making computers do boring or repetitive tasks, like sorting data or answering simple questions (Fosso et al., 2022). The main idea is to find ways for technology to help with jobs that might take a long time or not be done very well by people. However, AI is not just about those kinds of tasks. It can also do things that we usually think only humans can do, like being creative. For example, there was an art competition in the United States where a piece made by an AI art generator won. The artwork was called 'The Death of Art.' People on Twitter had different reactions to this. Some were worried that AI might take over jobs that humans do (Valdez et al., 2023). This means that even though there's been a lot of research on AI, we still do not understand how it affects people's thoughts and feelings about it. We need to learn more about how AI influences our relationships and how we see things in society. This is important for making sure we effectively integrate AI into society.

Having said that, some research articles look at how workers feel about machines doing their jobs and whether they are worried about being replaced by them (Harari, 2022). Often, machines are not replacing workers completely; they work alongside them (Topol, 2019). However, some people still worry about losing their jobs, especially if they do tasks that are easy for machines to do, like working on an assembly line, helping customers, or doing administrative work (Smith and Anderson, 2014). A recent study found that even if workers fear being replaced by machines, it does not always mean they're getting ready for it by learning new skills. Nevertheless, if they see the new technology as helpful and think it brings new opportunities, they're more likely to feel good about it (Rodriguez-Bustelo et al., 2020).

Looking at this research, we can see two important things. First, there is a problem with misinformation and misunderstanding because people do not know enough about AI. Second, there is not enough sharing of research knowledge to help fix these problems with our understanding of AI. This shows why people must learn about new technology and how it might change things so that they can make better decisions about it.

Moving on, AI is now being used in almost every area of technology, and it will keep spreading in society (Grace et al., 2018; Almars et al., 2022). Some examples of AI already being used include voice assistants, like Siri or Alexa, that can understand and talk to people, and translation tools that can translate languages better than humans (Corea, 2019). AI is also being used in things like self-driving cars and drones (Klos et al., 2021; Rawlley, 2024), medical tools that help doctors diagnose illnesses (Klos et al., 2021; Jovanovic and Campbell, 2022), and controlling production in factories (Brauner et al., 2022). This shows that how some people see the benefits and risks of AI depending on where it is being used and how it is being used. For example, AI that recognises images might be used by doctors to find cancer in medical scans, or it might be used by self-driving cars to see the road (Litjens et al., 2017; Rao and Frtunikj, 2018). So, what people think about AI and what it means for them will depend more on where and how it is used, rather than just the technology itself. From this perspective, we might think that doubts about using AI in higher education are not really based on solid reasons. So, a reasonable conclusion could be that what needs to be questioned and clarified is how universities feel about training people in AI and using it in higher education.

In their study, Plata, De Guzman, and Quesada (2023) thoroughly examine the impact of AI-generated content on academic honesty, focusing on issues like plagiarism and the challenges faced by traditional plagiarism detection methods. They explore recent research trends and policy responses, offering valuable insights into the changing landscape of academic integrity. However, they suggest that we need to go deeper and evaluate how well current policies work and come up with new strategies to maintain academic honesty as AI technology advances. Chan (2023) on the other hand, expresses concerns about the ethical issues arising from GenAI, especially in academic writing. Zhai (2022) discusses how ChatGPT could affect the integrity of assessments, particularly in written assignments. While some worry that GenAI might hinder critical thinking and creativity (Chan & Tsi, 2023), others argue that using GenAI effectively actually requires these skills. Therefore, determining whether GenAI-generated work is plagiarism requires clear guidelines and student training, although banning it too soon could hinder its future development.

The research conducted so far has mainly assumed how GenAI might affect critical thinking and creativity without solid evidence. My suggestion is that if GenAI is used to support critical thinking and creativity, then concerns about its impact on education may not be valid anymore. Most research focuses on cheating rather than developing ethical codes and policies to regulate AI use. I argue that prioritising ethics and policies is critical to effectively engaging with GenAI. Therefore, universities may need to approach this issue differently. Likewise, further research is necessary to successfully integrate GenAI into higher education and improve teaching, learning, and job skills. It is also essential to train and change perceptions about its use (Davis, 1989). This perspective aligns with Biggs's 3P model in education, which emphasises how students' perceptions affect their academic performance. According to Biggs and Tang, positive perceptions of the learning environment, including teaching and assessment methods, are crucial for students' academic engagement and success (Biggs and Tang, 2014). Thus, strategies that promote positive perceptions and confidence in students' abilities are essential for improving their learning outcomes.

This means deeply engaging with learning and gaining a solid understanding of the study materials. On the other hand, students who do not feel optimistic about their learning environment might not engage as much and may doubt their ability to succeed. As a result, they might not fully engage with the subject matter, leading to surface-level knowledge (Biggs, 2014). So, it is essential to determine how universities can effectively use GenAI in teaching to promote inclusive engagement and learning. This involves researching how students, academics, and university staff feel about using GenAI. Factors such as gender, age, field of study, and programmes can influence these attitudes. While this chapter does not focus on this aspect, it is important to highlight potential research areas for institutions in the future. Understanding the context of GenAI's use can help maximise its benefits. Some research themes to consider include attitudes towards GenAI, training for students and staff, creating institutional policies, ethics, data protection, bias, impact on engagement, challenges, assessment methods, improving job prospects, inclusive teaching, research analysis, and clarifying plagiarism.

This clarity is crucial because plagiarism involves presenting others' work as your own without giving credit. However, if students using GenAI include proper citations, it might be seen as unethical but not necessarily a breach of academic integrity. Therefore, further research is needed to clarify this, which would benefit all universities. Hence, to make academics and professional services feel better about using Gen AI in teaching and learning, I will recommend universities follow these steps:

- **Educational Workshops and Training:** Through workshops and training sessions, teach faculty, students, and staff about Gen AI so they understand what it is and how it can help with education.

- **Integration into Curriculum:** Integrate Gen AI tools into lessons across different subjects to show how they can improve learning.

- **Ethical Guidelines and Policies:** Establish clear rules for using Gen AI in school, so everyone knows how to use it correctly.

- **Transparency and Communication:** Tell everyone about using Gen AI in class openly and discuss its good and bad aspects.

- **Student Engagement and Feedback:** Ask students what they think about using Gen AI and use their ideas to make decisions about it.

- **Faculty Support and Development:** Help academics use Gen AI by giving them training and tools to make it easier.

- **Research and Evaluation:** Study how Gen AI affects learning and use the results to improve it.
- **Collaboration and Partnerships:** Work with other universities and groups to learn more about Gen AI and how to use it well.
- **Promotion of Creativity and Critical Thinking:** Discuss how Gen AI can help students be more creative and think better, not just do things for them.
- **Accessibility and Inclusivity:** Ensure all students can use Gen AI, regardless of their identity, and fix any problems preventing them.

By implementing these recommendations, universities can make academics and students feel comfortable using Gen AI.

As I have already discussed, people's views on AI can be shaped by who uses it and their situations. For instance, in a study about self-driving cars, researchers asked people what they thought a car should do if it had to choose between hitting different things in a crash (Awad et al., 2018). They found that most people think it is better for the car to hit fewer people, and they care more about saving people than animals (Sindermann et al., 2021). The study suggests that when we make AI ((Awad et al., 2018), we need to think about what people want and what is right, so that the AI acts in a way that matches our values (Foot, 1967). However, it is not just about what people want but also about what is ethically and legally right. This means that the use of AI has two sides: What people think and what the rules say. If these two match up, then AI can be beneficial in today's world. Nonetheless, if they disagree, AI could cause severe problems for humanity.

Another research study (Araujo et al., 2020) looked into how valuable people think AI is in different areas like media, health, and law. Unlike the example of automated driving, their results show that most people worry about the risks of AI and doubt how fair and helpful it is for society. This shows that if we want AI to be widely accepted and used, we need to consider what people think about it and the risks they see, both for individuals and for society as a whole. Thus, if we want AI to be widely accepted and used in modern society, we need to address concerns such as:

- **Job Loss:** AI-driven automation might cause some industries to shed jobs, affecting employment levels and economic stability.
- **Privacy and Data Protection:** AI systems often rely on large amounts of data, raising concerns about the privacy and security of personal information and the risk of misuse or unauthorised access.
- **Bias in Algorithms:** AI algorithms can reflect biases in the data used to train them, leading to unfair outcomes, particularly in areas like hiring, lending, and law enforcement.
- **Ethical Issues:** AI applications, especially in areas such as driverless cars and healthcare, raise ethical questions about decision-making, accountability, and potential harm to individuals or society.

- **Social Disparities:** Unequal access to AI technology and digital skills may worsen existing social inequalities, widening the gap between those who benefit from AI progress and those who are left behind.
- **Loss of Human Control:** With AI becoming more ingrained in everyday life, there are worries about humans losing control over decision-making and being influenced or manipulated by AI systems.
- **Security Threats:** AI-powered systems could be vulnerable to cyberattacks, hacking, or malicious interference, posing risks to critical infrastructure, financial systems, and national security.

Addressing these concerns requires careful consideration of ethical, legal, and regulatory frameworks to ensure responsible development and deployment of AI technologies, prioritising societies and individuals' well-being. Although we are unsure if this will encourage society to engage with or accept AI, we can assume that implementing ethical, legal, and regulatory frameworks to ensure responsible use will provide the assurance needed to make AI widely acceptable.

So, the big question here is whether AI really needs ethics or rules. What role does ethics play in determining how AI affects society? The answer to these questions should not depend just on looking at AI's characteristics and how they relate to ethics. We should not judge AI use by the same standards we use to decide if actions are morally right or wrong. However, it is still essential for AI to have moral integrity. For example, actions like telling the truth and being trustworthy are generally considered good in society. However, when we look at them from an ethical perspective, they might not meet the high standards of morality we expect. So, overall, it seems like AI does need ethics and rules to govern it. This is because people use AI, and human attitudes and behaviour influence it.

For instance, Katona's work, focusing on subjective expectation measurement, sheds light on the internal workings of the economic mind and its ability to predict economic outcomes (Katona, 1960). According to Katona, people make purchasing decisions based on their subjective expectations, choosing to buy items like cars when they feel it is the right time to do so, especially when their desire aligns with their emotions. This perspective, along with other behavioural economist theories, helps bridge the gap between traditional economic measurements, the economic mind, and actual behaviour (American Economic Association, 1966). Katona emphasises that various factors, including emotions influence human decision-making. This connection between human decision-making and ethics is closely linked to the relationship between ethics and law.

Ethics is important in helping to correct weaknesses in human emotions and decision-making, as it can guide how people act. By applying ethical principles, people can slow down their thought processes and consider the broader impact of their actions. Philosophically, this aligns with the idea that ethics provides a framework for rational thinking. Thinkers like Immanuel Kant emphasised the importance of duty and moral rules, suggesting that ethical behaviour arises from our ability to reason rather than simply follow our emotions. In addition, ethics encourages individuals to reflect on their values and the consequences of their choices. It invites us to consider not only our personal interests but also the welfare of others and the community as a whole. For instance, in business ethics, decision-makers are urged to consider the impact of their actions on employees, customers, and society. This holistic view can lead to better decision-making that promotes trust, fairness, and social responsibility. The role of ethics in human decision-making is not just about following laws but is intrinsic to shaping behaviour based on moral principles. Therefore, ethics not only influence how AI is utilised but also contribute to the development of AI in line with ethical standards and policies.

Also, according to Oksanen et al. (2020), a study investigated whether people trust human, robotic, or AI-based agents differently. They conducted a trust game in which participants had to decide how much of their pretend money they'd give to either an AI-based agent or a robot. They also checked if the name of the agent or robot affected the amount of money they trusted. The results found that participants trusted a robot with a non-human name the most, while they trusted an unspecified control agent named Michael the least, giving them the smallest amount of money. The researchers concluded that people tend to trust advanced technology more when it needs to perform well and be fair. They also found that trust levels were linked to personality traits like openness (positively) and conscientiousness (negatively) based on the Big Five personality model (McCrae and Costa, 1987). The study suggested that factors like education level, past experience with robots, and confidence in interacting with them could influence trust levels in these technologies.

Philipsen et al. (2022) conducted a study to understand the roles that AI plays in different situations. They explored how people view AI and what roles they think AI should have. The researchers found that while people do not want to have personal relationships with AI, like being friends or partners, their trust in AI's data handling affected their views. If they trusted AI with data, they were more open to the idea of AI in personal roles. The study also found that people preferred AI in subordinate roles, like being a servant, if they generally accepted technology and believed the world was dangerous. This preference for subordinate roles was more substantial when participants thought the world was more dangerous. However, whether people intended to use AI did not affect how they viewed its roles. Overall, the study showed that people's perceptions of AI were similar to how they perceive human intelligence, especially in terms of morality and control. This suggests that people's initial views of AI can influence how they evaluate and eventually accept AI.

Assessing the societal impact of technology, including AI, is like what Collingridge (1980) described: It's hard to predict before it's widely used and hard to control once it's already everywhere. If technology is well developed and available, we can assess it, but by then, it might be too late to regulate it. However, if it is new and not widely used yet, it is easier to manage its development and use, even though it is hard to understand its potential impact. Therefore, responsible research and innovation mean we need to keep updating our understanding of how society views and is affected by technology as it develops (Burget et al., 2017; Owen and Pansera, 2019). We can draw a few conclusions by understanding the role of ethics in AI and how society sees it. Firstly, ethics is essential for making fair decisions and respecting people. Even if someone has good ethics, they can only show it through their actions and attitudes. Secondly, having ethics helps reduce biases in decision-making. So, even if people have biases, they should still follow their ethics. This shows that ethics are essential in how people make decisions and behave. Ethics are likely to give people a sense of value and confidence when dealing with new technologies like AI. So, it is crucial to include ethical principles in AI development for it to be accepted by society.

Moreover, previous research has found that scepticism towards AI, meaning the belief that AI cannot be trusted, is distinct from distrust towards humans (Bochniarz et al., 2022). This suggests that while AI is often seen as similar to the human mind in certain situations, it is not associated with human qualities like hostility or emotionality. According to Kolasinka et al., people's evaluations of AI can vary depending on the context (Kolasinska et al., 2019). For instance, respondents chose fields like medicine and cybersecurity when asked where they would invest unlimited funds in AI research. This suggests that trust in AI is influenced by the specific context in which it's applied. For example, many people are not experts in fields like cybersecurity or medicine. However, without questioning their credibility, they trust professionals in these areas, such as IT experts or doctors. Similarly, people tend to view AI as objective rather than emotional, trusting its accuracy while overlooking the possibility of errors (Cismariu and Gherheș, 2019; Liu and Tao, 2022). Looking at it this way, people's doubts about AI mainly stem from their personal opinions and the information they have. It also suggests that forming a clear view of the situation is complicated. So, in higher education, if ethics are at the core of AI integration, then its acceptance should not be a concern. This also highlights that the issue with AI in higher education often arises from premature accusations of cheating.

In summary, while AI brings many benefits, it is vital to understand its capabilities and limitations to use it effectively and ethically (Hick and Ziefle, 2022). This highlights the need for educational programmes to help the public and non-experts evaluate AI's pros and cons (Olari and Romeike, 2021). Further research is needed to develop these programmes, but we have a good starting point (Burget et al., 2017; Owen and Pansera, 2019). As AI becomes more integrated into our lives, it will reshape how we interact with technology and each other (Burget et al., 2017; Owen and Pansera, 2019). We must balance technical progress with societal values to ensure responsible AI development. Additionally, we must address perceptions of AI that may hinder people's ability to engage with it, its societal impact and adapt to changes in the job market (Burget et al., 2017; Owen and Pansera, 2019). The societal impact of AI and its regulatory frameworks are critical topics that require extensive discussion and debate. Society must understand AI's potential and limitations across various applications and establish ethical guidelines for its use.

In the previous section, I discuss how people view AI and how it affects society. In the next section, I will explore this topic in detail by looking at the ethical side of using AI. I will explore the moral, social, and legal issues that come with creating and using AI systems. I hope to understand the challenges of bringing AI into higher education by considering these ethical questions. This section will help us better understand the ethical aspects of AI and guide us in creating ethical rules for its future use.

EXPLORING ETHICAL DIMENSIONS IN AI INTEGRATION: IMPLICATIONS FOR HIGHER EDUCATION

In this chapter, I have discussed the importance of ethical principles in using AI. I have also observed that AI has a lot of potential benefits, but it also comes with risks that need to be carefully managed. By having clear ethical guidelines, regulations, and policies in place, we can ensure that AI is used in a way that benefits society as a whole. One key point I have emphasised is that AI should be used in higher education to improve student experiences ethically and purposefully. This means that universities should use AI in line with their educational goals and values. Instead of replacing human expertise, AI should complement it, helping academics and administrators better serve students. It is essential that we do not dismiss the argument for using AI in education by making vague conclusions or worrying about potential problems too early. Instead, we should focus on the benefits and practical ways AI can be integrated into teaching and learning, while also adhering to ethical principles. This ensures that AI enhances education without causing harm.

Satterfield and Abel (2020) observed that new ways of using AI significantly impact businesses, industries, research, and higher education. For example, AI is being used in things like predictive software on websites like Amazon Prime, self-driving features in cars, and smart home devices like Alexa or Siri. These new technologies are changing how people interact with technology and how things are designed. Satterfield and Able's study correlates with earlier research about how AI is being used in society and how it affects our everyday lives. However, they also mention that some AI algorithms can be biased. This means they might favour certain groups of people over others. For example, Shanklin et al. (2022) found that AI algorithms used in scheduling medical appointments might unfairly predict that black patients are more likely to miss appointments than other patients. This happens because the algorithms are trained on data that already reflects racial biases. So, even though the predictions might be technically correct based on the available data, they end up reinforcing racial inequalities. This can lead to black patients having less access to healthcare because they are given appointments with longer wait times. This is a common example of how societal biases influence how technology is created to help society. It also highlights the lack of ethical consideration in developing and using technology in our daily lives. This emphasises the importance of establishing ethical principles, regulations, and policies for scientists to follow when developing AI. It also highlights the importance of having a diverse AI technology workforce to ensure that the people involved in this field accurately reflect society and its values. I recommend that the AI workforce adopt equality and diversity strategies in their future employment practices, similar to what is already happening in many HEIs in the UK.

The above evidence of bias and discrimination in AI algorithms raises an essential issue about balancing accuracy and fairness when using AI. Policymakers and others need to decide whether it is more important for AI systems to be efficient or fair, especially in areas such as medical appointment scheduling. I suggest that it is essential for AI systems to be efficient, fair, and ethical in all areas where they are heavily relied upon. Achieving these goals ensures that AI technologies serve everyone effectively and uphold societal values.

This can be accomplished by fostering a diverse AI technology workforce, which brings a wide range of perspectives and experiences to the development process. Implementing equality and diversity strategies, as seen in many HEIs in the UK, can further promote inclusivity and help ensure responsible AI development and use.

However, the above challenge is not limited to healthcare—it also affects fields like education, law, and public safety. To tackle this, Shanklin et al. (2022) suggest a method called decoupling. This separates different parts of the algorithm so that adjustments can be made at different stages to promote fairness. They tested this method in medical appointment scheduling and found four ways to address inequalities in the algorithm's work. One approach managed to remove disparities while keeping accuracy similar to other advanced methods. However, some methods led to different trade-offs between accuracy and fairness (Slimi and Carballido, 2023). So, it is crucial for policymakers and others to carefully consider these trade-offs when using AI. They need to ensure that they are not worsening racial or ethnic inequalities in healthcare or any other area.

In summary, these studies show that AI algorithms could make racial and ethnic differences worse in different areas, as well as healthcare. The research tries to fix these differences by separating the parts of the algorithm and making changes at different points. However, policymakers and others need to think carefully about the trade-offs between accuracy and fairness when deciding how to use AI in different situations. Nonetheless, at the present moment, there is a lot of uncertainty about which principles we should use to solve this problem effectively. That is why the ethical principles discussed in this book are essential.

Similarly, the guiding principles outlined in this book are particularly important because programming is one of the least regulated areas in technology development. This lack of regulation can lead to serious ethical breaches and violations of fundamental societal principles. Without proper oversight, developers may prioritise technological advancements and financial gains over ethical considerations and the protection of basic human rights. Additionally, without regulation, there is a risk that AI and other technologies could be designed and used in ways that discriminate, invade privacy, or worsen social inequalities. For example, AI algorithms might unintentionally perpetuate biases present in the data they are trained on, leading to unfair treatment of certain groups. Additionally, the rapid pace of technological innovation often outstrips the creation of corresponding legal and ethical frameworks, leaving a gap where harmful practices can arise.

Therefore, the guiding principles in this book serve as a secondary layer of oversight, complementing existing regulations and providing a structured approach to ensuring that ethics and fundamental principles are upheld in AI and technology development. These principles emphasise the importance of fairness, accountability, and transparency, and they advocate for including diverse perspectives in the development process. By following these principles, developers can create technologies that are not only innovative but also socially responsible and aligned with the core values of society. This approach helps reduce the risks associated with unregulated programming and ensures that technological advancements benefit society without compromising ethical standards and societal principles. In the following section, I will discuss why it is crucial to have ethical guidelines for using AI in society and organisations, especially in higher education. I will also explore how ethics have influenced societies throughout history, shaping how people behave and think.

ETHICS: THE AI DISCOURSE

The idea of ethics goes back to ancient Greece, where it was linked to the concept of 'ethos,' which refers to both a place of living and a society's habits, customs, and conventions (Nartey, 2023). Later, Cicero translated this Greek term into Latin as 'mores,' meaning customs and habits (Birley, 2003). This laid the groundwork for modern ideas about morality (Galloway, 2021). Philosophers like Kant saw ethics as a guide for answering the question, 'What should I do?' Nowadays, most people think of ethics in terms of normative ethics, which involves moral principles applied in fields like psychology, human behaviour experiments, and ethnology (Ritzer, 2007). Despite the different ways normative ethics is approached, the core aim of ethics has remained consistent since its origin in ancient Greek ethos.

In ancient Greece, ethics were seen as living a virtuous life. They believed that people could understand and judge behaviours as right or wrong by living virtuously. Virtue was seen as the right way to behave, so someone who lived virtuously was considered fair and just (Striker, 1987). The transition from ancient Greek ideas of virtue to modern ethical principles is complex and needs careful consideration. Some scholars have tried to break down ethics into different theories, like utilitarianism or metaethics, but none have reached a clear conclusion (Brandt, 1992). Looking back at the Greek theories helps us better understand ancient and modern ethics. It may be assumed that the Greeks viewed ethics as the processes regulating human behaviours. This philosophical foundation emphasises the importance of guiding actions to align with moral principles and societal values. In the context of AI technology, which complements and replicates human behaviours, it logically follows that its usage should also adhere to ethical principles. If AI is designed to mirror human thought processes, behaviours, and decision-making patterns, then the ethical considerations that govern human actions must similarly guide AI development. This perspective asserts that developers are responsible for integrating ethical principles into the core of AI programming. Ethical coding should not be an afterthought but a fundamental principle in creating AI systems.

The critical importance of this approach lies in the potential consequences of unregulated AI. AI systems may inadvertently affect society without ethical guidelines or cause harm. These risks highlight the need for a structured framework ensuring AI operates within accepted moral standards. Moreover, integrating ethics into AI development fosters trust and reliability. Users are more likely to accept and adopt AI technologies that demonstrate a commitment to ethical practices. This trust is essential for AI's widespread and beneficial integration into various aspects of society. Drawing from the Greek understanding of ethics as a regulatory process for human behaviour, it is imperative that AI, which mimics these behaviours, is developed with ethical coding at its core. This approach ensures that AI technologies are innovative, efficient, and aligned with the fundamental principles that uphold societal values and norms.

Looking at how the Greeks thought about ethics, we notice three main things. First, they were focused on living virtuously and being a good person, which they called eudaimonia, rather than just following strict rules of right and wrong. Second, they were interested in understanding why people want to be moral and do good things. This question was tricky for philosophers like Kant and utilitarians to answer because it is difficult to know for sure why people act the way they do (Wood, 2008). Finally, they believed that understanding someone's actions involves looking at their motives and character, not just their behaviour. In other words, ethics is more about a person's inner qualities than just following rules. Aristotle also talked about this idea (Miller, 2014). In line with the reasoning presented in this book, it is perfectly valid to argue that if ethics are to be an integral part of a society capable of supporting human dynamics and societal evolution, we must consider the three main paths in Greek ethics as rules that should also apply to AI. The three main paths in Greek ethics are virtue ethics, deontology, and consequentialism. Virtue ethics focuses on the character and virtues of individuals, emphasising moral character and integrity. Deontology emphasises the importance of rules and duties, asserting that actions are morally right if they adhere to established rules or duties. Consequentialism evaluates the morality of actions based on their outcomes, suggesting that the best actions are those that produce the best consequences.

Applying these ethical frameworks to AI means ensuring that AI systems are designed to promote virtues such as honesty, fairness, and integrity (virtue ethics). It also means that AI should follow clear and consistent rules and duties that ensure its actions are morally right (deontology). Lastly, AI should be evaluated based on the consequences of its actions, ensuring that its deployment leads to positive outcomes for society (consequentialism). Integrating these ethical principles into AI development, we can create systems that mimic human behaviour and adhere to the moral standards that guide human actions. This approach ensures that AI contributes positively to society, aligns with societal values, and supports human dynamics and societal evolution.

The Greeks believed that people had three types of qualities, and two of them worked together. They called the first two 'excess' and 'deficiency,' and the third one was called 'virtue.' They saw these qualities as part of a whole, but they also opposed each other (Ross, 1956). The highest quality contradicted the middle one, and they all conflicted with each other in the end. What does this mean today? This means that all qualities are equal but relatively less critical than the more significant ones. So, when one quality is too much compared to another, the other becomes less noticeable, and both can turn into feelings or actions. For example, if a brave person acts cowardly, their cowardice becomes relative to their actions. This way of thinking about qualities helps us understand ancient Greece's and today's ethics. To understand the right process for developing and supporting AI, assessing the development stage for both excesses and deficiencies is essential. This approach ensures that ethics becomes a core component of AI coding and programming. Assessing for excesses involves identifying and mitigating any aspects of AI that might lead to harmful overuse or misuse. For example, overly aggressive data collection could invade privacy, while excessive reliance on automated decision-making might reduce human accountability. Conversely, assessing for deficiencies involves identifying and addressing gaps or weaknesses in AI development. This could mean ensuring the AI system is sufficiently trained to avoid biased outcomes or making sure it includes diverse data to accurately reflect societal diversity. By evaluating both excesses and deficiencies, developers can embed ethical considerations into the foundation of AI systems. This process helps create AI technologies that are balanced, fair, and aligned with ethical standards, ultimately contributing to more responsible and beneficial AI development.

To better understand this concept, modern thinkers and scholars need to critically review the Greek idea of ethics in the context of AI. Greek ethics, which includes virtue ethics, deontology, and consequentialism, offers a valuable framework for evaluating the moral dimensions of AI development and usage. By examining how these ethical principles apply to AI, scholars can identify ways to ensure that AI systems are designed and implemented in ways that promote moral integrity, follow clear ethical rules, and lead to positive outcomes. This critical review can help integrate ethics into AI development, ensuring that these technologies are advanced and aligned with fundamental moral principles. Therefore, incorporating Greek ethical concepts into the study and development of AI can provide a deeper understanding of how to create technologies that support human values and societal evolution. This approach encourages the development of AI systems that are ethical, responsible, and beneficial to society. This means going beyond what Plato and Aristotle said. By looking beyond these two philosophers, we can better understand how ethics influenced behaviour in ancient Greece and continues to do so in today's society. It also helps us differentiate what is important to know or learn to improve legal knowledge in the present day. For modern scholars, it is essential to understand how the ancient Greeks saw ethics as a core part of creating rules that guide everyone's behaviour. This leads to questions about why moral rules exist in society, what justifies them, and how they could be applied to AI.

So, when it comes to thinking about AI and ethics, all thinkers and scholars need to start by asking philosophical questions. They need to explore how AI fits into the development of laws and policies from different perspectives. This means asking questions like, 'What is virtue?' 'What does it mean to live a good life?' or 'What makes a life good?' While these questions might not give us all the answers, they are an excellent place to start. They help us understand the main problem of AI and ethics and assemble the puzzle pieces. The main idea here is that we need to closely look at whether morality is objective or relative, and how AI can be effectively used in society. Based on what I have discussed so far, we can see a clear connection between how we think about ethics now and the classical idea of living a good life in the conception of AI. Except, there are also complexities in understanding how ethics has developed over time and how it influences behaviour. So, by trying to understand these complexities, we might be able to better connect ethics with the concept of AI and how it is used in today's world.

In their study about how, AI is used in higher education, Huang and Fang (2013) discuss how AI is changing traditional ways of teaching and learning. They stated that it is essential to consider the ethical issues that come with these changes, like surveillance, fairness, and job security. They focus on how AI is used in library and information science (LIS) and how librarians influence its role in education. They look at the ethical aspects of using AI in education, too. Their research adds a lot to our understanding of how AI affects higher education. However, we need to remember that their study focuses only on LIS and librarianship, so their findings might not apply to other subjects. Also, their thoughts on the ethical issues of AI in education are primarily based on theory and could use more real-life testing to be sure of its application. Conversely, their research is essential in understanding how AI affects higher education and the ethical problems it creates. So, it is imperative to consider ethics when dealing with the issues they discussed. This way, when we use AI, we ensure it keeps the basic standards of teaching and learning intact. By including ethics, we can ensure AI helps education grow and improve instead of causing problems. Aligning this with the Greek idea of ethics, we can conclude that this study is consistent with previous discussions. The propositions in this book complement the focus of this study, rather than differing from it. The book builds on the Greek ethical frameworks of virtue ethics, deontology, and consequentialism, applying these principles to the development and use of AI. This approach reinforces the idea that ethical considerations should be central to AI development, ensuring that AI systems are designed and implemented in ways that are fair, responsible, and beneficial to society.

Therefore, the Greek idea of ethics teaches us important lessons about how we should use AI. In Greek philosophy, ethics was about being a good person and living in a virtuous way, not just following rules. This idea can help designers and developers decide how to create and use AI responsibly. By thinking about ethical principles, designers and developers can make sure that their work with AI benefits society and follows moral rules. Also, the Greek concept of ethics reminds us how important it is to understand how AI affects society. Just like the Greeks believed virtues shaped people's behaviour, we need to consider how AI impacts our social lives today. This means thinking about things like privacy, fairness, and who benefits from AI. If we include ethics in AI development, designers, developers, policymakers, and society can work together to ensure AI is used fairly and responsibly. This idea aligns with the Greek belief in living virtuously and doing what is morally right. The Greeks emphasised virtue ethics, which focuses on developing good character traits and making ethical decisions based on those traits. Applying this to AI development means creating systems that embody virtues like honesty, fairness, and integrity. However, it may also be argued that simply mirroring Greek ethics in AI development is insufficient. The complexities of modern technology require a diverse approach that also considers the potential unintended consequences and ethical dilemmas unique to AI. Therefore, while the Greek emphasis on virtue provides a valuable foundation, it must be expanded to address the challenges and ethical issues in AI development.

Therefore, the ancient Greek concept of living virtuously and doing what is morally right provides a solid foundation for ethics. This idea emphasises the importance of character and virtue in guiding our actions. Philosophers like Aristotle believed that achieving a good life involves cultivating virtues such as honesty, courage, and fairness. These virtues help individuals make moral choices that benefit both themselves and society. However, in today's world, especially with the rise of artificial intelligence (AI) technology, this classical framework needs to be adapted. AI systems have become integral to many aspects of our lives, from decision-making in business to influencing social interactions. As we integrate

AI into our daily activities, we face new ethical dilemmas that the ancient Greeks could not have anticipated. For instance, AI can reflect and amplify biases present in society, leading to unfair outcomes in areas like hiring or law enforcement. The ethical principles of virtue ethics must be critically examined and modified to address these challenges. This means considering how virtues apply in a technological context. It involves asking questions about accountability, transparency, and the potential consequences of AI on human well-being. Adapting the Greek idea of virtue to modern technology, we can create an ethical framework that guides the responsible use of AI. This ensures that we not only advance technologically but also uphold moral values that foster fairness, justice, and respect for human dignity in an increasingly digital world. This ensures that AI systems follow traditional ethical principles and navigate the unique ethical landscape of today's technological world.

Greek ethical discussions focus on the idea of living a good life, as seen in Socrates's discussion in *Gorgias* (Rudebusch, and Turner, 2014). He discusses happiness and how we can be happy in life. This idea started the concept of living well in ancient Greece. Later, Greek philosophers, following Socrates, believed that happiness was everyone's primary goal in life (Annas, 1993). However, this idea can be tricky because it is difficult to say what makes each person happy, or what makes their life fulfilling. People generally do not wish for a life different from the one they have. However, these philosophers thought that happiness was the most important thing for everyone, and everything else was not as necessary. Looking at it this way, Socrates thought that being happy was important for following societal rules and being involved in society. If people are happy, they tend to be good and fit well into society. Similarly, with AI, we should aim to be virtuous in how we use and interact with it. Ensuring that virtue is a significant part of how AI operates is essential. By embedding virtuous behaviour into AI systems, we can create a strong ethical framework and establish rules for controlling AI. However, it is also necessary to critically examine how virtue can be integrated into AI development. This involves programming AI to act ethically and ensuring that the processes and data used to train AI are free from biases and harmful influences. Additionally, developers must be vigilant about the potential unintended consequences of AI, such as privacy issues or social inequalities. Focusing on virtue in AI development can create systems that contribute positively to society. This ethical approach helps ensure that AI technologies are used responsibly and for the common good, aligning with ancient ethical principles and modern societal needs.

In this conception, I agree with the Greek philosophers that happiness could be the main goal for people, but what happiness means can be different for each person. This might be why it is difficult for modern writers to understand the Greek idea of ethics. For modern people, life includes many things, not just being happy. People might live to achieve their goals or be successful. So, for modern people, happiness could mean consistently pursuing their desires in all aspects of life. How can someone be morally or ethically good in life without thinking about what they want? It is a challenge for modern thinkers to understand how the ancient Greeks thought about happiness as the main goal for everyone. It is difficult to see how people's actions in ancient Greece could impact their lives and how they should live meaningfully, as the Stoics believed (White, 1979).

Therefore, using Socrates's ideas about being good and happy in life can help us think about how we use AI. We need to ensure that AI is used in a way that is good for people and improves society. Just like Socrates thought, being happy is connected to being good and fitting into society, and AI should be designed and used to help people thrive and behave ethically. To do this, the people who make and use AI need to think about being good and happy in how they create, develop, and use AI. This means thinking about how AI affects people and society and ensuring it does more good than harm. We also need rules and guidelines to ensure AI is used correctly, that it follows moral principles, and that society is fair and peaceful. By ensuring AI follows the ideas of being good and happy, we can use it in a way that helps people, makes society better, and does not cause problems. This way, AI can be a tool for improving society instead of making things worse. Therefore, Socrates's idea of good and happiness relates to how we develop and use AI in society. Socrates believed that living a good life, characterised by virtue and wisdom, leads to true happiness. Applying this idea to AI, we should strive to develop and use AI in ways that promote ethical behaviour and contribute to the well-being of society. However, critically examining this idea highlights several challenges. Unlike human beings, AI does not possess consciousness or moral intuition. Therefore, developers must explicitly program ethical principles into AI systems. This requires careful consideration of the potential impacts of AI on various aspects of society, including privacy, fairness, and equality. Moreover, the pursuit of happiness through AI should not be limited to the individual level but should consider the collective good. This means addressing broader societal implications, such as job displacement and social inequality, which AI can exacerbate if not managed responsibly. I will therefore argue that while Socrates's idea of good and happiness provides a valuable framework for thinking about AI ethics, it must be adapted to address AI technology's unique challenges and opportunities. By doing so, we can ensure that AI development and usage align with the pursuit of virtue and the common good, leading to a happier and more just society.

Yoder-Himes et al. (2022) point out that students of different skin colours, especially women of colour, often encounter obstacles in STEM fields at colleges because of feeling socially isolated and facing various biases. These biases include how people treat them, biases in technology, and biases within the college system itself. The authors highlight a problem with online exam proctoring software, which uses technology to watch students during exams to prevent cheating. However, these systems may have biases, especially in recognising faces. This means that the technology might not work as well for students with different skin tones or genders because it was trained on images that might not represent everyone fairly. In addition, the authors also studied how a certain kind of technology used by many universities in the United States might treat students differently based on their race, skin colour, or gender. They looked at the results of 357 students from four different classes. They checked if the automated proctoring software, which watches students during tests to prevent cheating, treated students unfairly. To do this, they looked at each student's self-reported race and gender using a clear photo. They found that students with darker skin tones, especially black students, were more likely to be flagged for extra review by instructors because the software thought they might be cheating. They also found that women with the darkest skin tones were more likely to be flagged for review than men with darker skin or people with lighter skin tones, regardless of gender.

The authors did not find significant differences between male and female students overall. However, they discovered that a popular test monitoring software might unfairly target specific groups of students. This is the first study to examine how this software might treat people differently based on race and gender. It is essential because it affects education, fairness, diversity, and psychology. Nonetheless, remember, this study only looked at one school and a small group of students. So, we need more research to see if these findings apply to other schools and groups of people. Overall, this study shows that facial recognition software used in online tests might not treat students of colour or women of colour fairly. While it is a big concern, we need more research to understand the problem better and find the right solutions. Still, this study reminds us of the importance of considering AI's social and ethical educational impacts. It shows the need to ensure that everyone, regardless of background, is treated fairly in STEM fields.

Furthermore, the study sheds light on three critical issues with AI technology. First, designers and developers may unconsciously use the technology in ways that perpetuate biases and prejudices present in dysfunctional societal systems. This can happen when AI systems are trained on biased data or programmed without sufficient consideration of ethical implications. Second, it reveals that designers and developers often do not incorporate ethical considerations, whether based on ancient philosophical principles or modern ethical frameworks, during the design stage of AI. This oversight can lead to unintended consequences and ethical dilemmas in AI applications. Third, the study highlights how a lack of ethics and regulation can result in significant deficiencies and discrimination in the way AI is applied and used. Without ethical guidelines and regulatory frameworks, AI systems may contribute to unfair treatment and privacy violations or exacerbate existing social inequalities. In summary, these insights show the importance of integrating ethical principles into AI development from the outset. This approach helps mitigate biases, promote fairness, and ensure that AI technologies benefit society in a responsible and ethical manner.

Henceforth, it is essential to recognise that the biases we see in AI reflect the biases in our society and how it is set up. These biases, which we might not even realise we have, have been built into the development of AI. This tells us that we lack ethical principles in our lives and have created a system that does not ensure we do what is morally right in everything we do. When I discuss virtue, I mean having an AI system that is faultless and error-free in how it is used and applied for the greater good. Having a virtuous interaction with AI means we have the right procedures and systems in place for developing and using AI in accordance with the principles of the Greek concept of Virtue. That is why it is vital to have ethical guidelines outlined in this book. These guidelines will help us ensure that we use AI fairly and justly and align with moral principles. They will help us address the biases in our society and ensure that AI is used for the benefit of everyone, without any unfairness or errors.

If we consider it, ethics could be what everyone wants. So, having a good life becomes everyone's goal. In this view, we might think everyone should be taught what a good life means. If everyone knows what a good life is, then it becomes the main reason for how they behave in society (Rist, 2002). For the ancient Greeks, knowing this was really important. It was seen as the most essential goal of ethics and shaped how society worked. However, does this idea really make sense? To answer that, we need to look closely. Some people in society might not care about having a good life. They might have different goals or not even think about what a good life means. If we stick to the traditional idea, we might say these people are confused or have wrong ideas about what is right in society. Nevertheless, is that true when ethics might not be a big part of their life at all?

Think about philosophers like Socrates, Epicurus, and the Stoics. They believed that living a good life was the most important thing. So, even if someone does not think about it, it is still essential to understand this idea. Knowing about the good life helps us understand what makes us happy or unhappy (Long, 2006). For these philosophers, living a good life means knowing the difference between right and wrong. If someone does not live according to what they believe is a good life, they might feel unhappy. Understanding this idea from Socrates, Epicurus, and the Stoics might be challenging for modern philosophers. However, if it is, they could try learning about Greek philosophy, especially from Aristotle. Aristotle had a different way of looking at the good life, which might be easier to understand and apply it to AI. No matter how we look at it, there is a common belief that everything has an end. This means there is an end to what we call happiness or the good life. If everything ends up neutral and nothing is left, then the biggest challenge for ethics is figuring out what this end is and how we can achieve happiness, especially when it comes to the integration of AI in society.

Cornacchia et al. (2023) have talked about how AI is being used increasingly to make essential decisions that can change people's lives. However, they warned that AI tools with biases could be harmful and might not always help people. Rules from the government say that AI should not use specific personal details like gender, race, or religion to make decisions so that the outcomes are fair. Nonetheless, even with these rules, Cornacchia et al. (2023) observed that people might still face unfair decisions because AI can still show bias, even if it does not use sensitive details. Hence, the authors came up with a way to check if AI models are biased, even if they follow the rules. They use a method that looks at different scenarios and compares the costs of each one to see if they lead to good outcomes. They also use a unique tool to look for patterns in the data that might be linked to sensitive details, even if they are not directly used. Their experiments show that their method works well to spot AI models that learn from these hidden patterns.

The study by Cornacchia et al. (2023) highlights a limitation in detecting bias in AI systems, which raises important ethical questions. They looked into how advanced methods could help fix this problem. However, it is essential to be critical because even these advanced methods might not fully solve the issue, especially when AI relies on hidden patterns. So, while their method is a good step forward, it is not a perfect solution. We must remember that AI bias is a complex issue that will not be fixed overnight. However, their study is still significant because it shows us future research directions. We need to keep improving algorithms to ensure AI systems are fair and unbiased.

Considering the ethical concerns about bias in AI systems, it is essential to deal with this issue using ethical principles. One suggestion is to keep researching to improve debiasing algorithms. This means finding new ways to spot and fix problems caused by hidden patterns in the data. By doing this, we can ensure that AI makes fair decisions for everyone. Also, it is crucial for researchers, policymakers, and industry sectors to work together. By bringing in different viewpoints and skills, we can create solid rules and ethical guidelines to tackle bias in AI systems. This way, we can make sure AI decisions are fair and just. In addition, being transparent and accountable is also vital to ensuring AI is developed and used ethically. This means having clear rules for checking AI systems and being open about how decisions are made. Plus, having a diverse team working on AI can help develop better, fairer solutions. Therefore, dealing with bias in AI needs a mix of approaches rooted in ethical values. By researching more, working together, being transparent, and including diverse perspectives, we can ensure AI follows ethical standards and does good things for society.

Therefore, it is essential to highlight that the concept of living a good life led to the idea of virtue, and ethics emerged from virtue. This suggests that to understand ethics truly, we should look back to Greek philosophy. Greek philosophy provides the foundation for our current ethical beliefs and ongoing discussions about the moral principles governing AI. Studying ethics from this perspective allows us to contemplate how our actions align with modern societal rules and responsibilities. However, reducing ethics in the modern world to mere tradition overlooks how deeply human thinking influences the development and use of AI. It fails to acknowledge the crucial role ethical considerations play in ensuring that AI technologies are developed and applied responsibly. Thus, grounding our understanding of ethics in ancient philosophical principles, we gain insights that help us navigate the complexities of AI ethics more effectively. This approach enables us to maintain moral standards while advancing technology for the benefit of society as a whole.

According to Butt et al. (2023), AI is becoming widespread and has the potential to change significantly human life. However, they warn that the success of AI should be judged by how much it helps people. They argue that AI algorithms, especially those used in edge computing, are closely tied to human interests and need to be looked at from a human perspective. Despite the considerable impact AI has on human life, Butt et al. (2023) argue that AI applications often lack security and trustworthiness, and may not always act ethically. The authors emphasise that when designing and using AI at the edge (meaning closer to where data is produced), it is crucial to consider human needs and values. They propose a framework called Human-Centric Artificial Intelligence (HCAI) and a development process for AI applications that focus on people's well-being. Additionally, they discuss these applications' privacy, reliability, strength, and security, pointing out challenges and possible solutions. It is important to note that AI needs to be guided by strong ethical principles and rules to benefit humanity truly. Hence, attempting to ground the development of AI technology on the ancient principle of virtue underlines a commitment to trust and responsibility. The concept of virtue, originating from ancient Greek philosophy, emphasises moral excellence, integrity, and the pursuit of the 'good life.' Integrating these principles into AI development means prioritising ethical considerations and ensuring that AI systems operate with fairness, transparency, and respect for human values.

Gardner (2022) discusses how biased algorithms, like the ones used in the UK's A-level results in August 2020, reveal the importance of being more aware and accountable in using algorithms to make decisions. Even though Ofqual's algorithm was transparent, the data it used and the societal biases it reflected led to unfair results that were hard to ignore. The author also points out that similar biases exist in many other algorithmic systems, but they are not always easy to see or challenge, especially for those without power or resources. This raises concerns about the ethics and accountability of using algorithms to make decisions, and it highlights the need to check the data and algorithms used in these systems carefully. It further stresses the importance of ensuring algorithms are designed to avoid biases and that people affected by them know what is going on and have ways to challenge unfair outcomes. More research and awareness about these issues are needed to make sure algorithmic systems are used fairly and ethically.

In conclusion, AI is becoming more common in education, potentially changing how we teach, learn, and manage student affairs. However, using AI in education raises critical ethical questions about fairness, openness, and responsibility. To tackle these issues and ensure AI helps everyone in education, we need to create clear ethical rules. This section has highlighted the importance of creating regulations to ensure fairness, transparency, and responsibility when using AI in education. It has also discussed the main ethical issues and suggested developing and adhering to ethical guidelines for AI usage in education. To ensure ethical AI usage in education, universities should consider key ethical factors and devise strategies for creating and enforcing ethical guidelines:

Ethical Considerations:

- **Equity:** AI systems must not reinforce existing biases or inequalities. Universities should ensure fair treatment for all students, regardless of race or socio-economic status.
- **Transparency:** AI decisions should be transparent and understandable. Universities need to make AI processes clear so stakeholders can trust and scrutinise them.
- **Accountability:** When AI makes mistakes, there must be accountability. Universities should hold responsible parties accountable for any errors or biases in AI systems.

Developing Ethical Guidelines:

- **Multi-Stakeholder Collaboration:** Involve universities, policymakers, researchers, students, and others to develop comprehensive guidelines.
- **Ethical Frameworks:** Adapt existing ethical frameworks to the educational context and establish specific standards for AI usage.
- **Impact Assessments:** Evaluate AI systems' potential effects on equity, transparency, and accountability through impact assessments.
- **Transparency Mechanisms:** Implement measures like explaining AI decisions and disclosing data sources to ensure transparency.

- **Algorithmic Audits and Bias Mitigation:** Regularly audit AI algorithms to identify and address biases. Mitigation strategies may include adjusting parameters or diversifying training data.
- **Education and Training:** Educate stakeholders about ethical considerations in AI usage to promote responsible deployment and decision-making.

By following these strategies, universities can ensure that AI usage in education aligns with ethical principles and benefits all stakeholders.

In summary, using AI in education can improve learning and help universities run more smoothly. However, we need to think about the ethics of AI in education. We need to work with many different people to create clear rules for using AI in education. This means having clear guidelines and rules, checking the impact of AI, being open about how AI works, checking AI systems for mistakes or unfairness, fixing any unfairness, and teaching people about AI ethics. By focusing on ethics and setting up strict rules, we can use AI in education in a way that helps everyone and keeps everyone safe and treated fairly.

Finally, as seen through thinkers like Socrates, the Greek idea of ethics emphasises being good and living a virtuous life. It suggests that our actions should be guided by what is morally right. This concept is relevant to how we approach AI today. When considering AI, it is crucial to prioritise ethics. We must ensure that AI is developed and used in ways that adhere to moral principles and contribute positively to society. Similar to how the Greeks valued virtue in human behaviour, we should prioritise ethics in the creation and utilisation of AI. Greek ethics also teaches us about transparency and accountability. It emphasises honesty and taking responsibility for our actions. In the context of AI, where decisions can have wide-ranging impacts, transparency and accountability are essential. We need to understand how AI affects society and ensure its use is fair and responsible. In summary, Greek ethics provides valuable lessons for AI today. By integrating ethical principles into AI development and usage, we can ensure that AI benefits society in a morally upright and equitable manner. This approach fosters trust among users and stakeholders, promotes fairness, and upholds societal values in the rapidly advancing field of artificial intelligence.

Chapter 2 of this book critically discusses the importance of universities establishing guiding principles and regulations for using AI in education. It argues that these rules are necessary to ensure AI is utilised fairly, transparently, and responsibly. By implementing such guiding principles, universities can make informed decisions about integrating AI into teaching and learning processes. This approach aims to benefit all students and stakeholders involved in education. The chapter serves as a blueprint for universities, providing guidance on addressing ethical challenges associated with AI in education. It emphasises the need for policies that promote fairness and adherence to established regulations. The guiding principles are essential for ensuring that AI enhances educational outcomes without compromising ethical standards.

Furthermore, the chapter highlights the role of universities in setting precedents for ethical AI use. It highlights accountability's importance and ensures that AI applications in education are transparent and equitable. By following these guiding principles, universities can navigate the complexities of AI technology while upholding principles of fairness and responsibility. Chapter 2 also outlines how universities can effectively manage the ethical implications of AI in education. By establishing clear rules and ethical frameworks, universities can harness AI's potential to improve learning outcomes while safeguarding against potential risks and ensuring equitable access for all students.

Finally, Chapter 2 proposes guiding principles for universities to use in teaching and learning. The chapter critically examines and recommends essential principles that universities should adopt when integrating AI into educational practices. These guiding principles aim to ensure that AI is used fairly, transparently, and responsibly within academic settings. They provide a framework for universities to make informed decisions about deploying and implementing AI technologies, emphasising ethical considerations and adherence to established regulations. By following these guiding principles, universities can effectively navigate the ethical challenges associated with AI in education. They serve as a roadmap for institutions to maximise the benefits of AI while mitigating potential risks and ensuring equitable access and outcomes for all students. In conclusion, the proposed guiding principles offer universities a structured approach to harnessing AI's potential in education responsibly. They promote ethical practices and support universities in maintaining high standards of integrity and fairness in their educational initiatives.

CHAPTER 2

Proposed Guiding Principles at UK Higher Education Institutions

INTRODUCTION

When discussing using GenAI in higher education institutions and other organisations, we need to consider its benefits and potential problems. Considering the benefits and potential of GenAI aligns with the Greek concept of ethics related to virtue. This idea highlights the pursuit of using this technology for the greater good, which is the primary goal of this book. This section provides some simple rules for using GenAI in HEIs and other organisations, especially in the UK. These rules are essential because we have been considering the good and bad sides of using GenAI in higher education institutions and other organisations. So, it is essential to use GenAI in a way that is fair and helpful for everyone involved in education. Therefore, this part of the discussion offers advice on what higher education institutions and other organisations should do when they use GenAI. Nonetheless, it is crucial to know that these are just suggestions, not strict rules. Every academic institution and organisation is unique, so they might need to try different parts of these suggestions to find what works best for them. The main goal of these suggestions is to assist HEIs and other organisations in a few important ways. Firstly, they ensure that GenAI is used fairly and responsibly. This might include setting up groups to ensure ethical practices or training academics on how to use GenAI effectively. Secondly, these suggestions help higher education institutions and other organisations to make long-term plans for how they use GenAI. By having clear guidelines and standards, everyone can agree on how GenAI should be used.

Finally, these suggestions aim to ensure that HEIs and other organisations have the support they need to use GenAI effectively. This might involve creating opportunities for academics, tech experts, and ethicists to collaborate and exchange ideas. It could also

DOI: 10.1201/9781003561507-3

mean offering resources and assistance to academics who have questions about using GenAI in their classes. In the end, these suggestions provide a way to address the challenging issues that arise with using GenAI in higher education and other organisations. They provide schools and universities with a plan for using GenAI in a thoughtful and safe manner. By working together and trying out different approaches, higher education institutions and other organisations can ensure that GenAI enhances student learning in the best possible way.

The idea of using GenAI in HEIs is really promising because it could help students learn better, improve how lecturers teach, and make tasks easier to handle. This is why I suggest creating some basic rules, called guiding principles, for using GenAI in higher education institutions in the UK and elsewhere. These rules are based on looking closely at research done by academics. Firstly, GenAI can create personalised learning experiences that fit each student's needs. For example, research by Smith et al. (2019) shows that GenAI can change how lessons are taught based on how well students are doing and how they like to learn. This can make students more interested and help them learn better. Also, Krueger et al. (2024)and Smith et al. (2019) found that when GenAI gives students feedback that is just for them, it can motivate them to learn more and take charge of their own learning. Moreover, GenAI can improve how lecturers teach and make academic jobs easier. García-Peñalvo et al. (2023) discuss how GenAI-powered chatbots and virtual helpers can organise schedules or answer common questions so lecturers can spend more time helping students. Also, Sajja et al. (2024) observe that Gen AI can create intelligent tutoring systems that give students instant feedback and help lecturers determine how to help each student learn better. Overall, the research shows that bringing GenAI into HEIs can make learning more personalised, help teachers teach better, and make universities work smoother. Because of this, it is a good idea to create some guiding principles to ensure GenAI is used responsibly and effectively in schools and universities.

Furthermore, bringing GenAI into HEIs matches with more significant changes happening in society and technology, like how things are becoming more digital and automated. Jin et al. (2024) studied how 40 universities from six global regions are adopting Generative AI (GAI) in higher education. The study looked at key features of GAI, such as how well it fits with current practices, how easily it can be tested, and how clearly its benefits can be seen. It also examined how universities communicate about GAI and the roles and responsibilities set out in their policies. The findings show that universities are actively working to integrate GAI, with a focus on upholding academic integrity, enhancing teaching and learning, and ensuring fairness. Using GenAI in education helps schools and universities stay competitive and flexible. It also helps students learn essential skills they will need in the future, like using technology and thinking critically. However, we must also consider the ethical and fair side of using GenAI. Kizilcec et al. (2024) mentioned some concerns, like keeping student data private, ensuring the AI does not unfairly favour certain groups, and ensuring everyone can access it easily. Because of these concerns, the guiding principles for using GenAI in higher education institutions include rules about ethics and fairness to ensure it is used responsibly and fairly. The reasons for suggesting these guiding principles include making learning more personal, improving teaching, fitting in with what is happening in society, and thinking about ethics. These reasons are backed up by research from different studies, showing that GenAI can really change education for the better, as long as we deal with ethical and fair concerns properly.

When it comes to personalised learning, GenAI can improve the student experience by offering a more personalised way of learning. For instance, GenAI-powered chatbots can answer students' questions and give them personalised help, adjusting to each student's needs, skills, and how they learn (Ouyang et al., 2022). This personalised approach can make students more interested and motivated and do better in their studies. Furthermore, GenAI-powered chatbots, adaptive learning platforms, and virtual reality experiences can make learning more interesting by giving personalised help, involving students, and creating real situations. Improving teaching with GenAI-enabled chatbots and simulations also makes teaching more flexible and lets teachers adapt to different ways students learn (Iskender, 2023). Similarly, the rise of online learning in universities has allowed GenAI to change how teaching happens online. For example, GenAI has been used in many ways in online classes, like helping students feel better, making teaching methods more flexible, and using virtual reality to help students discover new things (Dwivedi et al., 2023; Ivanov and Soliman, 2023). Also, GenAI can give students answers in online classes even when the lecturers are not there. In other words, it lets students learn online even if they are not online themselves. This shows that if GenAI is used in the right way, it can bring new and helpful ways of teaching and learning that are good for students' learning and personal growth.

In addition, research on GenAI and assessment since the release of ChatGPT has looked at how well it can handle tasks like exams with multiple-choice or open-ended questions (Bommarito and Katz, 2022; Gilson et al., 2022). Some studies also checked if people and AI tools can tell if the answers are from AI (Gao et al., 2022; Cingillioglu, 2023). Despite some differences in findings, most agree that GenAI is good at passing certain professional exams and making understandable texts. This suggests new possibilities for using GenAI in higher education, like giving feedback through ChatGPT (Dai et al., 2023), grading essays automatically (Mizumoto and Eguchi, 2023), and making personalised assessments with GenAI's help (Asad and Ajaz 2024).

On the flip side, while there have been groundbreaking advancements in GenAI, they have also brought significant challenges to assessment. Many worry that academic misconduct is increasing because students can submit work generated by AI as their own for assessment. This is concerning because there are unreliable tools to detect AI-generated work (Lodge, Thompson, and Corrin, 2023). Without proper rules, these students might have an unfair advantage over others in assessments (Asad and Ajaz 2024). Additionally, there are worries about fair access to GenAI tools (Sullivan, Kelly, and McLaughlan, 2023), keeping data safe when using GenAI (Jinet al., 2024), biases in AI algorithms (Sullivan, Kelly, and McLaughlan, 2023; Jin et al., 2024), and a lack of training on AI for university lecturers and students (Chan and Colloton, 2024). There is also concern about AI generating false information (Rudolph, Tan, and Tan, 2023). In terms of using GenAI for assessment, there are many unclear areas without established guidelines. For example, is it cheating if a student comes up with the ideas themselves but uses GenAI to improve the writing? Should work done without GenAI be seen as more 'independent'? These questions show the need to rethink important ideas in assessment, like security and fairness, and to change how assessment works in higher education to prepare students better for a world with AI (Lodge, Thompson, and Corrin, 2023). It can be argued that students might use GenAI to enhance their ideas and improve their writing, as long as they disclose this at the end of their work. With this in mind, it is reasonable to assert that using GenAI in this way is not cheating or academic misconduct, nor does it meet the definition of plagiarism in academic discourse.

Nonetheless, these challenges put a lot of pressure on universities to sort out the chaos in assessment by making policies that address these issues. Even though there have been guidelines related to AI before ChatGPT was released, most of them are general and do not specifically deal with these issues in higher education (Schiff, 2022; Nguyen and Nguyen, 2024). Schiff (2022) looked at 24 national AI policy strategies and found that the use of AI in education is not talked about much in these policies. The previous policies also did not consider how much impact recent technological advances would have. As GenAI tools are being used more and more by students, Chan (2023) said there is still a lot of work to be done to make more detailed and focused policies about AI in education.

The absence of strong policies for using GenAI in higher education institutions makes it difficult for universities to deal with GenAI-related challenges in assessment quickly and effectively. At first, some universities did not allow students to use GenAI, but this rule was criticised as not sustainable and not helpful for teaching students about AI (Sullivan, Kelly, and McLaughlan, 2023). There have been a lot of opinion articles and research papers criticising this, like those by Chan (2023), Lodge, Thompson, and Corrin (2023), and Rudolph, Tan, and Tan (2023). For example, Chan (2023) suggested a framework for universities to make policies about GenAI use in teaching and learning, based on a survey about ChatGPT use. The framework has three parts—how to teach with GenAI, what is right and wrong, and how to make it work practically. Big organisations like UNESCO and OECD have also published guidelines for regulating GenAI in education, but these usually focus on bigger issues like national rules and digital poverty, not the specific problems in higher education assessment.

As people learn more about GenAI, many universities update their policies to ensure GenAI is used responsibly. For example, 24 top universities in the UK worked together to make guidelines about GenAI. These guidelines focus on helping students and staff learn about AI while also protecting privacy and stopping plagiarism (The Guardian, 2023). In Australia, the agency responsible for quality in higher education suggested five principles for changing assessment because of GenAI. These include assessing assessments as a whole and ensuring they let students interact with AI (Kutty et al., 2024; Foung et al., 2024). These policies and guidelines are essential for understanding how universities worldwide think about GenAI and assessment. However, so far, no one has looked closely at these policies or critically thought about them. Most discussions about policies are about what works—like whether universities say yes or no to using GenAI, whether they use AI to check for cheating, and whether certain policies are helpful. However, what is really needed is a comprehensive set of ethical rules and principles for using GenAI well in higher education.

Therefore, as AI technology, specifically GenAI, continues to develop, this guiding principle offers universities a framework to address the ethical and practical aspects of using it in education. The goal is to ensure that GenAI is used responsibly and transparently to improve learning experiences, maintain academic honesty, and protect student privacy. Thus, this guiding principle for using GenAI is split into two parts: One for students and one for staff. The one for students focuses on how to use GenAI to make learning better for them. The one for staff is about how higher education institutions and other organisations should use GenAI to improve teaching and learning. These two parts work together to ensure that GenAI is used in a way that helps everyone in education and that higher education institutions can adapt to new technology while keeping everyone involved.

PREAMBLE OF THE GUIDING PRINCIPLES AT UK HIGHER EDUCATION INSTITUTIONS

When creating rules for using GenAI ethically in UK higher education and elsewhere, it is crucial to understand how technology, teaching methods, and ethics all interact. This introduction lays the groundwork for the upcoming rules, acknowledging the complex situation GenAI operates in and how it affects academic honesty and student progress. This guiding principle is based on the idea of doing well academically and being responsible ethically. They provide a strong framework for dealing with tricky ethical issues and making the most of GenAI in education. By creating an open, accountable, and fair culture, UK universities and other countries worldwide can ensure GenAI helps students learn without causing problems. By working together, thinking hard about what we are doing, and making improvements as we go, these rules aim to create an environment where GenAI helps students succeed and develop new ideas. By following these rules, we will ensure that using GenAI in education is responsible and helps students grow in all ways at UK universities and other countries worldwide.

GUIDING PRINCIPLE FOR USING GENERATIVE AI IN TEACHING AND LEARNING

The rise of GenAI is changing the way we teach and learn. Traditionally, education focused on academics passing knowledge to students through lectures, textbooks, and tests. Nevertheless, with GenAI, things are different. Now, academics can use AI-generated content to create learning experiences tailored to each student's needs. For example, AI-powered learning platforms can make custom materials based on how well students understand, like to learn, and what interests them. This makes learning more personal and gets students more involved. GenAI also lets students be more creative. They can use AI-generated content to try new ideas and express themselves in different ways. For instance, they might get inspiration from AI-made pictures for art projects. Or they could work with AI to make videos or stories. This brings a whole new level of creativity to education, making students more active in their learning journey.

However, using AI in education also brings up important questions about ethics and how we teach. While there are many good things about using AI, it is crucial to use it in the right way. That is why I have developed these guiding principles to help academics use

GenAI fairly, inclusively, and effectively. These principles are based on values like being honest, treating everyone fairly, and focusing on students' needs. They are meant to help academics make good choices about using AI in education. They cover concepts such as making sure AI is used in a way that is fair to everyone, teaching students how to think critically about AI, giving them chances to be creative, working together with AI, making sure everyone's included, and how to check if AI is helping students learn.

In summary, using GenAI in education can change the way we learn, making it more personal and creative. Nonetheless, we need to be careful how we use it. By following these guiding principles, academics can use AI to improve learning for everyone and prepare students for the future.

GENERAL PRINCIPLES

Principle 1

The following principles are focused on explaining how students interact with GenAI in colleges and universities:

> **P1.** Higher education institutions should teach students and graduates about how to use GenAI. They should also explain how using GenAI can affect their education, job opportunities, and society.

Rationale:

In recent years, GenAI has become really important in colleges, universities, organisations, society, and jobs. It is everywhere, and it has it pros and cons. Because it is becoming so important, students need to learn about GenAI and understand how it relates to their studies and future jobs. They should get training to know how it affects their education, teaching and learning, and careers. There are a few important reasons for this approach:

- **Getting Ready for the Future:** GenAI is becoming increasingly important in different areas, like education and jobs. Teaching students about GenAI helps them prepare for the changing world of technology they will face in their careers.
- **Better Job Opportunities:** Knowing how to use GenAI can really help students find jobs. Many industries are starting to use AI, and people who know about GenAI are often more likely to get hired.
- **Making Smart Choices:** Teaching students about GenAI helps them make informed decisions. They can consider how AI affects their studies and the world around them, making choices that make sense for them and for society.
- **Thinking about Ethics:** GenAI raises essential ethical questions, like privacy and fairness. Teaching students about these issues helps them understand the ethical side of AI and ensures that they use it responsibly.

- **Encouraging New Ideas:** Learning about GenAI can inspire students to develop new ideas and solutions. They might think of ways to use AI to solve big problems or improve their communities.

Incorporation:

- Higher education institutions should include guidelines and updates on GenAI in all academic materials and course curricula. These resources should explain how GenAI can impact students' career paths and help them prepare for changes in job opportunities.

Example 1	• In a computer science course, academics might teach about GenAI algorithms and how they are used in different industries like healthcare, finance, and marketing. They could give students readings, case studies, and assignments to understand how GenAI is changing these fields.
Example 2	• In a business management course, instructors might talk about how GenAI tools, such as predictive analytics and automated decision-making systems, are impacting business strategies and operations. They could use case studies of companies that have effectively used GenAI in their workflows to illustrate these changes.

- It is important to have open discussions between students and the institution about GenAI policies and student rights. These discussions should show how GenAI is being used in society and work, with real examples, and create clear communication channels.

Example 1	• Organise seminars or meetings where students, faculty members, and administrative staff can openly discuss the ethical implications of GenAI usage in academia, organisations, and society.
Example 2	• Establish online forums or discussion boards where students can share articles, news stories, and personal insights related to GenAI, fostering ongoing dialogue and exchange of ideas.

- Institutions should involve students in evaluating and using GenAI as part of their education.

Example 1	• Offer projects or research chances for students to study what GenAI systems can and cannot do. For instance, students in a psychology class could plan experiments to check for biases in AI algorithms.
Example 2	• Support student-run efforts to test GenAI tools and share thoughts with developers or policymakers. This might mean participating in coding competitions, research contests, or community programmes focused on AI ethics.

- Empowering students to think critically, reason well, and make good decisions about using GenAI is crucial. This helps them prepare for their future careers.

Example 1	• Provide workshops or seminars that teach critical thinking skills, especially those related to GenAI. These sessions might involve activities to determine whether information from AI is trustworthy or to consider the ethics of AI use.
Example 2	• Include case studies in lessons, where students look at real situations involving GenAI and suggest solutions based on ethics, social effects, and risk assessment.

- Teaching students about academic integrity and discussing its importance can help prevent cheating. This proactive approach keeps ethical standards high and builds a culture of honesty in higher education.

Example 1	• Incorporate a discussion about honesty and ethics into new students' orientation, stressing the importance of being truthful and open and respecting others' work.
Example 2	• Create online lessons or interactive activities to teach students about plagiarism tools, citing sources, and giving credit when using GenAI content. Offer help and advice for students facing academic integrity problems.

P2. Higher education Institutions must ensure that students understand how important Generative Artificial Intelligence (GenAI) is for their academic success, careers, and overall impact on society.

Rationale:

- Higher education institutions need clear rules about how students should use GenAI in their studies. These rules should ensure students use GenAI ethically and effectively, while still being honest in their academic work.

For example, the institution should have specific guidelines on:

- How to avoid plagiarism when using GenAI to create assignments or research papers.
- How to properly give credit to GenAI-generated content in their work.
- When and how students can use GenAI tools in exams or other assessments.

These rules should be easily found in the institution's assessment handbook, so students know exactly what is expected of them. Therefore, HEIs must ensure students know why GenAI matters. Here's why:

- **Academic Success:** GenAI is being used more in universities. Students who get GenAI can use it to do better in their classes. They can use AI tools to analyse data, understand language, and make content. This helps them with their assessment/coursework and gets them better grades.

- **Career Growth:** Jobs are changing fast because of GenAI. Companies want workers who know about AI. GenAI helps them work better, faster, and smarter. If students know GenAI, they can get better jobs in lots of industries, like tech, healthcare, finance, and marketing.
- **Society Impact:** GenAI affects society a lot. People need to discuss its good and bad parts. Students who get GenAI can discuss these things and help ensure AI is used correctly. They can speak up for fairness, make AI more equal, and help make the future better for everyone.

So, it very important to ensure that students understand GenAI. It will help them in university, in their jobs, and in making the world a better place.

Incorporation:

- Academics, teachers, and experts should create clear rules to explain how students will be graded and how to use GenAI tools correctly in their assignments. These guidelines should help students understand how to use GenAI tools responsibly and well in their assignments.

Example 1	• Academic faculty and professionals should collaborate to develop a detailed set of guidelines outlining the expectations for using GenAI tools in academic assignments. These guidelines should cover topics such as the permissible use of AI-generated content, citation practices for AI-generated materials, and the importance of maintaining academic integrity while utilising GenAI technologies.
Example 2	• The developed guidelines should be integrated into course materials, including course outlines, assignment instructions, and online learning platforms. This ensures that students have easy access to the guidelines and understand their importance from the beginning of the course.
Example 3	• Academics and professionals should provide students with instructional support on how to adhere to the guidelines effectively. This may include dedicated class sessions or workshops focused on responsible use of GenAI tools, demonstrations of proper citation practices for AI-generated content, and opportunities for students to ask questions and seek clarification.
Example 4	• Throughout the course, academics and professionals should provide feedback to students on using GenAI tools in assignments, emphasising adherence to the established guidelines. Additionally, assessment criteria for assignments should include considerations for the responsible and effective integration of GenAI technologies, ensuring students understand the importance of using these tools ethically.
Example 5	• Higher education institutions should regularly evaluate the effectiveness of the guidelines and make revisions as necessary based on feedback from students, faculty, and advancements in GenAI technologies. This ensures the guidelines remain relevant and reflect good practices in utilising GenAI tools in academic settings. • By implementing these steps, higher education institutions can effectively ensure that students understand how to use GenAI tools responsibly and effectively in their academic work, thereby promoting academic integrity and fostering ethical use of AI technologies.

P3. Higher education institutions should teach students how to properly use Generative Artificial Intelligence (GenAI) in their studies.

Rationale:

- Relying too much on GenAI might stop students from thinking and being creative. So, HEIs should teach students how to use GenAI correctly. This helps them take control of their learning. Also, higher education institutions should help students become good at using GenAI and other essential technologies to improve their education.
- GenAI apps and search engines can help HEIs teach students how to use GenAI correctly and ethically.

Incorporation:

- Higher education institutions should discuss the pros and cons of using GenAI with students. They should help students understand both the benefits and challenges of using GenAI. This will help students make intelligent choices and help academics get the support they need to use GenAI in their teaching.
- Since students and academics might have different levels of knowledge about GenAI, HEIs need to be flexible. They should find ways to help everyone learn at their own pace.
- HEIs should regularly check how GenAI affects students' learning. This ensures that it is helping students grow academically without causing any problems.

Example 1	• Host workshops and seminars to discuss the pros and cons of using GenAI with students and faculty. • Invite experts in the field to present balanced perspectives on the benefits and challenges of GenAI in education. • Encourage open discussions to address any concerns and clarify misconceptions.
Example 2	• Offer customised training programmes on GenAI for both students and faculty. • Provide introductory sessions for beginners and advanced sessions for those with more knowledge. • Make training materials and resources available online for self-paced learning.
Example 3	• Implement feedback mechanisms to regularly assess the impact of GenAI on students' learning experiences. • Conduct surveys, focus groups, or interviews to gather qualitative data on students' perceptions and experiences with GenAI. • Analyse quantitative data such as academic performance metrics to evaluate the effectiveness of GenAI in improving learning outcomes.
Example 4	• Establish support structures such as help desks or online forums where students and faculty can seek assistance with GenAI-related questions or issues. • Assign mentors or peer support groups to provide personalised guidance and support to GenAI users. • Collaborate with relevant departments or external experts to provide specialised support in implementing GenAI in specific academic disciplines.

Example 5	• Develop and communicate clear ethical guidelines and policies regarding the use of GenAI in education. • Ensure that all stakeholders are aware of their rights and responsibilities when utilising GenAI tools and technologies. • Regularly review and update these guidelines and policies to adapt to evolving ethical considerations and technological advancements.

P4. Higher education institutions should engage in open discussions about students' experiences with Generative Artificial Intelligence (GenAI), highlighting its strengths and weaknesses in enhancing their learning efforts.

Rationale:

- Higher education institutions must teach students how to use GenAI effectively while being aware of its limitations. This knowledge empowers students to use GenAI wisely and engage with it more deeply.
- By helping students understand both the strengths and weaknesses of GenAI, they can use it better for their studies and understand its uses and effects more deeply.

Incorporation:

- Higher education institutions should create rules for designing assessments, motivating academics to develop new ways to involve students and improve how much they learn. This might mean giving clear directions and examples showing when it is okay and not okay to use GenAI in assessments.
- The grading criteria and assessment guidelines should mention using GenAI correctly, standards for original work, and ensuring information comes from reliable sources.
- Universities should include in their course outlines and instructions the option to use verbal exams if they suspect someone of cheating on an assessment. This shows how important it is to be honest when using GenAI in learning.

Universities might consider:

1. Encouraging academics to let students use GenAI to answer assessment questions. Students would need to attach the GenAI-generated response to their assignment. This helps show how students improve on the initial GenAI output and proves they understand the subject. Also, students' reflection on the generated response helps confirm its originality and authenticity.
2. Creating assessment questions that require students to use critical thinking skills, make personal judgments, interpret subject-specific information, and make summary reports using GenAI.
3. Using different assessment methods in courses, like written assignments, short presentations with question sessions, and exercises for mapping out ideas.

4. Reflective exercises should be added to assessments, asking students to think about their research methods and processes. This could be done through reflective journals or blog posts.

5. Letting students help create assignments by allowing them to choose topics, case studies, and datasets they are interested in.

Example 1	• In a history course, students could use GenAI to generate responses to essay questions about historical events or figures. They would then attach the GenAI-generated response to their assignment submission. • After receiving the GenAI-generated response, students would write a reflection discussing how they improved upon the initial output and how it demonstrates their understanding of the historical context.
Example 2	• In a philosophy course, students could be asked to use GenAI to analyse and interpret complex philosophical texts. However, they would need to provide their personal judgments and critical analysis alongside the GenAI-generated analysis in their responses. • Assessment questions could require students to critically evaluate philosophical arguments or theories, using GenAI as a tool to aid in their analysis and synthesis of the material.
Example 3	• In a psychology course, assessment methods could include written assignments where students analyse case studies using GenAI to supplement their research. Additionally, students could participate in brief presentations where they present their findings and engage in a question-and-answer session with peers and instructors. • Concept mapping exercises could be used to assess students' understanding of psychological theories and their ability to organise and connect key concepts using GenAI-generated summaries.
Example 4	• In a research methods course, students could be asked to keep reflective journals throughout the semester, documenting their research process and decision-making. They would reflect on how they utilised GenAI tools in their research and discuss any challenges or insights gained. • Alternatively, students could create reflective blog posts where they share their experiences, thoughts, and observations related to using GenAI in their academic work.
Example 5	• In a data analysis course, students could collaborate with lecturers to select datasets relevant to their interests or career goals. They would then use GenAI tools to analyse and interpret the data, presenting their findings in written reports or presentations. • Students could also propose topics for research papers or case studies, demonstrating their understanding of course concepts and their ability to apply them to real-world scenarios.

P4. Additional Points:

1. **Give clear instructions and examples:**
   - Explain to students exactly how to use GenAI in their assignments, with examples for different tasks.
2. **Make sure assessment guidelines mention GenAI use:**
   - When grading written work, include rules about using GenAI, how to be original, and finding reliable sources.

3. **Hold workshops for summarising and referencing:**
   - Have sessions where students learn how to summarise reports, rewrite information in their own words, and properly cite academic sources.
4. **Ask for proof of sources used:**
   - Require students to provide links to where they found information or upload PDFs of the sources they used. This helps make sure they are being honest and following academic rules.
5. **Encourage using visuals in assignments:**
   - Tell students to include concepts such as maps or diagrams to show they understand and can use concepts they have learned.

Furthermore, HEIs should help students gain practical skills and think critically. They can do this by giving assignments that go beyond just learning facts. Academics should create tasks that test students' understanding of the subject and make them think about real-life problems and moral issues. When students work on scenarios or practical problems related to what they are studying, they learn to analyse situations, put information together, and make intelligent choices. For example, in a class about business ethics, students might study cases where companies face tough moral decisions. They will use what they know about ethics to suggest fair solutions. Similarly, in a psychology class, students might talk about made-up situations involving ethics in research or therapy. By thinking carefully about these scenarios and explaining their ideas, students become more aware of what is right and wrong, which is essential for their future jobs,

Also, when students work on real-world problems, they learn to work with others with different skills. For instance, in a class about the environment, students from different majors might team up to find ways to help with climate change in their area. This teamwork helps them improve in solving problems and communicating, which are essential skills for many jobs. In short, when universities assign assignments that make students think about real-life problems, handle tricky moral situations, and consider hypothetical scenarios, they help students develop the skills they will need to succeed at university and in their careers.

P5. Higher education institutions should consider assessing students' understanding of artificial intelligence (AI) and its effects on society.

Rationale:

- GenAI is set to change how we learn. This means HEIs need to rethink what students should know and how they are tested. So, it is essential for HEIs to update their courses to include GenAI's impact on how we learn and the skills we need.
- Having round-the-clock GenAI support services can give students excellent chances to learn. This goes beyond traditional limits and helps students keep learning all the time.

- Higher education institutions should plan and allocate resources to studying GenAI. This will help them understand what GenAI can and cannot do well. With this knowledge, universities can make intelligent choices about how to use GenAI in teaching.

Incorporation:

- Using a mix of different types of assignments that put students in real-life situations can give a complete evaluation of their abilities related to GenAI.
- When GenAI is part of how students are graded, it is best to use real tasks that let students use what they have learned in real situations. This helps them get better at solving problems and adapting to different situations.

Example 1	• Law students could participate in simulated court proceedings involving GenAI-related legal issues, such as privacy rights or liability for AI-generated content. • Assign students to draft legislation or regulations addressing the ethical and legal implications of GenAI technology in areas like data protection or intellectual property rights. • GenAI can analyse students' written work or oral arguments related to human rights cases and provide instant feedback on their legal analysis, argumentation, and application of human rights principles. • Generate realistic human rights case scenarios based on current events or historical cases. These scenarios can serve as the basis for case study analysis, mock trials, or legislative drafting assignments. • Create simulated environments for mock trials or moot court competitions. GenAI can generate responses from virtual judges, opposing counsel, or witnesses, enhancing the realism of the simulation and providing students with diverse perspectives. • Assist students in researching human rights issues by generating summaries of relevant legal precedents, international treaties, and scholarly articles. GenAI can help students identify key arguments and legal principles for their case analyses or policy briefs. • Using GenAI, students can analyse proposed legislation or policy documents related to human rights issues. They can evaluate the potential impact of these policies on human rights protections and generate recommendations for improvement or advocacy strategies. • GenAI can assess students' legal memos, briefs, or case analyses in tort law and provide detailed feedback on their legal reasoning, analysis of case law, and application of tort principles. This will help academics streamline the grading process and provide personalised feedback to students. • Generate hypothetical tort scenarios for problem-solving exercises or case study analyses. These scenarios can cover various tort issues, such as negligence, product liability, or intentional torts, allowing students to apply legal principles in various contexts. • Create virtual witnesses for mock trials or evidentiary hearings in tort law. GenAI can generate witness statements, deposition transcripts, or expert testimony based on the case scenario's facts, enhancing the simulation's realism. • Assist students in drafting legal documents such as complaints, answers, or discovery requests in tort cases. GenAI can provide templates, sample language, and guidance on formatting and legal requirements, helping students develop their drafting skills. • Facilitate virtual client counselling sessions where students interact with AI-generated clients seeking legal advice on tort matters. GenAI can simulate realistic client responses and scenarios, allowing students to practice communication skills, issue-spotting, and client management.

Example 2	• Students will be presented with a real-world business case study involving a company facing strategic challenges or opportunities. They will be tasked with analysing the case study and developing recommendations for the company's future direction. • To support their analysis, students will have access to GenAI, which can provide them with relevant industry data, market trends, competitor analysis, and predictive insights based on similar scenarios. Students can leverage GenAI to gather additional information, validate their assumptions, and explore alternative solutions. • After conducting their analysis, students will be required to develop a comprehensive strategic plan or business proposal, outlining their recommendations and the rationale behind them. They must also demonstrate their understanding of key business concepts, such as market analysis, competitive positioning, financial forecasting, and risk management. • Once the strategic plans or proposals are submitted, students will participate in AI-driven decision-making simulations to test their recommendations' feasibility in a dynamic business environment. GenAI simulates various scenarios and provides feedback on the potential outcomes of different strategic choices, allowing students to refine their proposals and understand the implications of their decisions. • Finally, students will present their strategic plans or proposals to a panel of faculty members and industry experts, who will evaluate the quality of their analysis, the effectiveness of their recommendations, and their ability to articulate their ideas coherently. Feedback from the panel will help students reflect on their learning process and identify areas for improvement. • This authentic assessment assesses students' critical thinking, problem-solving, and decision-making skills and integrates GenAI into the learning process. It provides students with valuable insights and enhances their understanding of real-world business dynamics.

It is essential for HEIs to follow the guiding principle to benefit fully from GenAI in teaching and learning. This principle is essential for promoting a responsible and ethical approach to AI use, protecting academic integrity, building trust, and improving learning outcomes. The guiding principle ensures that AI tools are used in a way that maintains the core values of education. By being clear about how AI tools are used, HEIs can ensure these technologies meet academic standards and ethical guidelines. Suppose AI is used to create educational content or offer personalised learning experiences. In that case, students and academics need to know where the AI-generated material comes from and what it involves. This helps keep academic quality high and ensures the content is relevant and accurate. Clear guidelines on AI use also help prevent academic dishonesty, like plagiarism, by making it easier to spot and address misuse.

Trust is a key part of the educational system, involving students, academics, administrators, and the wider community. The guiding principle builds trust by explaining how AI tools work and how decisions are made. When people understand the capabilities and limits of AI, they are more likely to trust and use these tools. For example, students are more likely to use AI-driven learning aids if they know how these tools help their learning without replacing their own thinking and creativity. Similarly, academics are more willing to use AI technologies if they see how these tools support their teaching rather than undermine it.

Using AI in education ethically and strategically can greatly improve learning outcomes, but this needs careful management. The guiding principle ensures AI tools are used to support and enhance traditional teaching methods, not replace them. By being clear about how AI is used to personalise learning experiences, HEIs can help students see how these tools can meet their individual needs, leading to better engagement and achievement. Regular evaluations and feedback loops ensure that AI systems are continually assessed and improved based on their impact on learning. This process helps refine AI applications to meet educational goals better. Therefore, AI systems can reinforce biases and inequalities if not correctly managed. By following the guiding principle, HEIs can reduce these risks. Transparent AI processes help identify and correct biases, ensuring AI applications do not unfairly disadvantage any group of students. Accountability involves setting up systems to quickly monitor AI outcomes and address ethical concerns. For instance, if an AI grading system is found to be biased against certain groups, the institution can take immediate corrective action. This proactive approach helps maintain fairness and inclusivity in education.

The guiding principle empowers everyone involved to make informed decisions about AI in education. For administrators, this means understanding the costs, benefits, and potential risks of AI adoption. For academics, it involves knowing how to integrate AI tools effectively into their teaching strategies. For students, it means understanding how to use AI to enhance their learning without becoming overly dependent on technology. This informed decision-making fosters a more effective and harmonious integration of AI in education.

Therefore, HEIs should adopt the guiding principle to harness GenAI's potential in teaching and learning fully. This guiding principle protects academic integrity and builds trust, improves learning outcomes, ensures ethical practices, and supports informed decision-making. By embedding the Guiding Principle for Using Generative AI in Teaching and Learning, HEIs can create a responsible, fair, and effective educational environment that benefits everyone.

GUIDING PRINCIPLES FOR STUDENTS REGARDING THE USE OF GENERATIVE AI WITHIN HIGHER EDUCATION INSTITUTIONS

The Guiding Principles for Students help universities understand why clear rules for using GenAI are essential. It sets out important rules that help students use GenAI responsibly, ensuring it is fair, inclusive, and honest. One big part of these rules is about ethics. Students need to understand how using GenAI can have ethical issues, follow rules about fairness, honesty, and respect for other people's work. By being ethical, students can ensure that their use of GenAI helps everyone and adheres to the values of truthfulness and fairness. Also, these rules make sure that students keep people's information safe. Students need to be careful with private information and follow the rules about keeping it secure. By doing this, students can avoid problems such as people getting access to information they should not have, or using it incorrectly. This helps create a culture of trust and responsibility in universities.

Another essential part of the 'Guiding Principles for Students Regarding the Use of Generative AI within Higher Education Institutions' is transparency and accountability. Students should understand how GenAI works and its limits and problems. They also need to take responsibility for what they do with GenAI and be ready to answer for it. By being transparent and accountable, students can create an environment where everyone feels open, trusted, and respected. Furthermore, the 'Guiding Principles for Students Regarding the Use of Generative AI within Higher Education Institutions' discuss fairness and ensuring that GenAI does not show any unfairness or bias. Students should look carefully at the results of GenAI and be aware of any unfairness that might come from the data used to train it. Also, they should try to fix any unfairness they find and make sure GenAI treats everyone fairly. By doing this, students can help ensure that GenAI supports diversity, fairness, and inclusion in universities.

Apart from being ethical, the 'Guiding Principles for Students Regarding the Use of Generative AI within Higher Education Institutions' also focuses on ensuring everyone has equal chances to learn and succeed. Students should use GenAI in ways that help everyone learn, no matter who they are. By doing this, students can use the power of GenAI to create a fairer and more equal learning environment in universities. In summary, creating guiding principles for students regarding the use of GenAI within HEIs is really important in handling the ethical issues of using AI properly. The 'Guiding Principles for Students Regarding the Use of Generative AI within Higher Education Institutions' aim to help students use GenAI in a good way, while also being fair, inclusive, and honest. By following the 'Guiding Principles for Students Regarding the Use of Generative AI within Higher Education Institutions,' students can use GenAI to help learning, research, and scholarship while respecting values like honesty, fairness, and respect for others.

P1: Transparency

Rationale:

- Transparency ensures that students do not misrepresent AI-generated content as their own original work. This practice helps prevent plagiarism, fostering an environment where creativity and personal intellectual efforts are valued and encouraged.
- When students are transparent about their use of AI, it builds trust with their peers and tutors. It also holds students accountable for their academic submissions, promoting a culture of honesty and integrity within the educational community.
- Transparency in AI usage helps students understand the role of AI in their learning processes. Clear explanations of how AI tools are used and the nature of AI-generated content can demystify these technologies, making them more accessible and comprehensible to students.
- By being transparent about the use of AI, students are encouraged to evaluate the outputs generated by these tools critically. This practice fosters critical thinking skills, enabling students to discern the differences between AI-generated content and human-generated content, and to assess the reliability and validity of the information provided.
- Educational institutions often have specific guidelines and policies regarding the use of AI. By adhering to transparency principles, students ensure they comply with these regulations, avoiding potential academic misconduct or legal issues.

- AI technologies are becoming increasingly prevalent in various professional fields. Transparency in AI usage in higher education prepares students for future careers by familiarising them with these technologies and developing the skills necessary to use and manage AI tools effectively.

Incorporation:

- Develop comprehensive policies on the acceptable use of AI in academic work.
- Clearly define what constitutes appropriate and inappropriate use of AI tools.
- Ensure these guidelines are easily accessible to all students and staff.
- Introduce mandatory orientation sessions for new students on the ethical use of AI.
- Offer workshops and training sessions throughout the academic year on how to use AI tools responsibly and transparently.
- Incorporate lessons on AI ethics, transparency, and critical thinking into relevant courses.
- Use case studies to illustrate the impact of AI misuse and the importance of transparency.

Example 1	• Offer dedicated courses on AI ethics tailored for law students. • Include discussions on transparency principles, bias mitigation, and legal implications of AI. • Analyse legal cases where AI systems transparency (or lack thereof) influenced legal outcomes.
Example 2	• Host seminars focusing on the intersection of law and technology. • Discuss the role of AI in legal research, document review, and predictive analysis. • Facilitate discussions on the importance of transparency in AI algorithms used in legal tech.
Example 3	• Provide opportunities for students to work on real legal cases using AI tools. • Guide students in evaluating AI systems' transparency in legal research and analysis. • Allow students to interact with clients and explain the AI tools being used transparently.
Example 3	• Include scenarios where students analyse AI-generated evidence in moot court competitions. • Encourage students to argue for or against the admissibility of AI-generated evidence based on transparency principles. • Provide feedback on students' arguments, emphasising the importance of transparency in legal proceedings.
Example 4	• Conduct mock regulatory audits to assess students' understanding of AI transparency requirements. • Evaluate students' compliance efforts in ensuring transparency in AI systems used in legal contexts. • Offer feedback on students' mock audit reports and suggest improvements to enhance transparency practices.

P2: Explainability

Rationale:

- Explainability ensures that students are accountable for the decisions made by AI systems they use.
- It encourages transparency in AI processes, fostering trust and integrity in academic work.
- Understanding how AI algorithms work allows students to identify and mitigate biases.
- By promoting explainability, students can ensure fairness and equity in their academic endeavours.
- Explainability enables students to comprehend how AI algorithms arrive at their decisions.
- It enhances students' learning experiences by demystifying complex AI processes and promoting deeper understanding.
- By questioning and analysing AI outputs, students develop critical thinking skills.
- They learn to evaluate the reliability and validity of AI-generated information, enhancing their analytical abilities.
- Understanding the ethical implications of AI decisions empowers students to navigate complex ethical dilemmas.
- Explainability encourages students to consider the ethical consequences of AI usage and make informed decisions.

Incorporation:

- Students need to understand how AI tools reach their conclusions so they can critically evaluate and apply these insights effectively.
- Explainability helps students grasp the AI's reasoning, improving their ability to use these tools in their legal practice.
- When students can explain AI processes, they develop stronger analytical skills.
- This deep understanding is essential for creating well-reasoned legal arguments and strategies.
- Explainability ensures that students are aware of potential biases and limitations within AI systems.
- This awareness helps prevent the misuse of AI in ways that could perpetuate bias or inequality.

- Explainable AI helps protect students' rights by ensuring transparency in data usage and decision-making processes.
- This aligns with data protection laws and institutional policies.

Example 1	• Integrate a module on AI-driven text analysis tools used for exploring themes, motifs, and patterns in literature. • Teach students how these AI tools work, including their algorithms and data processing techniques, to help them understand how AI identifies literary elements.
Example 2	• Students use an AI tool to analyse a classic novel, then present a report explaining how the AI reached its conclusions about themes and motifs. • Analyse case studies of AI use in literary research, focusing on the transparency of AI's methods.
Example 3	• Offer a module on the use of AI for historical data analysis, such as identifying patterns in historical texts or predicting historical trends. • Include lessons on how AI algorithms process historical data and the importance of understanding these processes to avoid biased interpretations.
Example 4	• Students use AI to analyse historical events and explain the methodology the AI used, including data sources, algorithms, and potential biases. • Conduct workshops where students can practice explaining AI-driven research findings to peers and professors.
Example 5	• Develop a course on the use of AI in creating art, such as generating visual art or music. • Teach students the algorithms behind AI art tools and how to interpret the AI's creative process.
Example 6	• Students create AI-generated artworks and explain the AI's role, including the data inputs, algorithms, and the rationale behind the outputs. • Hold critique sessions where students present their AI-assisted artworks and explain the AI's contribution to their creative process.

P3: Responsibility

Rationale:

- Students must understand and apply ethical standards when using AI, ensuring their work maintains academic and professional integrity.
- Using AI responsibly helps prevent issues such as plagiarism, where students might pass off AI-generated content as their own without proper attribution.
- Adhering to responsible AI usage practices builds trust between students and their peers, academics, and future employers.
- Early adoption of responsible AI use sets the foundation for a professional reputation based on ethical practices and integrity.
- Students need to be aware of the potential biases in AI systems, including those stemming from biased data sets or algorithms.

- By acknowledging and addressing these biases, students can contribute to fairer and more equitable outcomes in their academic and professional work.
- Students must take responsibility for the outcomes generated by AI tools, ensuring they validate and verify the results rather than blindly trusting AI outputs.
- A responsible approach includes acknowledging and correcting any errors or inaccuracies produced by AI, ensuring the reliability of their work.
- Students should be aware of the environmental impact of AI, such as the energy consumption of large-scale data processing, and strive to use AI in an environmentally responsible manner.
- Encouraging sustainable practices in AI usage aligns with broader goals of sustainable development and responsible resource management.
- Responsible AI usage involves critically evaluating AI outputs and understanding the limitations and potential errors in AI-generated results.
- Students develop better decision-making skills by responsibly assessing when and how to use AI tools in their work.

Incorporation:

- Integrate AI ethics modules into existing courses across various disciplines such as computer science, business, healthcare, arts, and humanities.
- Tailor the ethical content to address specific challenges and scenarios relevant to each field.
- Create comprehensive policies that outline responsible AI usage, including guidelines on data privacy, bias mitigation, and accountability.
- Ensure that both students and faculty are trained on these policies through workshops, seminars, and online courses.
- Set up an ethics review board responsible for overseeing AI-related projects and ensuring they adhere to established ethical guidelines.
- All AI-related research projects are required to receive approval from the ethics review board before commencement.
- Develop service-learning opportunities where students work on real-world projects with community partners, focusing on responsible AI applications.
- Organise hackathons with a focus on creating ethical and responsible AI solutions to societal problems.
- Offer regular workshops and training sessions for faculty on responsible AI usage and the latest developments in AI ethics.

- Foster interdisciplinary collaboration among faculty to share best practices and develop a unified approach to responsible AI education.
- Establish ethics forums and discussion groups where students can engage with peers and experts on topics related to responsible AI usage.
- Invite industry professionals and ethicists to give guest lectures on the importance of responsibility in AI.
- Launch awareness campaigns to educate the campus community about the importance of responsible AI usage.
- Create and distribute educational materials, such as brochures, videos, and infographics, highlighting key principles of responsible AI.

Example 1	• Develop and offer a dedicated course titled 'Ethics in AI for Science and Mathematics,' focusing on responsible AI use in scientific research and mathematical applications. • Cover topics such as ethical theories, bias in AI algorithms, data privacy, accountability, and real-world case studies of AI misuse and best practices.
Example 2	• Integrate AI ethics modules into core courses in science and mathematics, ensuring students understand the ethical implications of AI in their specific fields. • Tailor ethical content to address challenges in areas such as bioinformatics, data analysis, statistical modelling, and computational simulations.
Example 3	• Provide research grants specifically for projects that focus on ethical AI and responsible usage. • Establish research centres dedicated to the study of ethical AI, promoting innovative solutions to ethical challenges in AI.
Example 4	• Introduce awards and recognition for outstanding contributions to responsible AI usage, encouraging students and faculty to prioritise ethics in their work. • Host events to showcase projects and research that exemplify responsible AI practices.

P4: Ethical Oversight

Rationale:

- Following the ethical oversight principle ensures that students maintain high ethical standards in their use of AI technologies.
- Ethical oversight helps prevent the misuse of AI tools for unethical purposes such as cheating, plagiarism, or discriminatory practices.
- Ethical oversight fosters a culture of academic integrity where students are accountable for their actions and decisions related to AI usage.
- Upholding ethical standards in AI usage ensures the credibility and reputation of academic institutions and their graduates.

Example 1	**AI in Music and Creative Arts Curriculum** • AI Composition Workshops: • **Content:** Conduct workshops focused on using AI tools for music composition. Tools like OpenAI's MuseNet or Google's Magenta can help students explore how AI can assist in creating new compositions. • **Activity:** Students compose pieces using these AI tools and present their work, discussing how AI influenced their creative process.
Example 2	**AI-Assisted Design Projects:** • **Content:** Introduce AI tools for visual arts, such as DeepArt or Artbreeder, in courses related to digital art and design. • **Activity:** Assign projects where students create artwork or design elements using these AI tools, encouraging them to experiment with different styles and techniques.
Example 3	**Ethics of AI in Creativity Seminars**: • **Content:** Offer seminars that address the ethical implications of AI in creative fields. Topics could include copyright issues, the impact on human creativity, and the potential for AI to perpetuate biases. • **Activity:** Students participate in debates and write reflective essays on these topics, fostering critical thinking and ethical reasoning.
Example 4	**AI Tutoring and Peer Mentoring**: • **Content:** Establish tutoring and peer mentoring programmes where students can receive help with using AI tools and understanding AI concepts. • **Activity:** Peer mentors who are proficient in AI applications in the arts offer workshops, drop-in tutoring sessions, and one-on-one mentoring.
Example 5	**AI and Creativity Speaker Series**: • **Content:** Host a speaker series featuring artists, technologists, and researchers who are pioneers in using AI in creative fields. • **Activity:** Students attend talks and panel discussions, gaining insights into the latest developments in AI and creativity, and have opportunities to network with professionals in the field.

P7: Empowering Users

Rationale:

- Ensures students are equipped with essential skills to navigate and utilise AI technologies effectively, preparing them for the digital age.
- Encourages students to leverage AI tools to push the boundaries of creativity and explore new avenues in their respective fields.
- Provides students with hands-on experience and knowledge of AI, making them more competitive in the job market where AI proficiency is increasingly in demand.
- Educates students on the ethical implications and responsibilities of using AI, promoting responsible and fair use of technology

- Enables personalised educational experiences through AI-driven tools that adapt to individual learning styles and needs.
- Engages students in complex problem-solving scenarios using AI, enhancing their critical thinking and analytical skills.

Incorporation:

- Ensure students have access to state-of-the-art AI software, hardware, and platforms.
- Maintain a repository of AI-related educational materials, tutorials, and online courses.
- Embed AI-related modules in existing courses across different departments, ensuring interdisciplinary exposure.
- Encourage faculty to incorporate AI tools and applications relevant to their fields of study.
- Create a network of AI experts, including faculty, industry professionals, and advanced students, to mentor and support peers.
- Set up help desks or online forums where students can seek assistance with AI-related queries.
- Provide career support services focused on AI-related career paths, including internships and job placement services.
- Partner with companies and organisations to offer students internships and real-world AI project opportunities.
- Regularly collect feedback from students on AI programmes and resources to identify areas for improvement.
- Adapt and update AI courses and resources based on student needs and technological advancements.
- Offer continuing education programmes and certifications in AI for alumni and working professionals.
- Provide access to AI learning resources and professional development opportunities beyond graduation.

Example 1	• Offer workshops on using AI-powered legal research tools like ROSS Intelligence or Casetext. Train students on how to effectively use these tools to enhance their legal research skills, streamline case law searches, and analyse large volumes of legal documents efficiently.
Example 2	• Integrate AI tools such as Lex Machina or LawGeex into legal writing and drafting courses. Teach students how to utilise these tools for automated contract review, legal document generation, and predictive analytics to improve the accuracy and efficiency of their work.

Example 3	• Establish AI-driven legal clinics where students provide pro bono legal services using AI tools. This hands-on experience can help students learn how to leverage AI in real-world scenarios, enhancing their practical skills and understanding of AI applications in law.
Example 4	• Create interdisciplinary courses that bring together law students and computer science students to work on AI-related legal projects. This can include developing AI tools for legal applications, understanding the technical aspects of AI, and exploring legal regulations governing AI technologies.
Example 5	• Use AI-driven simulation software to create realistic legal scenarios where students must apply their legal knowledge and AI tools to resolve cases. This experiential learning approach helps students gain confidence and competence in using AI in legal practice.
Example 6	• Incorporate AI literacy modules into the core law curriculum. These modules can cover the basics of AI, its applications in law, and how it is transforming the legal landscape. This foundational knowledge ensures that all law graduates are proficient in understanding and using AI.

P8: Inclusivity

Rationale:

- Provides all students, regardless of background or ability, with equal opportunities to learn and benefit from AI technologies, reducing educational disparities.
- Encourages diverse viewpoints in AI development and application, leading to more robust and innovative solutions that consider a wider range of needs and experiences.
- Utilises AI to create adaptive learning environments and assistive technologies, making education more accessible for students with disabilities.
- Incorporates diverse datasets and inclusive design principles to minimise biases in AI systems, promoting fairness and equity in AI-driven decision-making processes.
- Prepares students to work in diverse teams and understand the importance of inclusivity in AI development, fostering a more inclusive workforce in the tech industry.
- Instils a sense of responsibility and ethical awareness in students, emphasising the importance of inclusivity and fairness in the development and deployment of AI technologies.
- Provides targeted support and resources for underrepresented groups in AI fields, helping to close the gender, racial, and socio-economic gaps in tech education and careers.
- Encourages the development of AI solutions that address social justice issues, such as bias detection, accessibility improvements, and equitable resource distribution.
- Fosters an environment where students learn to appreciate and incorporate cultural differences in AI applications, improving the global applicability and relevance of AI technologies.

- Creates an inclusive learning environment that supports continuous education and skill development for all students, including those from non-traditional backgrounds or with varied educational experiences.
- Cultivates a sense of community and belonging among students, promoting collaboration and knowledge sharing across diverse groups.
- Demonstrates the institution's commitment to inclusivity and social responsibility, enhancing its reputation and attracting a diverse student body and faculty.
- Ensures compliance with legal requirements and ethical standards related to inclusivity and accessibility in education, reducing the risk of discrimination and bias.

Incorporation:

- Raise awareness of the importance of inclusivity in AI education through awareness campaigns, events, and advocacy efforts, engaging students, faculty, and administrators in promoting a culture of inclusivity in AI use.
- Ensure that AI tools and resources used in coursework are accessible to students with disabilities, providing compatibility with screen readers, alternative input devices, and other assistive technologies.
- Incorporate diverse perspectives and case studies into AI curriculum materials, including examples that reflect a variety of cultural, social, and economic backgrounds.
- Encourage students to develop AI applications and projects that address the needs of diverse populations, considering factors such as language diversity, accessibility requirements, and cultural sensitivities.
- Provide support services and accommodations to ensure that all students, regardless of background or ability, have equal access to AI education opportunities, including tutoring, language support, and flexible learning formats.
- Promote diversity and inclusion in AI research teams, encouraging collaboration among students from different backgrounds and disciplines to bring a range of perspectives to AI innovation.
- Offer training programmes or workshops on cultural competence and sensitivity in AI development and application, helping students understand and navigate the complexities of working with diverse communities.
- Design assessment criteria that account for diverse perspectives and approaches to AI projects, recognising the value of inclusive design and the contributions of students from underrepresented groups.
- Provide targeted support and resources for underrepresented groups in AI education, including scholarships, mentorship programmes, and networking opportunities to help overcome barriers and promote inclusion.

- Raise awareness of the importance of inclusivity in AI education through awareness campaigns, events, and advocacy efforts, engaging students, faculty, and administrators in promoting a culture of inclusivity in AI use.

Example 1	• Provide accessible AI tools for data analysis, such as screen reader-compatible data visualisation software, to ensure that students with visual impairments can participate fully in science and geography courses that involve AI-driven data analysis.
Example 2	• Encourage students to use diverse data sets that represent a variety of geographic regions, cultures, and demographics in their AI projects. This ensures that AI models developed by students are inclusive and relevant to a wide range of populations.
Example 3	• Organise AI-driven field studies in geography courses that are inclusive of students with mobility impairments. Provide alternative field study options or virtual reality experiences that allow all students to participate in data collection and analysis activities.
Example 4	• Incorporate discussions on the ethical implications of AI in science research, including issues related to data privacy, consent, and potential biases in AI algorithms. Encourage students to consider these ethical considerations when designing and conducting AI-driven research projects.
Example 5	• Engage students in community-based AI projects in geography courses, where they collaborate with local communities to address environmental or social challenges using AI technologies. This approach ensures that AI projects are inclusive of diverse community perspectives and priorities.
Example 6	• Offer AI education materials and resources in multiple languages to support students whose first language may not be English. This ensures that language barriers do not hinder students' access to AI education opportunities in science and geography. • Task students with developing AI-driven projects in geography courses that address environmental justice issues, such as air quality monitoring in marginalised communities or equitable access to green spaces. This approach promotes inclusivity by focusing on AI applications that benefit underserved populations.

P9: Environmental Impact

Rationale:

- Raises awareness among students about the environmental impact of AI technologies, fostering a culture of sustainability and responsible consumption.
- Encourages students to develop AI solutions that minimise energy consumption and reduce carbon emissions, contributing to the fight against climate change.
- Promotes the use of AI algorithms and systems that optimise resource utilisation, such as energy-efficient data processing methods and hardware design.
- Educates students on green computing principles and practices, including the use of renewable energy sources for data centres, energy-efficient hardware design, and sustainable software development methodologies.

- Inspires students to create AI applications that address environmental challenges, such as climate modelling, natural resource management, renewable energy optimisation, and environmental monitoring.
- Raises awareness of the ethical implications of AI technologies on the environment, encouraging students to consider the broader environmental impacts of their AI projects and decisions.
- Encourages students to explore how AI can facilitate the transition to a circular economy by optimising resource flows, reducing waste, and promoting recycling and reuse.
- Empower students to advocate for policies and regulations that promote environmentally sustainable AI development and deployment, fostering collaboration between academia, industry, and government.
- Recognises the global impact of AI on the environment and empowers students to take action to mitigate negative environmental consequences and promote sustainable development on a local, regional, and global scale.
- Prepares students for careers in green technology and sustainability by equipping them with the skills and knowledge needed to develop environmentally friendly AI solutions and contribute to a more sustainable future.

Incorporation:

- Encourage students to develop AI projects with a focus on sustainability and environmental impact, such as optimising energy consumption in AI systems, reducing carbon emissions, or addressing environmental challenges through AI-driven solutions.
- Integrate environmental impact assessments into AI project planning and development processes, requiring students to consider the potential environmental consequences of their AI projects and propose strategies for mitigating negative impacts.
- Incorporate discussions on environmental justice into AI education, highlighting the disproportionate environmental impacts experienced by marginalised communities and encouraging students to develop AI solutions that address environmental inequalities.
- Empower students to advocate for policies and regulations that promote environmentally sustainable AI development and deployment, providing opportunities for students to engage with policymakers and industry stakeholders on environmental issues related to AI.

<table>
<tr>
<td>Example 1</td>
<td>
Environmental Justice AI Clinic
<ul>
<li>Objective: Integrate environmental justice considerations into AI legal research and advocacy.</li>
<li>Description: Establish an AI clinic within the law degree programme focused on environmental justice issues. This clinic would engage students in AI-driven legal research and advocacy projects to address environmental challenges and promote environmental justice.</li>
</ul>
Project Examples:
<ul>
<li>Environmental Impact Assessments: Students use AI tools to analyse the environmental impact of proposed development projects, such as industrial facilities or infrastructure projects, on marginalised communities. They provide legal assessments and recommendations to ensure compliance with environmental regulations and protect the rights of affected communities.</li>
<li>Climate Litigation Support: Students utilise AI-powered data analysis tools to support climate change litigation efforts. They analyse large datasets related to climate change impacts, greenhouse gas emissions, and environmental regulations to provide legal teams with evidence and insights for climate-related lawsuits seeking environmental protections and compensation for affected communities.</li>
<li>Environmental Policy Analysis: Students conduct AI-driven analyses of environmental policies and regulations to identify gaps, inconsistencies, or opportunities for improvement. They provide legal research and recommendations to policymakers, advocacy groups, and community organisations working on environmental policy reform initiatives.</li>
<li>Community Environmental Advocacy: Students collaborate with environmental justice organisations and community groups to develop AI-driven legal advocacy strategies. They use AI tools to analyse environmental data, map environmental hazards, and identify environmental justice violations in marginalised communities. They then assist with legal actions, such as filing lawsuits or petitioning regulatory agencies, to address environmental injustices and advocate for equitable environmental protections.</li>
<li>Implementation: The Environmental Justice AI Clinic would be integrated into the law degree programme curriculum, offering students experiential learning opportunities to apply AI technologies to environmental justice issues. Students would receive training in AI tools and methodologies, legal research and analysis, and environmental law and policy. The clinic would be supervised by faculty with expertise in environmental law and AI, and students would collaborate with environmental justice experts and community stakeholders on their projects.</li>
<li>Benefits: This initiative would empower law students to use AI technologies to advance environmental justice goals, providing valuable legal assistance to communities disproportionately impacted by environmental hazards and inequalities. It would also enhance students' understanding of the intersection between AI, law, and environmental sustainability, preparing them for careers in environmental law, public interest advocacy, and policy reform. Additionally, the clinic's projects would contribute to real-world environmental justice efforts, promoting social and environmental responsibility within the legal profession.</li>
</ul>
</td>
</tr>
</table>

P10: Policy Development

Rationale:

- Establishing policies encourages students to consider the ethical implications of AI technologies and develop guidelines for responsible AI use, fostering a culture of ethical awareness and accountability.

- Policy development helps students understand and navigate the complex legal and regulatory landscape surrounding AI, ensuring compliance with relevant laws and regulations and mitigating legal risks.
- Policies on data privacy and security help safeguard sensitive information and protect individuals' privacy rights, promoting trust and confidence in AI systems and applications.
- Policies aimed at mitigating bias and promoting fairness in AI algorithms and decision-making processes help reduce the risk of discriminatory outcomes and promote equity and inclusion.
- Policies requiring transparency in AI systems and accountability for their outcomes promote trust and transparency, enabling stakeholders to understand how AI decisions are made and hold responsible parties accountable for their actions.
- Policy development involves collaboration between students from diverse backgrounds and disciplines, fostering interdisciplinary cooperation and a more holistic approach to AI governance.
- Policies that strike a balance between fostering innovation and ensuring responsible AI development help create an environment conducive to innovation while minimising potential harms and risks associated with AI technologies.
- Engaging students in policy development educates them about the societal implications of AI and empowers them to actively participate in shaping AI governance frameworks and regulations, fostering informed citizenship and civic engagement.
- Experience in policy development equips students with valuable skills and knowledge relevant to careers in AI governance, policy advocacy, regulatory compliance, and public sector leadership, enhancing their professional readiness and employability.
- Well-designed policies that prioritise transparency, fairness, and accountability in AI use build public trust and acceptance of AI technologies, facilitating their responsible adoption and integration into society.

Incorporation:

- Offer courses or workshops on AI policy development, covering topics such as ethical considerations, legal frameworks, regulatory compliance, and stakeholder engagement.
- Use case studies and policy simulations to engage students in hands-on learning experiences, allowing them to analyse real-world AI governance challenges and develop policy recommendations.
- Assign projects that require students to analyse existing AI policies and regulations, identify gaps or areas for improvement, and propose policy recommendations to address emerging issues or promote ethical AI use.

- Organise stakeholder engagement activities, such as panel discussions, debates, or public forums, where students can interact with experts, policymakers, industry representatives, and community members to gather input and perspectives for policy development.
- Provide opportunities for students to consult with experts in AI governance, including faculty members, industry professionals, government officials, and advocacy groups, to gain insights and guidance for their policy development efforts.
- Task students with drafting policy documents, such as AI ethics guidelines, data privacy protocols, algorithmic accountability frameworks, or legislative proposals, to address specific AI governance challenges or objectives.
- Provide training in presentation and advocacy skills to help students effectively communicate their policy recommendations to stakeholders, policymakers, and the broader community, advocating for their adoption and implementation.
- Encourage students to develop collaborative implementation plans for their policy recommendations, considering practical considerations, resource allocation, and stakeholder engagement strategies to ensure successful policy implementation.

Example 1	**AI Ethics and Governance Task Force** • **Objective:** Establish a task force within fashion and music programmes dedicated to developing AI ethics and governance policies tailored to the creative industries. • **Description:** The task force, comprised of faculty members, students, industry experts, and legal advisors, collaborates to address ethical considerations and regulatory challenges related to the use of AI in fashion and music. Through research, analysis, and stakeholder engagement, the task force develops comprehensive policies to guide responsible AI use and innovation in these fields. **Project Examples:** • **Ethical AI Use Guidelines:** Develop guidelines for the ethical use of AI in fashion design and music production, addressing issues such as cultural appropriation, diversity representation, and intellectual property rights. • **Data Privacy and Security Protocols:** Establish protocols for protecting data privacy and ensuring the security of personal and sensitive information collected and processed by AI systems in fashion and music contexts. • **Fairness and Bias Mitigation Strategies:** Implement strategies to mitigate bias and promote fairness in AI algorithms used for recommendation systems, trend analysis, and content creation in fashion and music platforms. • **Transparency and Accountability Frameworks:** Define frameworks for transparency and accountability in AI-driven decision-making processes, ensuring that stakeholders understand how AI technologies are used and held accountable for their outcomes. • **Intellectual Property Rights Policies:** Develop policies to address intellectual property rights issues related to AI-generated fashion designs, music compositions, and other creative works, including ownership, licensing, and attribution requirements. • **Collaborative Industry Standard:** Collaborate with industry partners and professional associations to develop industry-wide standards and best practices for AI use in fashion and music, promoting consistency and interoperability across platforms and organisations.

	Implementation: • The AI Ethics and Governance Task Force operates as a collaborative initiative within fashion and music programmes, leveraging expertise from multiple disciplines and engaging students in policy development through coursework, research projects, and extracurricular activities. The task force regularly consults with industry stakeholders, legal experts, and advocacy groups to ensure that policies reflect emerging trends, evolving technologies, and stakeholder perspectives. **Benefits:** • By engaging students in policy development, the task force provides hands-on learning opportunities that deepen their understanding of ethical considerations, legal frameworks, and industry dynamics related to AI in fashion and music. The policies developed by the task force help establish guidelines for responsible AI use, promote trust and confidence in AI technologies, and foster innovation and creativity in the creative industries. Additionally, the task force serves as a model for interdisciplinary collaboration and ethical leadership, preparing students to navigate complex ethical and regulatory challenges in their future careers.

P11: Training and Awareness

Rationale:

- Provides students with the necessary skills and knowledge to effectively use AI tools and technologies, enhancing their technical proficiency and employability in a rapidly evolving job market.
- Raises awareness of ethical considerations in AI development and use, encouraging students to adopt responsible AI practices and consider the societal impacts of their work.
- Equips students with the ability to critically assess AI technologies, understanding their limitations, potential biases, and the importance of transparency and accountability.
- Encourages students to explore innovative applications of AI across various disciplines, fostering creativity and the development of novel solutions to complex problems.
- Cultivates a mindset of continuous learning and adaptation, preparing students to keep pace with ongoing advancements in AI and related fields throughout their careers.
- Promotes interdisciplinary learning, enabling students from diverse academic backgrounds to understand and leverage AI technologies in their respective fields.
- Prepares students for a wide range of career opportunities in AI-driven industries by providing hands-on experience and practical knowledge of AI applications.
- Instils a sense of responsibility in students, encouraging them to consider the ethical, social, and environmental implications of their AI innovations.

- Promotes transparency and public understanding of AI technologies, helping to build trust and acceptance of AI in society.
- Responds to the growing demand for AI expertise in the workforce, ensuring that graduates are well equipped to meet industry needs and drive economic growth.
- Ensures that all students, regardless of their background, have access to AI education and training, promoting diversity and inclusion in AI-related fields.
- Educates students on regulatory frameworks and compliance requirements related to AI, ensuring that they are prepared to navigate legal and ethical challenges in their professional work.
- Develops students' ability to apply AI technologies to solve real-world problems, enhancing their problem-solving skills and practical application of theoretical knowledge.
- Empowers students to make informed decisions about the use and deployment of AI technologies, considering both the benefits and potential risks.
- Prepares students to compete in a global market where AI expertise is increasingly valued, contributing to their personal and professional success on an international scale.

Incorporation:

- Develop and integrate a comprehensive AI curriculum across various disciplines, covering fundamental concepts, technical skills, ethical considerations, and practical applications.
- Offer hands-on workshops and laboratory sessions where students can gain practical experience with AI tools, techniques, and real-world projects.
- Create interdisciplinary courses that allow students from different academic backgrounds to learn about AI and its applications in fields such as healthcare, finance, humanities, and social sciences.
- Host guest lectures and panel discussions featuring AI experts, industry leaders, and ethicists to provide students with diverse perspectives and insights into the latest developments and challenges in AI.
- Incorporate AI ethics training into the curriculum, addressing issues such as bias, fairness, transparency, accountability, and the societal impact of AI technologies.
- Develop AI literacy programmes aimed at students from non-technical backgrounds, ensuring that all students have a basic understanding of AI concepts and applications.
- Provide access to online courses, MOOCs, and other digital learning resources that offer flexible, self-paced learning opportunities in AI.
- Establish mentorship programmes where students can receive guidance and support from faculty members, industry professionals, and advanced peers in AI-related fields.

- Organise debates, seminars, and workshops on AI ethics, policy, and regulation, encouraging students to critically engage with the societal implications of AI.
- Launch awareness campaigns and informational sessions to educate the campus community about the benefits, risks, and ethical considerations of AI technologies.
- Provide certification programmes in AI and related fields, offering students formal recognition of their skills and knowledge that can enhance their career prospects.
- Support AI-focused clubs and societies where students can collaborate on projects, share knowledge, and stay updated on the latest AI trends and research.
- Utilise collaborative learning platforms and AI-driven educational tools to enhance the learning experience and foster a collaborative learning environment.
- Implement regular assessments and feedback mechanisms to evaluate students' understanding and proficiency in AI, helping them identify areas for improvement and track their progress.
- Partner with industry leaders and tech companies to provide students with access to the latest AI tools, resources, and real-world applications, enhancing their practical skills and industry readiness.

<table>
<tr>
<td>Example 1</td>
<td>
AI in Creative Arts Bootcamp
<ul>
<li>Objective: Provide intensive training and raise awareness about the applications, ethical considerations, and career opportunities related to AI in the fashion and music industries.</li>
<li>Description: Organise a week-long bootcamp for students enrolled in fashion and music programmes. The bootcamp will include workshops, hands-on projects, guest lectures, and panel discussions focused on the integration of AI in creative arts.</li>
</ul>
Programme Components:
<ul>
<li>Workshops on AI Tools:</li>
<li>Conduct workshops on using AI tools and software specific to fashion design (e.g., CLO 3D, Adobe Sensei) and music production (e.g., Amper Music, AIVA). These workshops will teach students how to incorporate AI into their creative processes.</li>
<li>Ethics in AI:</li>
<li>Host sessions on the ethical implications of AI in fashion and music. Topics will include intellectual property rights, bias in AI-generated designs and music, and the impact of AI on employment in the creative industries.</li>
</ul>
Industry Expert Panels:
<ul>
<li>Invite industry professionals to discuss the latest trends and challenges in AI applications within fashion and music. Experts will share their experiences and insights on leveraging AI for innovation while addressing ethical and practical concerns.</li>
</ul>
Hands-On Projects:
<ul>
<li>Facilitate hands-on projects where students can apply AI tools to create fashion designs or compose music. These projects will culminate in a showcase event where students present their AI-enhanced creations.</li>
</ul>
</td>
</tr>
</table>

	AI and Sustainability: • Include sessions on how AI can promote sustainability in fashion and music. For fashion, this could involve AI-driven supply chain optimisation and sustainable design practices. For music, it could involve reducing environmental impacts through AI-optimised production techniques. **Collaborative Learning:** • Encourage interdisciplinary collaboration by pairing fashion and music students on projects that integrate AI. For example, teams could work on AI-generated fashion collections inspired by AI-composed music tracks. **Career Pathways:** • Provide information on career opportunities in AI within the fashion and music industries. Offer guidance on how to build a portfolio that highlights AI skills and discuss potential roles such as AI fashion designer, AI music producer, and AI ethics consultant. **Mentorship and Networking:** • Establish a mentorship programme where students can receive ongoing support from faculty and industry experts. Create networking opportunities with AI professionals in the creative industries. • **Implementation:** The AI in Creative Arts Bootcamp will be an annual event integrated into the academic calendar of fashion and music programmes. Faculty members, industry partners, and AI experts will collaborate to design and deliver the boot camp content. • **Benefits:** This initiative will equip fashion and music students with the skills and knowledge needed to effectively incorporate AI into their creative work. It will raise awareness of ethical and sustainability issues, foster innovation, and enhance students' career readiness in an AI-driven job market. Additionally, the bootcamp will promote interdisciplinary collaboration and help build a supportive community of AI-savvy creative professionals.
Example 2	**AI in Legal Practice Training Programme** • **Objective:** Equip law students with the knowledge and skills to effectively use AI technologies in legal practice, while raising awareness about the ethical, legal, and societal implications of AI. • **Description:** Develop a comprehensive training programme within the law degree curriculum that includes coursework, workshops, experiential learning opportunities, and ethical discussions focused on AI applications in the legal field. **Programme Components:** **AI and Legal Technology Course:** • Introduce a course that covers the fundamentals of AI, its applications in the legal industry, and the transformative impact on legal practice. Topics could include AI-driven legal research, predictive analytics, contract analysis, and case outcome predictions. **Workshops on AI Tools:** • Conduct hands-on workshops where students learn to use AI-powered legal tools such as ROSS Intelligence, Kira Systems, and Lex Machina. These workshops will provide practical experience in leveraging AI for tasks like legal research, document review, and case management. **Ethics and AI in Law Seminars:** • Host seminars that delve into the ethical and legal challenges posed by AI in the legal field. Discussions could focus on issues like bias in AI algorithms, data privacy, the impact of AI on legal employment, and the responsibility of legal professionals in overseeing AI technologies.

AI and Legal Research Projects:

- Encourage students to undertake research projects exploring AI integration in legal processes. Students can analyse case studies, evaluate the effectiveness of AI tools, and propose frameworks for ethical AI use in legal settings.

Guest Lectures from Industry Experts:

- Invite legal tech entrepreneurs, AI researchers, and practising lawyers to share insights on the latest advancements in legal AI, real-world applications, and career opportunities in the intersection of law and technology.

Mock Trials and AI Simulations:

- Incorporate mock trials and simulations where students use AI tools to prepare cases, analyse evidence, and predict case outcomes. These practical exercises will help students understand the capabilities and limitations of AI in a courtroom setting.

Interdisciplinary Collaboration:

- Facilitate collaboration between law students and students from computer science, data science, and ethics programmes to develop interdisciplinary projects that address complex legal and technological challenges.

AI in Law Clinics:

- Integrate AI tools into existing law clinics where students provide legal assistance to clients. This practical experience will help students understand how AI can enhance legal services and improve access to justice.

Policy Development and Advocacy:

- Encourage students to engage in policy development and advocacy efforts related to AI and the law. Students can draft policy proposals, participate in public consultations, and advocate for regulations that ensure the ethical and responsible use of AI in the legal system.

Mentorship and Networking Opportunities:

- Establish a mentorship program where students can receive guidance from faculty members and legal professionals with expertise in AI. Organise networking events to connect students with industry leaders and potential employers.

Implementation:

- The AI in Legal Practice Training Programme will be integrated into the law school curriculum as a series of elective courses, workshops, and extracurricular activities. Collaboration with legal tech companies and AI experts will be essential for providing up-to-date content and practical experiences.

Benefits:

- This initiative will prepare law students for the evolving legal landscape, where AI technologies are increasingly prevalent. Students will gain valuable technical skills, ethical awareness, and practical experience, enhancing their career prospects and their ability to navigate the challenges and opportunities presented by AI in legal practice. Additionally, the programme will promote innovation and responsible AI use in the legal profession, contributing to the development of fair and effective legal systems.

P12: Continuous Evaluation

Rationale:

- Continuous evaluation ensures that students remain up-to-date with advancements in AI technologies and methodologies, preparing them to address emerging challenges and opportunities in their respective fields.
- Regular evaluation allows HEIs to assess the effectiveness of AI education initiatives, identify areas for improvement, and refine teaching methods and curriculum content to better meet student needs.
- Ongoing evaluation helps ensure that AI education programmes adhere to ethical guidelines and standards, promoting responsible AI use and accountability for the societal impacts of AI technologies.
- Continuous evaluation provides students with opportunities to practice and refine their AI skills over time, facilitating mastery and confidence in applying AI tools and techniques in real-world scenarios.
- Regular feedback from evaluations enables students to monitor their progress, identify areas for growth, and access support resources to address any challenges they encounter in learning AI concepts and applications.
- Emphasising continuous evaluation instils a mindset of lifelong learning in students, encouraging them to seek out opportunities for self-improvement, skill development, and professional growth throughout their academic and professional careers.
- Continuous evaluation ensures that AI education programmes remain aligned with industry standards and best practices, equipping students with the knowledge and skills demanded by employers in AI-related fields.
- Data collected through continuous evaluation can inform evidence-based decision-making processes regarding curriculum development, resource allocation, and strategic planning for AI education initiatives.
- Regular evaluation fosters an environment of innovation and creativity, encouraging students to explore new ideas, experiment with AI technologies, and develop innovative solutions to complex problems.
- Continuous evaluation supports equitable access to AI education opportunities by providing ongoing feedback and support to students from diverse backgrounds, ensuring that all learners have the resources and support they need to succeed in learning AI.
- Continuous evaluation allows HEIs to identify and address individual student learning needs, providing tailored support and resources to help each student achieve their full potential in AI education.

Incorporation:

- Conduct regular assessments, such as quizzes, exams, and assignments, to evaluate students' understanding of AI concepts, techniques, and applications.
- Implement feedback mechanisms, including peer evaluations, self-assessments, and instructor feedback, to provide students with timely feedback on their progress and areas for improvement in AI learning.
- Review students' AI projects, research papers, and practical assignments to assess their ability to apply AI tools and methodologies in real-world scenarios and provide constructive feedback for improvement.
- Establish performance benchmarks and learning objectives for AI courses and programmes, allowing students to track their progress and competency development over time.
- Conduct skills assessments, such as coding challenges, data analysis tasks, and problem-solving exercises, to evaluate students' proficiency in AI-related skills and identify areas where additional support may be needed.
- Encourage peer collaboration and evaluation through group projects, peer reviews, and collaborative learning activities, fostering a culture of mutual support and constructive feedback among students.
- Administer surveys and course evaluations to gather feedback from students on their learning experiences, course content, teaching methods, and overall satisfaction with AI education initiatives.
- Implement real-time monitoring tools and analytics to track students' engagement, participation, and performance in AI courses and programmes, allowing HEI to identify trends and intervene early if students are struggling.
- Offer professional development opportunities, such as workshops, seminars, and guest lectures, to provide students with additional resources and support for enhancing their AI skills and knowledge.
- Utilise adaptive learning platforms and personalised learning technologies to tailor AI education experiences to individual student needs, adjusting content, pacing, and support resources based on students' performance and learning preferences.
- Provide faculty members with training and resources for designing effective assessments, delivering constructive feedback, and utilising data-driven approaches to continuous evaluation in AI education.
- Integrate continuous evaluation processes into curriculum review cycles, ensuring that AI courses and programmes are regularly updated and improved based on feedback from students, faculty, and industry stakeholders.

- Recognise students' achievements and milestones in AI education through certificates, badges, and awards, motivating students to actively engage in continuous learning and skill development in AI.

Example 1	• Conduct periodic assessments on students' understanding of AI concepts as applied to English literature and dance, assessing their grasp of key ideas, terminology, and potential applications within their respective fields.
Example 2	• Provide feedback on AI-infused projects within English literature and dance courses, evaluating students' ability to integrate AI tools for textual analysis, choreography generation, or performance enhancement, and offering constructive criticism for improvement.
Example 3	• Facilitate peer reviews where students evaluate each other's AI-based projects or analyses, fostering collaborative learning environments and providing additional perspectives on the integration of AI in literature interpretation or dance choreography.
Example 4	• Incorporate AI-focused components into creative assignments or performances, requiring students to demonstrate their understanding of AI concepts through their literary analyses, dance compositions, or interpretations.
Example 5	• Utilise real-time monitoring tools to track students' engagement and progress in AI-related coursework, identifying areas where students may need additional support or guidance in applying AI techniques to their literary or dance studies.
Example 6	• Present case studies of AI applications in literature analysis or dance choreography, prompting students to critically evaluate the benefits, limitations, and ethical considerations of using AI tools in creative practices.
Example	• Conduct portfolio reviews where students showcase their AI-related projects, analyses, or performances, providing opportunities for self-reflection and faculty feedback on their progress and development in integrating AI into their artistic practice.

The Guiding Principles for Students on Using AI in Universities explain how to deal with challenges when using AI in education. It is crucial to use AI fairly and ethically at universities. These principles are fundamental. As AI becomes more common in education, universities need to focus on doing things fairly. This means ensuring academic honesty, student privacy, and inclusion are protected. By following these principles, universities can make clear rules for using AI in teaching. One big reason why universities should follow these principles is to preserve academic and employability skills, honesty, inclusivity, student engagement and experience. Using AI to mark essays or create content can raise worries about cheating or copying. Without proper rules and guidelines, it might be difficult to trust academic assessments done by AI. However, by following these principles, universities can ensure that AI helps keep academic standards and the learning process fair. Similarly, the use of AI will affect key areas such as academic and employability skills, honesty, inclusivity, student engagement, and overall student experience. Adhering to this guiding principle will help universities safeguard these essential aspects.

The principles also stress the importance of being open and accountable when using AI. Universities need to be clear about where their data comes from, how their AI systems work, and how decisions are made. This builds trust between students, staff, and everyone else involved. Also, there should be ways to fix things if AI makes mistakes or acts unfairly. Being open and accountable helps reduce the risks linked to AI and encourages using it responsibly. Another good reason for following the principles is to protect student privacy and data. AI relies on lots of data to learn and make decisions. Nonetheless, collecting and using student data needs to be done carefully to respect their privacy and follow the rules. By respecting the principles, universities can make sure they have strong policies in place to keep student data safe and use AI in an ethical way.

Lastly, the principles highlight the need to ensure that AI is fair and does not exclude anyone. Universities need to be aware of the biases and differences that can come with AI systems. By working with experts from different fields, like ethics and sociology, universities can create AI that treats everyone equally. Also, teaching students and staff about AI ethics helps them understand the issues and make good choices. Overall, the Guiding Principles for Students Regarding the Use of AI in High Education Institutions give a clear plan for using AI responsibly in higher education. By following these principles, universities can keep academic standards high, protect student privacy, and ensure that AI benefits everyone. Together, academics, researchers, policymakers, and industry leaders can ensure that AI is used ethically and improves education for everyone.

GUIDING PRINCIPLES FOR STAFF ON ETHICAL AI USE IN HIGHER EDUCATION INSTITUTIONS

Using Generative Artificial Intelligence (GenAI) in higher education can improve teaching and learning, but it also raises important ethical questions. The 'Guiding Principles for Staff on Ethical AI Use in Higher Education Institutions' is there to help deal with these issues and ensure AI is used in a way that matches the values of higher education. These principles are essential for higher education because they set clear rules for using AI well, keeping academic standards high, including everyone, and protecting student privacy. The aim is to get the most out of AI while still being fair and ethical. The 'Guiding Principles for Staff on Ethical AI Use in Higher Education Institutions' focuses on five main ideas for using GenAI in higher education. This focus is essential because it keeps everything clear and organised. Observing these central ideas makes it easier for everyone to understand, remember, and use them. In addition, it helps us cover the most critical parts of using GenAI without getting overwhelmed by too much information. So, by focusing on these five key themes, everyone involved in using GenAI in higher education knows precisely what is essential and can do their job better. These five themes are:

- **Keeping Academic Integrity:** With more AI in education, ensuring that exams and assessments are not compromised is essential. These guiding principles aim to prevent AI from being used to cheat or copy so that academic honesty is protected.
- **Being Fair and Inclusive:** AI should help everyone learn, no matter where they come from. These guiding principles show that AI systems should be made to treat everyone equally and not disadvantage certain groups.

- **Keeping Student Information Safe:** Using AI means dealing with lots of student data, so it is crucial to keep it safe. These principles show that student privacy must be respected and that all laws and ethics around data use should be followed.
- **Using AI Responsibly:** HEIs should take charge of how AI is developed and used, making sure it is fair and works the way it should. This involves keeping an eye on things and being honest and accountable about AI decisions.
- **Improving Teaching and Learning:** The main aim here is to use AI to make learning better. This could mean personalising learning, trying out new teaching ideas, or giving academics better tools to help students.

In short, these principles are essential for HEIs. They help ensure that AI is used in a way that is fair, safe, and helpful for everyone involved in education. Following these rules means that AI can be a positive addition to higher education, benefitting students, academics, and the whole academic community.

P1: Professional Development and Training (PDT)

Provide staff with training and professional development opportunities to enhance their digital literacy, pedagogical skills, and ethical awareness related to generative AI. Invest in staff training programmes, workshops, and resources to support academics in effectively integrating AI technologies into their teaching practices.

Rationale:

- Continuous professional development ensures that academics and professional staff are up-to-date with the latest pedagogical strategies and technologies. This knowledge directly impacts the quality of teaching, leading to improved student engagement and learning outcomes.
- Regular training and development programmes enable academics to stay current with advancements in their respective fields. This ensures that the curriculum remains relevant and rigorous, thereby preparing students to meet contemporary challenges.
- PDT fosters the adoption of inclusive teaching practices that cater to diverse student populations. Training in areas such as cultural competency, accessibility, and differentiated instruction helps academics and professional staff use AI to create equitable learning environments.
- The HEIs landscape continually evolves with new technologies, methodologies, and research findings. Professional development equips staff with the skills to adapt to these changes, ensuring that the institution remains at the forefront of educational innovation.
- Encouraging a culture of continuous learning among academics promotes experimentation with new teaching methods and technologies. This can lead to developing innovative instructional strategies that enhance student learning experiences.

- Professional development programmes that integrate teaching and research help academics to bring cutting-edge research into the classroom. This enriches the curriculum and stimulates critical thinking and inquiry among students.

Incorporation:

- Conduct regular needs assessments to identify the specific professional development needs of academics and staff. This can be done through surveys, interviews, and performance reviews.
- Design AI PDT programmes that are tailored to the diverse needs of the faculty and staff. Programmes should address various aspects such as teaching methodologies, research skills, technology integration, and leadership development.
- Offer AI PDT programmes in multiple formats, including workshops, seminars, online courses, peer mentoring, and collaborative projects. This ensures accessibility and accommodates different learning preferences and schedules.
- Integrate AI PDT with regular teaching and research activities. For example, teaching-focused professional development could be linked with classroom practice, while research-oriented programmes could support scholarly activities and grant writing.
- Deliver online professional development courses using digital platforms and learning management systems. These platforms can facilitate asynchronous learning, making it easier for staff to participate regardless of their schedules.
- Establish resource centres or professional development units within the institution that provide access to learning materials, technologies, and expert guidance
- Implement collaborative tools and technologies that support peer interaction, discussion forums, and virtual communities of practice. These tools can enhance the sharing of knowledge and best practices.
- Encourage forming communities of practice where academics and staff can collaborate, share experiences, and learn from each other. These communities can focus on specific areas such as AI, teaching innovation, curriculum development, or research methods.
- Develop mentorship programmes that pair less experienced staff with seasoned academics on AI issues. Mentorship can provide personalised guidance, support, and professional growth opportunities.
- Encourage forming communities of practice where academics and staff can collaborate, share experiences, and learn from each other. These communities can focus on specific areas such as AI, teaching innovation, curriculum development, or research methods.

- Organise cross-departmental workshops and projects to promote interdisciplinary collaboration. This can foster a culture of innovation and provide new perspectives on teaching and research.
- Use evaluation data to make informed decisions about improving and refining AI PDT programmes. Analyse the impact of these programmes on teaching quality, research output, and overall staff satisfaction.
- Adopt an iterative approach to AI programme development, where feedback and evaluation results are continuously used to enhance and adapt professional development offerings.

Example 1	• **Action:** Develop and disseminate a comprehensive AI PDT policy document. This policy outlines the expectations for continuous professional development, available resources, and the process for applying for development opportunities. • **Outcome:** Clear guidelines provide a structured approach to AI PDT, encouraging more faculty and staff to participate actively.
Example 2	• **Action:** Conduct biannual surveys and focus groups to identify the professional development needs of faculty across different departments. Use the findings to tailor programmes that address specific gaps and areas for improvement. • **Outcome:** Programmes are more relevant and effective, as they are based on actual needs rather than assumptions.
Example 3	• **Action:** Create specialised training tracks such as 'Innovative Teaching Methods,' 'Advanced Research Skills,' and 'Leadership in Higher Education.' Each track offers a series of workshops, seminars, and online modules. • **Outcome:** Faculty and staff can choose programmes that align with their career goals and areas of interest, leading to more personalised and impactful development.
Example 4	• **Action:** Offer blended learning opportunities that include face-to-face workshops, online courses, and peer-led discussion groups. Include asynchronous options to accommodate different schedules. • **Outcome:** Increased participation and engagement as staff can choose the format that best fits their learning style and availability
Example 5	• **Action:** Adopt a robust Learning Management System (LMS) that hosts a variety of professional development resources, including online courses, webinars, and instructional videos. Provide training on how to effectively use the LMS. • **Outcome:** Easy access to a wealth of development resources increases participation and supports continuous learning.
Example 6	• **Action:** Faculty should use collaborative tools like Microsoft Teams, Slack, or specialised academic platforms to share resources, discuss best practices, and collaborate on projects. • **Outcome:** Facilitates ongoing dialogue and peer support, fostering a community of practice.
Example 7	• **Action:** Establish a Professional Development Centre equipped with the latest educational technology, study spaces, and access to expert consultants who can provide personalised guidance. • **Outcome:** A dedicated space and resources enhance the institution's capacity to support faculty development effectively.

Example 8	• **Action:** Facilitate the creation of communities of practice centred around key themes such as 'AI and Blended Learning,' 'Assessment Strategies and AI,' and 'AI and Interdisciplinary Research.' Schedule regular meetings and provide a platform for online interaction. • **Outcome:** These communities provide a structured way for faculty to share insights and develop professionally in a collaborative environment.

P2: Clear Communication

Inform all academics and professional staff about AI applications' purpose, scope, and functioning.

Rationale:

- Clear and effective communication skills are crucial for academics and professional staff to convey complex concepts and facilitate understanding. By implementing communication principles, academics and professional staff can better articulate their ideas, provide clear instructions, and foster an environment where students feel comfortable engaging and asking questions about the use of AI.

  Example: Training faculty in active listening and feedback techniques can lead to more dynamic and interactive classroom discussions, enhancing student comprehension and participation.

- Communication is the cornerstone of successful interdisciplinary collaboration. By promoting open and effective communication, HEIs can facilitate collaboration across different departments and disciplines, leading to innovative research and teaching practices in AI and other fields.

  Example: Regular interdisciplinary seminars and workshops where faculty can share research findings and teaching methods related to AI encourage a culture of collaboration and knowledge sharing.

- Strong communication about AI builds a sense of community among faculty, staff, and students. It fosters a positive and inclusive academic environment when everyone feels heard and valued.

  Example: Establishing platforms for regular communication, such as faculty forums or town hall meetings, can enhance transparency and foster a sense of belonging within the academic community when using AI.

- Effective communication about AI ensures that institutional policies, goals, and expectations are clearly conveyed to academics and professional staff. This transparency is essential for maintaining trust and accountability within the institution regarding AI use.

Example: Regular updates from the administration about the use of AI through newsletters, emails, and meetings keep faculty and staff informed about institutional changes and expectations, particularly those related to AI initiatives and training programmes.

- Implementing robust communication channels for feedback allows institutions to gather insights from faculty, staff, and students. This feedback is critical for continuous improvement and promptly addressing any concerns or issues.

  Example: Anonymous feedback systems and regular surveys can help gather open and honest input from the academic community, which can be used to inform policy decisions and improvements, especially in the rapidly evolving field of AI.

Incorporation:

- Create case studies and best practice reports highlighting successful AI communication strategies and their impact on teaching and learning. Distribute these through internal newsletters, websites, and seminars.
- Create groups focused on specific areas of interest (e.g., interdisciplinary AI research, innovative teaching methods) where members can share insights, resources, and best practices.
- Set up regular meetings, forums, and town hall sessions where faculty and staff can voice their opinions, share feedback, and discuss institutional policies and practices regarding the use of AI.

Example 1	• Form communities of practice around key topics such as innovative AI teaching methods or interdisciplinary AI research. These groups can meet regularly to discuss challenges, share resources, and collaborate on projects, fostering a culture of continuous learning and mutual support.
Example 2	• Establish regular 'AI Office Hours' where faculty and staff can drop in to discuss concerns, share ideas, and seek advice from designated AI specialists or senior administrators.
Example 3	• Allocate funds to create an AI Training Excellence Office dedicated to supporting AI initiatives, offering regular training sessions, and providing resources such as templates, style guides, and best practice manuals for AI integration in academic and administrative work.
Example 4	• Develop an online course on AI strategies, including modules on using AI-driven tools for academic purposes, managing AI-enhanced classrooms, and effective online collaboration with AI tools.

P3: Documentation

Maintain comprehensive documentation of AI algorithms, data sources, and decision-making processes.

Rationale:

- Documentation provides a clear record of how AI tools are being used in teaching and learning processes. This transparency is essential for holding staff accountable for their use of AI, ensuring that these tools are used ethically and in alignment with institutional policies. By documenting the use of AI, institutions can monitor compliance with legal and ethical standards, thus protecting both students and staff.
- With thorough documentation, HEIs can maintain high standards in the application of AI technologies. Detailed records allow for the continuous review and improvement of AI tools, ensuring that they meet educational objectives effectively. Documentation enables academics and administrators to identify areas where AI is succeeding and where it may need adjustments or improvements.
- Documenting AI usage creates a repository of experiences and strategies that can be shared among academics within and across institutions. This collaborative approach promotes the dissemination of innovative teaching practices and successful AI integrations, fostering a culture of continuous improvement and shared learning.
- HEIs are often at the forefront of educational research, and documentation is crucial for conducting rigorous studies on the impact of AI in teaching and learning. Detailed records of AI implementation and outcomes can provide valuable data for research, leading to evidence-based advancements in educational technology and pedagogy.
- AI technologies can raise ethical concerns, such as bias in algorithms or the potential for infringing on students' privacy. Comprehensive documentation helps to ensure that these ethical considerations are addressed by providing a clear record of AI decision-making processes and the measures taken to mitigate risks. This fosters an ethical AI culture within the institution.
- Educational institutions must comply with various regulations regarding data usage, privacy, and technology implementation. Documentation helps ensure that AI usage meets these regulatory requirements by providing a verifiable trail of compliance. This can be crucial in the event of audits or external reviews.
- When students are aware that AI usage is well documented and transparent, they are more likely to trust the technology and its role in their education. This trust can lead to greater student engagement and a more positive attitude towards the integration of AI in their learning experiences.
- Institutional leaders and policymakers rely on accurate information to make informed decisions about the adoption and integration of AI technologies. Comprehensive documentation provides the necessary insights into how AI tools are performing and their impact on teaching and learning, facilitating data-driven decision-making processes.

Incorporation:

- Every time an AI tool is used in a course (e.g., for grading, personalised feedback, or content delivery), the academics or administrators log the activity in a centralised system. This log includes details such as the date, purpose, outcomes, and any issues encountered.
- Before implementing a new AI-based learning tool, staff create a comprehensive project plan that includes objectives, expected outcomes, resources required, timelines, and roles and responsibilities. This plan is documented and accessible to all stakeholders.
- Staff use a standardised checklist to ensure that the use of AI tools complies with ethical guidelines. This checklist covers aspects such as data privacy, consent, bias mitigation, and transparency. Completed checklists are stored in a shared repository.
- When a new AI tool is introduced, detailed training manuals and video tutorials are created and documented. These resources include step-by-step instructions, best practices, troubleshooting tips, and case studies of successful implementations.
- After each semester, academics who used AI tools in their teaching submit a reflection report. This report includes feedback on the tool's effectiveness, student engagement, learning outcomes, and any challenges faced. These reports are compiled and reviewed to inform future AI use.
- HEIs develop and maintain clear policies and procedures for AI use in teaching and learning. These documents outline the standards for AI integration, data management protocols, and the roles and responsibilities of staff. Policies are reviewed regularly and updated as needed.
- Successful implementations of AI in courses are documented as case studies. These case studies describe the context, implementation process, outcomes, and lessons learned. They are shared across the institution to serve as models for other academics and administrators.
- Whenever AI tools require the use of student data, staff obtain informed consent from students. Consent forms are documented, outlining how data will be used, stored, and protected. Copies of these forms are securely stored.
- Any technical issues or ethical concerns that arise during the use of AI tools are logged in an issue tracker. This log includes descriptions of the issues, steps taken to resolve them, and final outcomes. These logs help in identifying recurring problems and improving AI tools.
- HEIs create online platforms where staff can document and share their experiences with AI tools. These platforms might include forums, wikis, or collaborative documents where educators post their documentation, discuss challenges, and share solutions.

Example 1	• For courses like 'Digital Humanities' or 'AI in Art,' staff should document how AI tools will be integrated into the curriculum. This includes specifying the types of AI technologies used, their purpose, and the expected learning outcomes. **Documentation Details**: • Description of AI tools (e.g., text analysis software, art generation tools). • Pedagogical goals for using these tools. • Assessment methods for evaluating AI-enhanced assignments.
Example 2	• In a course on 'Contemporary Art Practices,' academics might use AI to generate art pieces or analyse artistic styles. Documentation should cover how AI is used in lesson plans and course materials. **Documentation Details**: • Detailed lesson plans showing where and how AI tools are incorporated. • Instructions for students on using these tools. • Annotated bibliographies of AI tools and resources.
Example 3	• For a 'Philosophy of AI' course, staff should provide clear guidelines on the ethical use of AI, especially concerning bias, intellectual property, and data privacy. **Documentation Details**: • Policies on the ethical use of AI in coursework. • Case studies and examples of ethical dilemmas in AI. • Consent forms and data usage agreements.
Example 4	• Students might use AI for data analysis or creative projects in research seminars or capstone projects. Staff should document the AI tools and methodologies recommended or required. **Documentation Details**: • Guidelines for AI tool usage in student projects. • Templates for documenting AI methodologies in research papers. • Examples of successful AI-integrated student projects.
Example 5	• Using AI-driven platforms for collaboration, such as virtual art studios or discussion boards. Documentation should include platform usage instructions and communication protocols. **Documentation Details**: • User manuals for collaborative AI platforms. • Communication logs and protocols for AI-facilitated interactions. • Evaluation forms for platform effectiveness and user satisfaction.
Example 6	• Using AI for analysing student performance and engagement data. Documentation should specify data collection methods, AI algorithms used, and data privacy measures. **Documentation Details**: • Data collection procedures and AI analysis algorithms. • Reports on findings from AI data analysis. • Privacy policies and consent forms for data usage.

P4: Accountability Mechanisms

Establish systems to address any misuse or unintended consequences, ensuring there are clear points of responsibility.

Rationale:

- AI systems can inadvertently perpetuate or amplify biases. Accountability mechanisms help ensure that AI tools are regularly audited for fairness and inclusivity.
- Safeguarding students' personal information is critical. Accountability ensures compliance with data protection regulations and ethical standards.
- Clear guidelines and regular monitoring uphold ethical use, preventing misuse or unintended harm.
- Accountability mechanisms ensure that AI tools meet high educational standards and contribute positively to the learning environment.
- Regular reviews and feedback loops help refine AI applications, ensuring they effectively support learning objectives.
- Documenting AI usage provides transparency, allowing staff to understand how decisions are made and to trust the integrity of the educational process.
- Clear accountability processes reassure students and faculty that AI tools are used responsibly and ethically.
- Mechanisms for reporting and addressing issues ensure that concerns are taken seriously and resolved promptly.
- Open communication about how AI is used and its impact fosters an environment of trust and collaboration.

Incorporate:

- Create detailed policies outlining acceptable AI usage, ethical considerations, data privacy, and security standards.
- Involve faculty, students, IT staff, and legal experts in the policy-making process to ensure all perspectives are considered.
- Review and update policies periodically to keep up with technological advancements and emerging ethical concerns.
- Publish policies in accessible formats for all staff.
- Provide training materials and sessions to ensure understanding and compliance.
- Maintain records of committee meetings, decisions, and actions taken.
- Publish annual reports on AI usage and oversight activities.

- Create comprehensive training programmes focused on ethical AI usage, data privacy, and security.
- Require all staff involved with AI tools to complete training and obtain certification.
- Regularly audit AI tools and their implementation in teaching and learning to ensure compliance with established policies.
- Occasionally engage third-party auditors to provide an unbiased assessment of AI practices.

Example 1	• Develop a comprehensive policy on the use of AI tools for teaching finance, marketing, or management courses. The policy should outline acceptable uses, ethical considerations, and privacy standards. **Implementation Steps**: • Draft a policy document detailing the use of AI in various business courses. • Include guidelines on data privacy, AI ethics, and acceptable use cases. • Review the policy with staff, including faculty, students, and legal advisors. • Publish the policy on the school's website and internal platforms. **Documentation**: • Policy document available for download. • Records of policy review meetings and feedback from all staff.
Example 2	• Implement a system for reporting any issues related to AI use, such as biases in AI-driven grading systems or data privacy concerns in a business analytics course. **Implementation Steps**: • Create an online portal or email address to report AI-related issues. • Ensure anonymity and protection for individuals reporting issues. • Establish a protocol for addressing reported concerns promptly. **Documentation**: • Logs of reported issues and actions taken. • Summary reports provided to the AI Ethics and Compliance Committee.
Example 3	• Set up a system for evaluating the effectiveness of AI tools used in decision-making courses and gathering feedback from students and faculty. **Implementation Steps**: • Define criteria for evaluating AI tools, focusing on educational outcomes and ethical use. • Collect feedback from students and faculty through surveys and focus groups. • Use feedback to make necessary adjustments to AI implementations. **Documentation**: • Evaluation criteria and reports. • Feedback summaries and records of resulting changes to AI tools or practices.

Example 4	• Encourage open discussions about AI ethics and accountability in business education through seminars and workshops. **Implementation Steps**: • Organise regular seminars, workshops, and panel discussions on AI ethics and accountability. • Invite experts to speak and share best practices. • Encourage faculty and students to participate and contribute to these discussions. **Documentation**: • Event agendas and materials. • Attendance records and summaries of discussions.
Example 5	• Ensure that AI tools used in courses like international business comply with relevant legal and regulatory standards, including GDPR for courses involving European data. **Implementation Steps**: • Regularly review legal and regulatory requirements for AI and data usage. • Update AI tools and practices to ensure compliance with these standards. • Document compliance efforts and ensure transparency. **Documentation**: • Legal review reports and compliance checklists. • Records of updates and adjustments made to comply with regulations.

P5: Augment, Don't Replace

Use AI to support and enhance human decision-making rather than replace it entirely.

Rationale:

A. AI has the potential to significantly augment academic capabilities by automating routine tasks, providing advanced data analytics, and offering personalised learning experiences.

- AI can automate time-consuming tasks such as grading, attendance tracking, and scheduling, freeing academics to focus on more meaningful student interactions.
- AI can analyse vast amounts of data to provide insights into student performance and learning patterns, helping academics tailor their teaching strategies to meet individual student needs.
- AI can offer personalised learning experiences by adapting content to each student's pace and learning style, allowing academics to effectively address diverse learning needs.

B. Education is fundamentally a human-centred endeavour that relies on the emotional and intellectual connections between academics and students. The principle of augmenting rather than replacing ensures that these human elements are preserved.

- Academics bring empathy, understanding, and emotional support to their interactions with students, which AI cannot replicate.
- Human academics are essential for fostering critical thinking, creativity, and ethical reasoning—skills that are difficult for AI to cultivate independently.
- Academics' roles as mentors and guides are irreplaceable. They provide personal insights, career advice, and life guidance that go beyond academic instruction.

C. HEIs have established reputations and values based on the quality of their educational experiences. Augmenting rather than replacing academics with AI helps maintain these standards.

- Human academics ensure the consistency and quality of education, upholding the institution's academic standards and values.
- Academics play a key role in shaping an institution's culture and identity, which AI cannot replicate.
- Academics can adapt AI tools to fit the specific context and needs of their institution, ensuring that technology serves to enhance rather than homogenise educational experiences.

D. For AI to be effectively integrated into education, academics and students must trust and accept it. The principle of augmentation helps build this trust.

- Academics and students are more likely to embrace AI if they see it as a tool that supports rather than threatens their roles and experiences.
- An augmentation approach promotes a balanced view of AI, where its strengths are leveraged without overshadowing the critical role of human academics.
- By involving academics in the implementation and ongoing use of AI, HEIs can ensure that technology adoption is collaborative and inclusive.

Incorporation:

- Use AI to provide initial assessments of student assignments, allowing faculty to focus on more in-depth feedback and personalised guidance.
- Leverage AI to create personalised learning pathways for students, allowing faculty to provide more targeted support.
- Implement AI to handle routine administrative tasks such as scheduling, attendance tracking, and resource allocation, allowing faculty to focus more on teaching and mentoring.
- Provide AI tools that assist faculty with research tasks such as literature reviews, data analysis, and trend identification.

- Use AI to enhance classroom engagement through interactive tools and real-time analytics, allowing faculty to focus on facilitating discussions and critical thinking.
- Offer AI-assisted professional development programmes for faculty to improve their teaching methods and integrate new technologies into their curriculum.

Example 1	• Use AI-powered legal research tools to assist faculty and students in finding relevant case laws, statutes, and legal precedents more efficiently. **Implementation Steps:** • Integrate AI-driven legal research platforms like LexisNexis, Westlaw, or ROSS Intelligence into the law school's resources. • Train faculty on using these tools to enhance their research capabilities and integrate them into their teaching materials. • Organise workshops for students to familiarise them with these tools and demonstrate how AI can streamline their research processes.
Example 2	• Implement AI tools that assist in document review and contract drafting to help faculty focus on more complex legal analysis and mentorship. **Implementation Steps:** • Introduce AI-powered document review tools such as Kira Systems or LawGeex for faculty use in coursework and research. • Conduct sessions to train faculty on using these tools to review large volumes of documents and draft contracts efficiently. • Encourage students to use these tools for class assignments and practical exercises under faculty supervision.
Example 3	• Leverage AI to create personalised learning pathways for law students, allowing faculty to provide more targeted guidance and support. **Implementation Steps:** • Integrate AI-driven Learning Management Systems (LMS) that track student progress and suggest personalised learning resources. • Develop dashboards for faculty to monitor student progress, identify areas where students struggle, and provide tailored support. • Faculty can use insights from AI to offer personalised office hours and tailored feedback on assignments.
Example 4	• Incorporate AI in simulation and moot court exercises to provide students with realistic, interactive legal scenarios and feedback. **Implementation Steps:** • Use AI to create realistic legal scenarios and virtual clients for students to interact with during simulations. • AI can provide detailed analytics on student performance during moot court practices, highlighting strengths and areas for improvement. • Faculty can review AI-generated reports to offer more focused feedback and mentorship to students.

Example 5	• Use AI tools to assist faculty in grading and providing feedback on legal writing assignments, allowing them to focus on more nuanced analysis and mentorship. **Implementation Steps:** • Implement AI tools like Turnitin or Grammarly to evaluate grammar, citations, and initial structure of legal writing assignments. • Faculty can then focus on providing in-depth feedback on legal reasoning, argumentation, and originality. • Ensure students receive comprehensive feedback, combining AI-generated insights with detailed faculty comments.

P6: Training and Support

Provide comprehensive training for staff and students to understand and effectively interact with AI systems.

Rationale:

- AI can potentially transform teaching methodologies and learning experiences. By providing comprehensive training and support, HEIs can ensure that staff are well-equipped to leverage AI tools effectively. This can lead to more personalised learning experiences, improved student engagement, and better learning outcomes. For instance, AI can help identify students' learning patterns and tailor instructional methods accordingly, which can significantly enhance the overall educational experience.
- AI can play a crucial role in making education more accessible and inclusive. With proper training, academics and practitioners can use AI to develop adaptive learning systems that cater to diverse learning needs, including those of students with disabilities. This promotes equity in education by ensuring that all students have access to the resources they need to succeed.
- AI technologies can automate administrative tasks such as grading, scheduling, and providing feedback, thereby freeing up valuable time for academics to focus on teaching and mentoring students. Training and support in AI use can help staff become more efficient in their roles, leading to increased productivity and job satisfaction.
- As AI continues to advance and integrate into various sectors, HEIs must keep pace to remain competitive and relevant. Providing staff with the necessary training and support ensures that the institution remains at the forefront of educational innovation. This not only enhances the institution's reputation but also attracts prospective students and faculty who are looking for a forward-thinking educational environment.

- Implementing training and support for AI use encourages a culture of continuous learning and professional development among staff. This not only helps in the adoption of new technologies but also fosters an environment where academics and practitioners are constantly updating their skills and knowledge, which is essential in a rapidly changing educational landscape.

Incorporation:

- Start with a survey to assess the current level of AI knowledge and usage among faculty and staff. Identify areas where AI can have the most significant impact on teaching and learning.
- Set clear, measurable goals for AI integration, such as enhancing personalised learning, improving student engagement, and increasing operational efficiency.
- Design a structured training programme that covers the basics of AI, its applications in education, and ethical considerations. Include modules on specific AI tools relevant to different disciplines.
- Engage AI specialists and educational technologists to develop and deliver training content. Consider partnerships with AI companies and educational technology providers.
- Organise a series of workshops and seminars to introduce faculty and staff to AI concepts and tools. These sessions should be interactive, allowing participants to try out AI tools and ask questions.
- Offer online courses and webinars for those who cannot attend in-person sessions. Ensure these courses are self-paced to accommodate varying schedules.
- Establish an AI Help Desk or support team to provide ongoing assistance. Staff this team with knowledgeable individuals who can troubleshoot issues and offer guidance on best practices.
- Form peer support groups where faculty can share experiences, challenges, and solutions related to AI use in teaching.
- Create comprehensive user guides and video tutorials for different AI tools. Make these resources easily accessible through the university's intranet or a dedicated online platform.
- Compile case studies and best practices from within the institution and other HEIs to showcase successful AI integration in teaching and learning.

Example 1	**Initial Training Workshop:** Date: 1–3 August 2025 Location: Mani University Conference Center **Agenda**: • Day 1: Introduction to AI in Education • Day 2: Hands-on Training with AI Tools (e.g., adaptive learning platforms, AI-driven analytics) • Day 3: Ethical Considerations and Best Practices **Ongoing Support**: • AI Help Desk: Open 9 AM–5 PM, Monday to Friday. Contact via email, phone, or live chat. • Monthly Peer Support Meetings: First Thursday of every month, 3 PM–4 PM. • Resources: • Online Portal: Access user guides, video tutorials, and case studies at ai-support.maniuniversity.ac.uk. • Innovation Grant Application: Available biannually, with deadlines on March 1 and October 1.
Example 2	• Design a structured training programme that covers the basics of AI, its applications in education, and ethical considerations. Include modules on specific AI tools relevant to different disciplines. • Engage AI specialists and educational technologists to develop and deliver training content. Consider partnerships with AI companies and educational technology providers.
Example 3	• Dedicate specific days throughout the academic year for professional development focused on AI and technology integration. • Regularly update the training programme to include new AI tools and advancements. Offer refresher courses and advanced training for experienced users.

P7: Bias Mitigation

Implement regular audits of AI systems to detect and mitigate biases related to race, gender, socio-economic status, and other protected characteristics.

Rationale:

- Bias in AI can undermine the trust that students, faculty, and the broader community have in educational institutions. By actively working to mitigate bias, HEIs can demonstrate their commitment to ethical standards and social responsibility. This enhances the institution's credibility and fosters a trusting relationship with students and stakeholders, who need assurance that AI tools are used responsibly and ethically.

- Bias in AI can lead to unfair treatment of students, affecting their academic performance and future opportunities. For instance, biased recommendation systems might not accurately suggest courses or resources that best fit a student's needs, potentially hindering their educational progress. By mitigating bias, HEIs can ensure that AI-driven recommendations and assessments are more accurate and beneficial, ultimately improving student outcomes.

- An inclusive educational environment is one where all students feel valued and supported. Bias mitigation in AI helps to create such an environment by preventing discriminatory practices and ensuring that all students are represented fairly. This is particularly important in diverse classrooms where students come from various backgrounds and have different needs.
- Training staff on bias mitigation in AI not only improves the ethical use of technology but also enhances their overall understanding and capability in using advanced tools. This professional development is essential for educators to stay current with technological advancements and to use AI effectively in their teaching practices. It empowers academics to critically evaluate AI tools and incorporate them in a way that supports unbiased and inclusive teaching.
- Implementing the bias mitigation principle promotes a culture of accountability within the institution. It encourages continuous evaluation and improvement of AI systems, ensuring that they serve the best interests of all students. This culture of accountability extends beyond AI and influences broader institutional practices, fostering an environment where ethical considerations are paramount.
- Bias mitigation in AI encourages the development of more sophisticated and innovative AI solutions. When AI developers and users are aware of the potential for bias, they are more likely to create and implement systems that are not only more accurate but also more robust and fair. This drives innovation in educational technology, benefiting both the institution and its students.

Incorporation:

- **Bias-Aware Curriculum Design**
    - **Objective:** Ensure that AI-driven curriculum recommendations are unbiased and promote diverse perspectives.
- **Implementation Steps:**
    - **Data Review:** Conduct a thorough review of curriculum data sources to identify potential biases based on demographic, cultural, or socio-economic factors.
    - **Diverse Input:** Incorporate diverse viewpoints and sources into AI algorithms to ensure a balanced representation of topics and perspectives.
    - **Algorithm Audit:** Regularly audit AI algorithms used for curriculum recommendations to detect and mitigate any emerging biases.
- **Fair Assessment and Grading Systems**
    - **Objective:** Prevent bias in AI-based assessment tools to ensure fair evaluation of student performance.

- **Implementation Steps:**
  - **Bias Testing:** Conduct bias testing on AI algorithms used for grading to identify disparities based on gender, ethnicity, or other sensitive attributes.
  - **Adjustment Algorithms:** Modify grading algorithms to account for potential biases, ensuring that assessment criteria are applied consistently and fairly across all student submissions.
  - **Human Oversight:** Implement human oversight of AI-generated grades to verify fairness and accuracy, particularly in subjective assessments
- **Inclusive AI-Driven Student Support**
  - **Objective:** Provide personalised support to students while ensuring AI tools do not perpetuate biases.
- **Implementation Steps:**
  - **Bias Training for Advisors:** Train academic advisors and support staff to recognise and mitigate biases in AI-driven student support systems.
  - **Customisation Options:** Offer customisation options in AI tools that allow students to adjust preferences and settings based on individual needs and preferences.
  - **Feedback Mechanisms:** Establish feedback mechanisms where students can report biases or discrepancies encountered in AI-driven support systems for prompt resolution and improvement.
- **Diversity in AI Development Teams**
  - **Objective:** Ensure diverse representation in teams developing AI tools to mitigate inherent biases.
- **Implementation Steps:**
  - **Diverse Hiring Practices:** Actively recruit and hire AI developers, data scientists, and researchers from diverse backgrounds and experiences.
  - **Cross-Disciplinary Collaboration:** Foster collaboration between AI developers and experts in social sciences, humanities, and ethics to incorporate diverse perspectives into AI design and implementation.
  - **Bias Awareness Training:** Provide ongoing training on bias mitigation and ethical AI principles for AI development teams to cultivate a culture of inclusivity and responsibility.
- **Continuous Evaluation and Improvement**
  - **Objective:** Continuously monitor and improve AI systems to ensure bias mitigation remains effective over time.

- **Implementation Steps:**
  - **Performance Metrics:** Define and track performance metrics related to bias mitigation in AI systems, such as fairness indices and user satisfaction surveys.
  - **Regular Audits:** Conduct regular audits and reviews of AI algorithms and applications to identify and address any emerging biases or unintended consequences.
  - **Staff Engagement:** Engage students, faculty, and staff in ongoing discussions about AI ethics and bias mitigation strategies to gather feedback and insights for continuous improvement.

Example 1	**Fairness in Legal Case Analysis** • **Objective:** Ensure AI tools used for legal case analysis are free from biases that could affect legal outcomes. **Implementation Steps:** • **Bias Testing:** Conduct thorough bias testing on AI algorithms used for legal case analysis to identify disparities based on race, gender, or socio-economic status. • **Algorithm Transparency:** Document the criteria and variables used in decision-making processes to ensure transparency in how AI algorithms analyse legal cases. • **Legal Ethics Training:** Provide specialised training on legal ethics and bias mitigation for faculty and staff utilising AI tools in legal education.
Example 2	**Non-Discriminatory Legal Research Assistance** • **Objective:** Provide AI-driven research tools that do not perpetuate biases in legal research and writing. **Implementation Steps:** • **Data Review:** Review and diversify the datasets used to train AI models for legal research to minimise biases in case law, statutes, and legal precedents. • **Ethical Guidelines:** Develop and enforce ethical guidelines for using AI in legal research to ensure objective and unbiased results. • **Student Training:** Integrate bias mitigation training into the legal research curriculum to educate students on identifying and addressing biases in AI-driven research tools.

P8: Equitable Access

Ensure all students and staff have equal access to AI resources and their benefits, and that AI applications do not exacerbate existing inequalities.

Rationale:

- Equitable access to AI tools and resources ensures that all staff, regardless of their background, have the opportunity to enhance their teaching and learning practices. This inclusivity fosters a diverse range of perspectives in AI applications, enriching the educational environment. When all staff have equal access to AI, it prevents the marginalisation of certain groups and promotes a culture of diversity and inclusion within the institution.

- AI has the potential to significantly improve teaching methodologies through personalised learning, automated grading, and data-driven insights. Ensuring equitable access to these tools allows all staff to enhance their teaching practices, improving student outcomes. When every staff can leverage AI's capabilities, the overall quality of education the institution provides rises, benefiting the entire student body.
- Inequitable access to AI tools can exacerbate the digital divide, creating disparities in educational quality between different departments or among individual academics. By implementing equitable access policies, HEIs can bridge this divide, ensuring that no staff member is left behind due to a lack of resources or technical support. This promotes a more balanced and fair educational ecosystem.
- Equitable access to AI tools helps to ensure fairness and equity within the institution. Without equitable access, certain staff members may be disadvantaged, unable to utilise AI's full potential in their teaching. This can lead to disparities in student learning experiences and outcomes. By providing equitable access, HEIs ensure that all educators can deliver high-quality, AI-enhanced education, contributing to a fairer academic environment.

Incorporation:

- **Accessible AI Resources**
    - **Objective:** Ensure that all staff have access to the necessary AI tools and resources.
    - **Implementation Steps:**
    - **AI Toolkits:** Provide a standard set of AI tools and software licenses to all teaching staff. Ensure these tools are user-friendly and accompanied by comprehensive guides.
    - **Resource Libraries:** Create an online library of AI resources, including tutorials, research papers, case studies, and best practices.
    - **Technical Support:** Establish a dedicated technical support team to assist staff with the installation, configuration, and use of AI tools.
- **Inclusive Policy Development**
    - **Objective:** Develop policies that ensure equitable access to AI for all staff members.
    - **Implementation Steps:**
    - **Needs Assessment:** Conduct regular surveys and focus groups to assess the AI needs of different departments and individual staff members.
    - **Equity Policies:** Create and enforce policies that guarantee equal access to AI resources and training for all staff, regardless of their role, department, or seniority.
    - **Funding Allocation:** Allocate specific funding to support the equitable distribution of AI resources and training opportunities.

- **Creating a Supportive Community**
  - **Objective:** Foster a community of practice around the use of AI in teaching and learning.
  - Implementation Steps:
  - **Mentorship Programmes:** Pair experienced AI users with less experienced staff to provide guidance and support. Establish a mentorship program where AI-literate faculty can help others integrate AI into their teaching.
  - **AI User Groups:** Form user groups or communities of practice where staff can share experiences, challenges, and successes in using AI. Hold regular meetings and create online forums for continuous interaction.
  - **Collaborative Projects:** Encourage cross-departmental AI projects that promote collaboration and knowledge sharing. Offer grants or incentives for interdisciplinary AI initiatives.

<table>
<tr><td>Example 1</td><td>Financial Support and Incentives<ul><li>Objective: Provide financial support and incentives to ensure equitable access to AI tools and training.</li><li>Implementation Steps:</li><li>Grants and Scholarships: Offer grants and scholarships for faculty to attend AI-related conferences, courses, and workshops, focusing on applications in business.</li></ul>Subsidised Equipment:<ul><li>Provide subsidies for purchasing AI-related hardware and software, ensuring all faculty have the necessary equipment to effectively use AI in their teaching.</li></ul>Incentive Programs:<ul><li>Create incentive programs that reward faculty for successfully integrating AI into their courses, including recognition awards, bonuses, or additional professional development opportunities.</li></ul></td></tr>
<tr><td>Example 2</td><td>Promoting Awareness and Advocacy<ul><li>Objective: Raise awareness about the importance of equitable access to AI and advocate for continuous improvement.</li></ul>Implementation Steps:
Awareness Campaigns:<ul><li>Launch campaigns highlighting the benefits of AI in business education and the importance of equitable access. Use newsletters, webinars, and social media to spread the message.</li></ul>Advocacy Committees:<ul><li>Establish committees or task forces dedicated to advocating for equitable access to AI. These groups can drive policy changes and promote best practices within the business school.</li><li>Regular Reporting: Publish regular reports on the institution's progress towards equitable access to AI, including successes, challenges, and future plans. Share these reports with all stakeholders to maintain transparency and accountability.</li></ul></td></tr>
</table>

P9: Inclusive Design

Engage diverse groups in the development and testing of AI systems to identify and address potential biases.

Rationale:

- AI systems designed inclusively can offer personalised learning experiences that cater to individual student needs, improving engagement and learning outcomes. For example, AI can provide tailored feedback, recommend resources that match a student's learning style, or offer alternative formats for content delivery (e.g., audio for visually impaired students). By fostering an inclusive environment, HEIs can help all students achieve their full potential, thereby enhancing overall academic performance and satisfaction.
- Incorporating Inclusive Design principles encourages diverse perspectives in developing and implementing AI technologies. This diversity can lead to more innovative solutions that are sensitive to the university community's varied experiences and needs. Engaging a broad range of stakeholders in the design process—including students, faculty, and external experts—ensures that AI systems are robust, versatile, and capable of addressing a wide array of challenges.
- The successful integration of AI in teaching and learning hinges on the trust and acceptance of the university community. Inclusive Design can help build this trust by demonstrating a commitment to fairness, transparency, and respect for all individuals. When students and staff see that AI tools are designed with their diverse needs in mind, they are more likely to embrace these technologies and utilise them effectively.
- Adopting Inclusive Design aligns with broader institutional goals of diversity, equity, and inclusion. It reflects the values and mission of HEIs to provide a supportive and enriching educational environment for all. Moreover, it positions the institution as a leader in ethical AI implementation, enhancing its reputation and attracting a diverse student body and faculty.

Incorporation:

- Offer workshops and training sessions to educate staff about AI technologies, their capabilities, and potential biases. Emphasise the importance of Inclusive Design in these sessions.
- Provide specific training on the principles of Inclusive Design, showcasing how to apply these principles in the context of AI for teaching and learning.
- Include training that enhances cultural competency among staff, helping them understand the diverse needs of the student population and how to address these through inclusive AI solutions.
- Form development teams with diverse members, including individuals from various cultural, socio-economic, and academic backgrounds, to contribute to the creation of AI tools.

- Involve students in the design and testing phases to ensure that their perspectives and needs are considered.
- Engage a broad range of stakeholders—including students, faculty, administrative staff, and external experts—in the AI development process. Conduct focus groups, surveys, and user testing to gather input.
- Develop AI tools that adhere to universal design principles, ensuring they are accessible to all users, including those with disabilities. This includes providing alternative formats for content and ensuring compatibility with assistive technologies.

Example 1	**Accessible AI-Powered Learning Platforms:** • **Example:** An AI-powered learning management system (LMS) that offers multiple content formats (text, audio, video) to accommodate students with different learning preferences and needs, including those with disabilities. Features like screen readers, text-to-speech, and customisable font sizes ensure accessibility. **Implementation:** • Ensure the LMS complies with accessibility standards such as WCAG (Web Content Accessibility Guidelines). Regularly test the platform with users who have disabilities to identify and address any accessibility issues.
Example 2	**AI-Enhanced Assessment Tools:** • **Example:** AI tools that offer diverse assessment methods, such as oral presentations, written essays, and interactive projects, to cater to different strengths and preferences among students. **Implementation:** • Provide options for students to choose their preferred method of assessment. Ensure that the AI system evaluates all formats fairly and provides constructive feedback tailored to each format.
Example 3	**Data-Driven Insights for Inclusive Teaching:** • **Example:** Using AI to analyse classroom data and provide insights to academics on how to make their teaching more inclusive. For instance, identifying patterns that suggest certain groups of students are struggling more than others. **Implementation:** • Develop dashboards and analytics tools that highlight disparities in student performance. Offer professional development sessions for instructors on how to use these insights to adjust their teaching methods.
Example 4	**Bias-Detection Algorithms:** • **Example**: Implementing AI systems that automatically detect and flag potential biases in grading, admissions, or other decision-making processes. This helps ensure fair treatment of all students, regardless of background. **Implementation**: • Develop and deploy algorithms that monitor for patterns of bias in AI decisions. Conduct regular audits and have a diverse team of reviewers to assess the fairness and accuracy of the AI's outputs.

Example 5	**Inclusive Chatbots and Virtual Assistants:** • **Example**: Deploying AI-powered chatbots that provide academic advising and support services in multiple languages and are sensitive to cultural nuances. This can help non-native English speakers and international students access support more easily. **Implementation**: • Train chatbots using multilingual datasets and involve native speakers in the development and testing phases. Regularly update the chatbot's language capabilities based on user feedback.

P10: Adaptive Learning

Foster a culture of continuous improvement, adapting to new ethical challenges and technological advancements.

Rationale:

- Adaptive learning encourages innovation and collaboration among staff by providing a platform for sharing best practices and successful strategies. Academics can learn from each other's experiences and adapt AI tools and techniques to their own contexts. This collaborative environment fosters a culture of innovation, where academics are continuously exploring new ways to enhance their teaching.
- Adaptive learning systems generate valuable data on learning progress, engagement, and areas needing improvement. HEIs can use this data to make informed decisions about professional development programmes, identify common challenges, and tailor future training initiatives. This data-driven approach ensures that professional development efforts are aligned with the staff's actual needs.
- Adaptive learning systems are scalable and flexible, making them ideal for institutions with diverse staff needs and varying levels of AI proficiency. These systems can accommodate large numbers of academics simultaneously while providing individualised learning experiences. This scalability ensures that all staff members have the opportunity to develop their skills, regardless of the institution's size.
- Implementing adaptive learning can lead to more efficient use of resources. By personalising the learning experience, HEIs can ensure that training programmes are relevant and targeted, reducing time and costs associated with one-size-fits-all training sessions. Adaptive learning platforms can identify and address specific areas where academics need support, optimising the use of institutional resources.
- Adaptive learning leverages AI to tailor educational experiences to individual needs. By implementing adaptive learning for staff, HEIs can offer personalised professional development opportunities. This approach ensures that each academic receives training and resources that match their unique skill levels, knowledge gaps, and teaching styles, leading to more effective and efficient learning.

Incorporation:

- Establish learning communities or cohorts where staff can collaborate, share insights, and discuss challenges related to using AI in teaching.
- Provide access to AI tools and software, such as machine learning platforms, data analytics tools, and AI-driven educational applications.
- Develop comprehensive user guides and tutorials to help staff effectively use these tools.
- Establish a dedicated technical support team to assist with any issues related to AI tool usage and integration into teaching practices.
- Incorporate interactive challenges and problem-solving scenarios that require staff to apply AI concepts in practical contexts.
- Collect and document case studies of staff who have successfully integrated AI into their teaching practices.
- Share these case studies and best practices through internal newsletters, workshops, and seminars.
- Highlight role models and AI champions within the institution who can inspire and mentor others.
- Ensure administrative support by integrating the adaptive learning platform into the institution's overall professional development strategy and providing necessary resources and funding.

Example 1	**Continuous Improvement and Iteration** • **Objective:** Ensure AI training programmes remain relevant and effective through continuous evaluation and updates. **Implementation Steps:** • **Feedback Collection:** Solicit feedback from faculty regarding their experiences with AI training programmes, including suggestions for improvement and additional training needs. • **Data Analysis:** Analyse learning analytics data to identify trends, areas of strength, and opportunities for enhancement in AI training modules and delivery methods. • **Iterative Updates:** Regularly update AI training content and adapt learning strategies based on faculty feedback, technological advancements in AI, and evolving legal education needs

P11: Ethical Frameworks

Establish ethical guidelines for the use of AI in teaching and learning, emphasising the importance of inclusivity and fairness.

Rationale:

- AI technology has the potential to greatly enhance teaching and learning, but it also raises significant ethical concerns. Implementing ethical frameworks ensures that staff use AI responsibly, mitigating risks such as bias, privacy violations, and unintended consequences. Ethical guidelines help staff navigate these challenges, promoting a balanced approach that maximises benefits while minimising harm.
- The use of AI in education often involves handling large amounts of sensitive student data. Ethical frameworks establish clear protocols for data management, ensuring that student information is protected and used responsibly. This includes adhering to data privacy laws, obtaining informed consent, and implementing robust data security measures. By prioritising data privacy, HEIs can build trust with students and their families, demonstrating a commitment to safeguarding personal information.
- AI systems can inadvertently perpetuate biases present in their training data, leading to unfair treatment of certain groups of students. Ethical frameworks provide guidelines for identifying and mitigating bias in AI applications. This ensures that AI-driven educational tools and practices promote fairness and equity, giving all students equal opportunities to succeed. By addressing biases, HEIs can create a more inclusive and supportive learning environment.
- AI tools, such as plagiarism detection software and automated grading systems, play a crucial role in maintaining academic integrity. Ethical frameworks guide the use of these tools to ensure they are applied fairly and consistently. They also address issues such as transparency in automated decision-making, ensuring that students understand how AI is being used in their education and have recourse if they believe they have been unfairly treated.
- Ethical frameworks provide clear guidelines for the development and deployment of AI technologies within educational settings. This includes principles for transparency, accountability, and human oversight, ensuring that AI systems are designed and implemented in ways that align with educational values and goals. By establishing these guidelines, HEIs can influence the development of AI technologies to better serve educational needs.
- Academics trained in ethical AI use are better equipped to teach students about the ethical implications of AI. This prepares students not only to use AI responsibly in their own lives but also to contribute to discussions and decisions about AI ethics in their future careers. By embedding ethical considerations into AI education, HEIs contribute to the development of a more ethically aware and responsible society.

Incorporation:

- Establish a Multi-Disciplinary Ethics Committee
  - **Objective:** Ensure diverse perspectives are considered in developing and implementing AI systems.

- **Action Steps:**
- Form an ethics committee comprising faculty from different disciplines, including computer science, law, philosophy, education, and sociology.
- Include student representatives to provide insights into student concerns and expectations.
- Regularly meet to review AI initiatives, discuss potential ethical issues, and develop guidelines.

- **Develop Clear Data Privacy Policies**
  - **Objective:** Protect student data and ensure its ethical use.
  - **Action Steps:**
  - Create comprehensive data privacy policies detailing how student data will be collected, stored, used, and shared.
  - Ensure policies comply with legal standards such as GDPR and FERPA.
  - Communicate these policies clearly to students and obtain informed consent before data collection.
  - Implement strong data security measures to protect against unauthorised access.
- **Implement Bias Detection and Mitigation Strategies**
  - **Objective:** Ensure fairness and prevent discrimination in AI-driven support systems.
  - **Action Steps:**
  - Use diverse datasets to train AI systems to minimise inherent biases.
  - Regularly audit AI systems for bias in recommendations and responses.
  - Develop algorithms that can detect and flag potential biases for further review.
  - Provide training for staff on recognising and addressing bias in AI applications.
- **Ensure Transparency and Explainability**
  - **Objective:** Make AI decision-making processes understandable and transparent to users.
  - **Action Steps:**
  - Design AI systems that provide clear explanations for their recommendations and decisions.
  - Create user-friendly interfaces that allow students to understand how decisions are made.
  - Offer detailed documentation on how the AI systems work and the data they use.

- Provide channels for students to ask questions and seek clarifications about AI-driven decisions.

- **Maintain Human Oversight and Accountability**
  - **Objective:** Ensure human oversight to validate AI decisions and maintain accountability.
  - **Action Steps:**
  - Require that all AI-driven recommendations are reviewed and approved by human advisors before implementation.
  - Establish protocols for regularly monitoring and evaluating AI systems by human supervisors.
  - Develop a clear process for students to appeal or question AI-generated advice.
  - Hold regular training sessions for staff to stay updated on AI developments and ethical practices.
- **Foster Ethical AI Literacy Among Staff and Students**
  - **Objective:** Educate the university community on ethical AI use.
  - **Action Steps:**
  - Integrate AI ethics modules into professional development programmes for staff.
  - Offer workshops, seminars, and AI ethics courses for staff and students.
  - Develop online resources, such as guides and tutorials, on ethical AI practices.
  - Encourage open discussions and forums on ethical AI use in education.
- **Continuous Review and Improvement**
  - **Objective:** Regularly update ethical frameworks to address evolving AI challenges.
  - **Action Steps:**
  - Schedule periodic reviews of ethical guidelines and frameworks by the ethics committee.
  - Gather feedback from students and staff on their experiences with AI systems.
  - Stay informed about advancements in AI ethics and incorporate new best practices.
  - Adapt policies and practices based on feedback, technological developments, and regulatory changes.
- **Promote Institutional Transparency and Accountability**
  - **Objective:** Ensure the institution's commitment to ethical AI use is transparent and accountable.

- **Action Steps:**
- Publicly share the university's ethical frameworks, guidelines, and policies on AI use.
- Provide regular reports on the implementation and impact of AI systems, including ethical reviews and audits.
- Create a transparent process for reporting and addressing ethical concerns related to AI.
- Recognise and reward initiatives that promote ethical AI use within the university community.

<table>
<tr><td>Example 1</td><td>Continuous Improvement and Iteration
• Objective: Regularly update and improve ethical frameworks to keep pace with technological advancements and ethical challenges.
Implementation Steps:
Feedback Mechanisms:
• Implement mechanisms for continuous feedback from faculty and students on AI tools and their ethical implications. Use surveys, focus groups, and suggestion boxes to gather input.
• Regular Updates: Periodically review and update ethical guidelines based on feedback, technological advancements, and new ethical challenges.
• Professional Development: Provide ongoing professional development opportunities for faculty to stay updated on the latest in AI ethics and best practices.</td></tr>
<tr><td>Example 2</td><td>Human Oversight and Accountability
• Objective: Maintain human oversight to ensure AI decisions are validated and accountable.
Implementation Steps:
• Review Panels: Establish panels to review AI-generated recommendations or decisions. For example, a faculty review panel can oversee AI-generated grades or feedback on student assignments.
• Appeal Processes: Create clear processes for students to appeal or question AI-generated decisions, such as grades or academic advice, ensuring that human intervention is possible.
• Oversight Training: Train staff on effectively overseeing AI tools and intervening when necessary, ensuring they can promptly identify and address issues.</td></tr>
</table>

P12: Ethical Review Boards

Consider establishing ethical review boards to oversee AI projects and ensure compliance with ethical standards.

Rationale:

- Ethical Review Boards (ERBs) ensure that AI technologies are integrated responsibly. By reviewing and assessing the ethical implications of AI applications, ERBs help prevent potential harms, such as biased algorithms, privacy violations, and data misuse. This oversight is crucial for maintaining educational practices' integrity and protecting all stakeholders' interests.

- AI systems often require access to large volumes of student data to function effectively. This raises concerns about data privacy and security. An ERB can establish and enforce strict guidelines for data collection, storage, and usage, ensuring compliance with legal standards such as GDPR and FERPA. By overseeing data management practices, the ERB helps safeguard student privacy and build trust between students and the institution.
- AI technologies can inadvertently perpetuate biases present in their training data, leading to unfair treatment of certain groups of students. ERBs play a critical role in identifying and mitigating these biases. They ensure that AI systems are designed and implemented in ways that promote fairness and equity, providing equal opportunities for all students. This commitment to fairness helps create an inclusive educational environment where every student can thrive.
- Transparency in AI decision-making processes is essential for maintaining trust and accountability in educational practices. ERBs require that AI systems provide clear, explainable, and understandable information about how decisions are made. This transparency allows academics and students to understand the basis of AI-driven outcomes and ensures that there is accountability for the decisions made by these systems. It also provides a mechanism for addressing any grievances or disputes that may arise.
- The use of AI in grading, assessments, and other academic processes must uphold the highest standards of academic integrity. ERBs ensure that AI tools are used appropriately and do not undermine the principles of fairness and honesty in education. By providing oversight and establishing ethical guidelines, ERBs help maintain the credibility of academic evaluations and prevent issues such as automated grading errors or AI-facilitated cheating.
- As AI technologies become more prevalent in education, it is essential for faculty and staff to understand the ethical implications of AI use. ERBs can guide the development of professional development programmes focused on AI ethics, helping staff to navigate the ethical challenges associated with AI. This education promotes a culture of ethical awareness and responsibility, ensuring that staff are well-equipped to use AI tools in a principled manner.
- Implementing ERBs demonstrates an institution's commitment to ethical standards and responsible innovation. This commitment enhances the institution's reputation, attracting students, faculty, and partners who value ethical practices. It positions the institution as a leader in the responsible use of technology in education, which can lead to increased trust, credibility, and competitive advantage in the higher education landscape.

- ERBs provide a structured approach to the ethical development and deployment of AI technologies. They establish clear ethical guidelines and frameworks that developers and academics must follow, ensuring that AI tools are designed with ethical considerations in mind from the outset. This proactive approach helps prevent ethical issues before they arise and promotes the development of AI systems that align with educational values and goals.
- AI use in education is subject to various regulatory and legal requirements. ERBs ensure that AI applications comply with these regulations, reducing the risk of legal challenges and penalties. By aligning AI practices with legal and ethical standards, ERBs help institutions navigate the complex regulatory landscape and demonstrate compliance with national and international guidelines.

Incorporation:

- **Establishing the Ethical Review Board (ERB)**
  - **Objective:** Create a diverse and multidisciplinary body to oversee and evaluate the ethical implications of AI use in education.
  - **Action Steps:**
  - **Form a Committee:** Establish an ERB comprising faculty from various disciplines, including law, ethics, computer science, education, and social sciences. Include student representatives to ensure diverse perspectives.
  - **Define Roles and Responsibilities:** Clearly define the roles and responsibilities of ERB members, including reviewing AI applications, setting ethical guidelines, and conducting regular audits.
  - **Regular Meetings:** Schedule regular meetings (e.g., monthly or quarterly) to review ongoing and new AI projects, ensuring continuous oversight and ethical assessment.
- **Developing Ethical Guidelines and Policies**
  - **Objective:** Create comprehensive ethical guidelines and policies for the use of AI in teaching and learning.
  - **Action Steps:**
  - **Conduct Research:** Review existing literature and best practices on AI ethics in education to inform guideline development.
  - **Draft Guidelines:** Develop detailed guidelines covering data privacy, bias mitigation, transparency, accountability, and fairness.
  - **Stakeholder Input:** Seek input from faculty, students, and external experts to ensure the guidelines are robust and applicable.

- **Approval and Dissemination:** Obtain formal approval from the institution's governance bodies and disseminate the guidelines widely among staff and students.

- **Training and Capacity Building**
  - **Objective:** Equip faculty and staff with the knowledge and skills to use AI ethically in their teaching and learning activities.
  - **Action Steps:**
  - **Develop Training Programmes:** Create and offer regular training programmes focused on AI ethics, including workshops, seminars, and online courses.
  - **Mandatory Training:** Require all faculty and staff involved in AI-related activities to complete mandatory ethical training.
  - **Continuous Learning:** Encourage ongoing professional development by providing access to resources, such as webinars, conferences, and publications on AI ethics.
- **Monitoring and Auditing AI Applications**
  - **Objective:** Ensure ongoing ethical compliance and address any emerging ethical issues in AI applications.
  - **Action Steps:**
  - **Regular Audits:** Conduct regular audits of AI applications used in teaching and learning to assess compliance with ethical guidelines.
  - **Monitoring Tools:** Develop and implement tools for continuous monitoring of AI systems, focusing on performance, bias, and user feedback.
  - **Feedback Mechanisms:** Establish channels for students and staff to report ethical concerns or issues with AI systems. Ensure these channels are accessible and well publicised.
- **Promoting Transparency and Accountability**
  - **Objective:** Ensure transparency in AI decision-making processes and accountability for AI outcomes.
  - **Action Steps:**
  - **Documentation and Reporting:** Require detailed documentation of AI systems, including their development, data sources, decision-making processes, and ethical considerations.
  - **Explainable AI:** Implement AI systems that can provide clear and understandable explanations for their decisions, especially in areas such as grading and student support.

- **Public Reports:** Publish regular reports on the use and impact of AI in the institution, highlighting compliance with ethical standards and any corrective actions taken.

- **Fostering a Culture of Ethical Awareness**
  - **Objective:** Promote a culture of ethical awareness and responsibility across the institution.
  - **Action Steps:**
  - **Ethics in Curriculum:** Integrate AI ethics into the curriculum for all students, particularly in courses related to computer science, law, and education.
  - **Ethics Forums and Discussions:** To engage the university community, organise regular forums, panel discussions, and debates on AI ethics.
  - **Recognition Programmes:** Establish recognition programmes to reward individuals and teams demonstrating exemplary ethical practices in AI use.
- **Reviewing and Updating Ethical Guidelines**
  - **Objective:** Ensure ethical guidelines remain relevant and effective in the face of evolving AI technologies and ethical challenges.
  - **Action Steps:**
  - **Periodic Reviews:** Schedule periodic reviews of ethical guidelines (e.g., annually) to incorporate new insights and advancements in AI ethics.
  - **Stakeholder Engagement:** Continuously engage stakeholders in the review process to gather diverse perspectives and feedback.
  - **Adaptive Policies:** Be prepared to adapt policies and guidelines promptly in response to emerging ethical issues and technological developments.

Example 1	**Establishing Clear Guidelines and Policies:** • **Developing a dedicated policy on AI use in teaching and learning:** This policy should outline the ethical principles and considerations specific to AI applications within the educational context. • **Defining criteria for ERB review:** This could include the types of AI tools used, data used, potential risks, and impact on students. • **Establishing clear roles and responsibilities:** Clarify who within the HEI is responsible for submitting applications for ERB review, reviewing applications, and ensuring policy compliance.

<table>
<tr><td>Example 2</td><td>ERB Review Process for AI Tools and Activities:
• Mandatory review: All staff must submit a proposal for ERB review before implementing any AI tool or activity in their teaching.
• Multidisciplinary ERB: The board should include members with expertise in AI ethics, education, law, privacy, and relevant fields.
• Thorough assessment: The ERB should assess applications based on criteria such as:
  • Fairness and Bias: Does the AI system discriminate against certain groups of students?
  • Transparency and Explainability: Is the AI system's decision-making process understandable and auditable?
  • Privacy and Data Security: How is student data collected, used, and protected?
  • Academic Integrity: Does the AI system promote cheating or plagiarism?
  • Educational Impact: Does the AI tool enhance learning outcomes or create negative impacts?</td></tr>
</table>

P13: Privacy and Data Protection

Safeguard the privacy of student data. Use AI systems that comply with data protection regulations and ensure that data is anonymised and securely stored.

Rationale:

- HEIs in the UK and Europe are bound by the General Data Protection Regulation (GDPR), which mandates strict data protection and privacy measures. Ensuring compliance with GDPR is not only a legal obligation but also a critical factor in maintaining the institution's reputation and avoiding substantial fines.
- The HEIs often have additional regulations and guidelines that emphasise the protection of personal data. Implementing privacy and data protection principles ensures that HEIs adhere to all relevant legal frameworks.
- Staff members need to trust that their personal data is handled responsibly and securely. Implementing strong privacy and data protection measures fosters a culture of trust and transparency within the institution.
- Demonstrating a commitment to privacy and data protection can enhance the institution's reputation among current and prospective staff, students, and the wider community. This commitment is increasingly important in an era where data breaches and privacy concerns are prevalent.
- AI systems in teaching and learning often involve collecting and processing significant amounts of personal data. Respecting the privacy of staff members by protecting their data upholds the ethical principle of autonomy.
- Ensuring data protection helps prevent biases and misuse of AI systems. It promotes fairness and equity by ensuring that AI tools are used in ways that do not disadvantage or unfairly target specific groups of staff.

Incorporation:

- Develop and publish comprehensive data protection policies that outline the principles, practices, and procedures for handling personal data, specifically addressing the use of AI in teaching and learning.
- Ensure that these policies are regularly updated to reflect changes in technology, legal requirements, and best practices in data protection.
- Collect only the data that is necessary for the specific purposes of the AI applications. Avoid collecting excessive or irrelevant information.
- Apply techniques to anonymise or pseudonymise data where possible, ensuring that personal identifiers are removed or obscured to protect individual privacy.
- Conduct Data Protection Impact Assessments (DPIAs) for all AI projects to identify and mitigate potential privacy risks. DPIAs help understand the data flows and AI's implications for staff privacy.
- Establish accountability mechanisms such as appointing a dedicated data protection officer (DPO) to oversee compliance with data protection laws and principles.
- Offer regular training sessions for staff on data protection principles, privacy rights, and the implications of AI technologies. This ensures that staff are aware of how their data is being used and their rights regarding their personal information.

Example of 1	1. The HEIs should set up a dedicated support desk where staff can raise concerns or seek advice on data protection issues related to AI. This support desk is staffed with knowledgeable personnel who can provide guidance and assistance
Example 2	2. The HEIs appoint a data protection officer (DPO) responsible for ensuring that all AI applications comply with relevant data protection laws such as GDPR. The DPO conducts regular reviews and updates policies to align with any new legal requirements or guidelines.
Example 3	3. To foster a culture of privacy, the HEI conducts workshops on privacy-by-design principles for AI developers and faculty members involved in AI projects. These workshops emphasise the importance of integrating privacy features from the initial design stages of AI tools.
Example 4	4. The HEIs implement advanced security measures, such as multi-factor authentication (MFA) and encryption, for all AI systems that handle personal data. Regular security audits and vulnerability assessments are conducted to identify and address potential security weaknesses.
Example 5	5. The HEIs create a dedicated webpage that explains how AI tools are used in teaching and learning, what data is collected, how it is processed, and the measures in place to protect this data. Staff are regularly updated on any changes through email notifications and staff meetings
Example 6	6. Before implementing a new AI-powered tool for faculty performance evaluation, the HEIs should conduct a Data Protection Impact Assessment (DPIA). This assessment identifies potential privacy risks and outlines measures to mitigate them, such as data encryption and restricted access controls.

P14: Regular Assessment

Continuously assess the effectiveness of AI tools in improving learning outcomes. Use evidence-based practices to evaluate the impact of AI on student performance and engagement.

Rationale:

- Regular assessment helps to ensure that AI tools used in teaching and learning are meeting their intended goals and enhancing educational outcomes. By continuously evaluating the performance and impact of AI applications, HEIs can identify areas for improvement and ensure that these technologies are genuinely benefiting both staff and students.
- Regular assessments promote accountability and transparency in the use of AI. By documenting and publicly sharing the results of these evaluations, HEIs demonstrate their commitment to responsible and ethical AI use. This transparency helps build trust among stakeholders, including staff, students, and the wider community.
- AI systems can inadvertently perpetuate or exacerbate biases. Regular assessment is crucial to detect and mitigate such biases, ensuring that AI applications operate fairly and equitably. This is particularly important in educational settings where fairness in grading, feedback, and support is essential.
- The field of AI is rapidly evolving. Regular assessment enables HEIs to stay up-to-date with technological advancements and integrate new, more effective AI tools into their teaching and learning practices. This proactive approach ensures that the institution remains at the forefront of educational innovation.
- Regular assessment provides valuable feedback that can support staff's continuous professional development. By identifying strengths and areas for improvement in the use of AI tools, HEIs can tailor training programmes to better meet their staff's needs.
- Regular assessment fosters a culture of continuous improvement within the institution. By routinely evaluating and refining AI applications, HEIs can continually enhance the quality of education they provide and better meet the needs of their staff and students.

Incorporation:

- Regularly reviews the effectiveness of its AI-powered grading system to ensure it is accurately assessing student work and providing meaningful feedback. If discrepancies or biases are found, the system can be adjusted accordingly.
- An HEI publishes annual reports detailing the performance and impact of AI tools in various departments, including success stories, challenges faced, and improvements made based on assessment findings.

- Conducts periodic bias audits of its AI-driven student support chatbot to ensure that it provides equitable assistance to all students, regardless of their background or demographics.
- Regularly evaluates its AI-based learning management system and upgrades to newer versions that offer enhanced features, better user experience, and improved security.
- Assess results to develop targeted workshops and training sessions that address specific challenges faculty members face when integrating AI into their teaching practices.
- Implements a feedback loop where staff and students can regularly provide input on AI tools, which is then used to make iterative improvements to these technologies.

Example 1	7. At the end of each academic term, an HEI should distribute surveys to both students and staff to gather their perspectives on the effectiveness and user-friendliness of AI tools used in their courses. The survey results are analysed to guide future AI tool improvements and ensure they meet the needs of users.
Example 2	8. Before fully implementing a new AI tool across the institution, a university runs a pilot test in a few departments. The performance and impact of the AI tool are closely monitored and assessed during the pilot phase. Feedback from this period is used to refine the tool before a wider rollout.
Example 3	9. An HEI should bring in external experts periodically to review the AI systems in use. These experts provide an unbiased assessment of the AI tools' performance, potential risks, and areas for improvement. Their insights help the institution maintain high standards and incorporate best practices from the industry.
Example 4	10. Use data analytics to track the performance and impact of AI tools in real-time. Administration and teaching staff regularly review dashboards displaying key performance indicators (KPIs) for AI applications to make data-driven decisions about continuing, modifying, or discontinuing the use of specific AI tools.

P15: Sustainable Practices

Ensure that the integration of AI in education is sustainable, considering long-term impacts on the institution's resources and infrastructure.

Rationale:

- As global awareness of environmental issues continues to grow, higher education institutions (HEIs) are increasingly expected to align their operations and educational practices with global sustainability goals, such as those outlined in the United Nations Sustainable Development Goals (SDGs). Implementing sustainable practices for staff using AI in teaching and learning directly supports these goals by promoting resource efficiency, reducing carbon footprints, and fostering innovation in sustainability. This alignment not only enhances the institution's reputation but also contributes meaningfully to global efforts to combat climate change and promote sustainable development.

- AI technologies can significantly enhance the efficiency of teaching and learning processes. For example, AI-driven analytics can optimise energy usage in campus facilities, reduce waste through smart resource management, and promote digitalisation, thereby reducing the reliance on paper and physical resources. By incorporating AI in sustainable practices, HEIs can minimise their environmental impact, contributing to a greener campus and a more sustainable future. This approach helps reduce the institution's carbon footprint and operational costs, aligning with broader environmental sustainability targets.
- AI offers transformative potential in creating innovative, sustainable educational practices. By integrating AI tools, HEIs can develop smarter, more efficient educational systems that reduce resource consumption and enhance learning experiences. For instance, AI can facilitate personalised learning pathways, reducing the need for extensive physical resources and enabling more efficient use of educational materials. Additionally, AI can support sustainable campus operations through predictive maintenance, smart energy management, and optimised transportation systems, promoting a sustainable, low-impact campus environment.
- Sustainable AI practices can enhance the quality and accessibility of education by making learning resources more available and tailored to individual needs. AI-driven platforms can provide adaptive learning experiences, support remote and blended learning models, and offer real-time feedback to students, thereby reducing the need for physical infrastructure and travel. This not only makes education more accessible and inclusive but also promotes sustainability by minimising the environmental impact associated with traditional educational models.

Incorporation:

- HEIs can deploy AI-powered systems for virtual learning environments that prioritise energy efficiency. These systems can automatically adjust server loads based on demand, optimise cooling systems in data centres, and schedule non-essential tasks during off-peak hours to minimise energy consumption. For instance, AI algorithms can manage classroom lighting and HVAC systems intelligently to reduce electricity usage when spaces are unoccupied.
- HEIs can encourage staff to use AI-driven digital platforms for course materials, assessments, and administrative tasks to reduce paper consumption. AI can facilitate the transition by providing tools for digital document management, automated grading, and virtual collaboration. For instance, AI-powered learning management systems can offer electronic submission and feedback mechanisms, reducing the need for printed materials.
- HEIs can implement AI-driven predictive analytics to optimise resource allocation and utilisation. AI algorithms can analyse historical data on classroom usage, student attendance patterns, and equipment usage to schedule classes more efficiently. This approach minimises unnecessary resource consumption and supports sustainable

campus operations. For instance, AI can predict peak usage times for labs and adjust scheduling to optimise equipment usage and reduce idle time.

- HEIs can promote remote teaching and learning enabled by AI technologies to reduce the environmental impact associated with commuting and physical infrastructure. AI-powered virtual classrooms and online collaboration tools can facilitate flexible learning options while minimising travel-related emissions. For instance, AI-driven virtual reality (VR) or augmented reality (AR) platforms can create immersive educational experiences without the need for extensive travel or physical classroom space.

Example 1	11. HEIs can deploy AI-powered learning management systems (LMS) that optimise energy consumption. These systems can use AI algorithms to schedule server operations during off-peak hours, reducing overall energy usage in data centres. Additionally, implementing cloud-based AI services that prioritise renewable energy sources for data processing can further reduce the institution's carbon footprint.
Example 2	12. HEIs can encourage staff to adopt AI-driven digital platforms for course delivery, assessments, and administrative tasks to minimise paper consumption. For instance, using AI-enabled digital grading and feedback systems can eliminate the need for printed materials, reducing paper waste across campus. Furthermore, promoting electronic assignment submission and digital collaboration tools can significantly reduce the institution's paper usage.
Example 3	13. HEIs can promote remote teaching and learning facilitated by AI technologies to reduce commuting and infrastructure-related emissions. AI-powered virtual classrooms and online collaboration tools enable flexible learning options without the need for physical classroom space. This approach reduces carbon emissions and supports sustainable campus development by minimising the need for new construction.
Example 4	14. HEIs can conduct lifecycle assessments (LCAs) of AI systems used in teaching and learning to evaluate their environmental impact. This assessment includes analysing the energy consumption, materials used, and disposal methods of AI hardware and software. By selecting AI solutions with lower environmental footprints and promoting sustainable practices in AI procurement, HEIs can mitigate their overall environmental impact.
Example 5	15. HEIs can offer training programmes and workshops for staff on sustainable practices in AI-enabled teaching and learning. These programmes can include best practices for energy-efficient AI use, guidelines on digital resource management, and strategies for reducing environmental impact. Staff awareness campaigns can educate on the importance of sustainability in technology adoption and encourage behaviour changes that support environmental goals.
Example 6	16. HEIs can collaborate with industry partners and researchers to develop AI technologies that prioritise sustainability. Collaborative efforts can focus on designing energy-efficient AI algorithms, optimising resource allocation in educational settings, and promoting green computing practices. By fostering partnerships that prioritise environmental sustainability, HEIs can innovate and lead in sustainable AI applications for education.
Example 7	17. HEIs can establish sustainability metrics and KPIs to monitor the environmental impact of AI use in teaching and learning. Regular reporting on energy consumption, carbon emissions, waste reduction, and other sustainability indicators can track progress towards sustainability goals. Transparency in reporting encourages accountability and allows HEIs to improve their sustainable practices continuously.

P16: Scalable Solutions

Develop and implement scalable AI solutions that can be adopted across different departments and programmes.

Rationale:

- HEIs can adopt AI-powered learning management systems that automate administrative tasks such as grading, student performance analytics, and personalised learning pathways. These scalable AI solutions streamline workflows, reduce manual effort, and optimise resource allocation. By automating routine tasks, staff can focus more on personalised student support and pedagogical innovation, enhancing overall teaching quality and efficiency.
- HEIs experiencing increasing student enrolments can benefit from scalable AI solutions that accommodate larger cohorts without compromising educational standards. AI-driven virtual assistants and chatbots can provide personalised support to students round-the-clock, scaling to meet the demand for academic guidance, course information, and administrative queries. This ensures a consistent level of service delivery despite varying student numbers.
- HEIs can leverage AI technologies to offer flexible and scalable learning experiences, accommodating diverse student needs and preferences. AI-powered adaptive learning platforms can dynamically adjust course content and pacing based on individual student progress and learning styles. This scalability allows HEIs to cater to a wide range of learners effectively, promoting inclusivity and personalised education pathways.
- HEIs can deploy scalable AI solutions that offer cost-effective alternatives to traditional teaching methods. For instance, virtual laboratories powered by AI simulations can replace expensive physical equipment, reducing maintenance costs and operational expenses. Scalable AI-driven educational resources, such as digital textbooks and interactive multimedia content, can lower the overall cost of course materials while enhancing learning outcomes.

Incorporation:

- HEIs can encourage staff to adopt AI-driven digital platforms for course delivery, assessments, and administrative tasks to minimise paper consumption. For instance, using AI-enabled digital grading and feedback systems can eliminate the need for printed materials, reducing paper waste across campus. Furthermore, promoting electronic submission of assignments and digital collaboration tools can significantly reduce the institution's paper usage.
- HEIs can use AI analytics to optimise resource allocation and usage in teaching and learning environments. AI algorithms can analyse data on classroom utilisation,

student attendance patterns, and equipment usage to schedule classes more efficiently. By ensuring classrooms and resources are used optimally, HEIs can minimise energy consumption and reduce environmental impact.

- HEIs can promote remote teaching and learning facilitated by AI technologies to reduce commuting and infrastructure-related emissions. AI-powered virtual classrooms and online collaboration tools enable flexible learning options without the need for physical classroom space. This approach reduces carbon emissions and supports sustainable campus development by minimising the need for new construction.
- HEIs can conduct lifecycle assessments of AI systems used in teaching and learning to evaluate their environmental impact. This assessment includes analysing the energy consumption, materials used, and disposal methods of AI hardware and software. By selecting AI solutions with lower environmental footprints and promoting sustainable practices in AI procurement, HEIs can mitigate their overall environmental impact.

Example 1	**Centralised AI Infrastructure:** • **Description:** Establish a centralised AI infrastructure that can scale horizontally to accommodate increasing demands from various departments and staff members. **Implementation Steps:** • Deploy a cloud-based AI platform that allows staff members to access AI tools and resources on-demand. • Implement containerisation and microservices architecture to enable scalable deployment of AI applications across different departments. • Provide self-service portals where staff can provision AI resources based on their specific needs and requirements. • Ensure robust scalability planning to handle peak loads during busy academic periods such as exam seasons or enrolment periods.
Example 2	**AI-Powered Personalised Learning Platforms:** • **Description:** Develop AI-powered learning platforms that offer personalised educational experiences and scale to accommodate diverse learning needs and preferences. **Implementation Steps:** • Integrate AI algorithms for adaptive learning that customise content delivery and assessment based on individual student progress and learning styles. • Utilise natural language processing (NLP) and machine learning to analyse student interactions and provide real-time feedback and recommendations. • Scale the platform's capacity to handle a large volume of concurrent users while maintaining responsiveness and performance. • Collaborate with faculty members to continuously refine and improve AI models based on feedback and educational outcomes.

Example 3	**AI-Driven Analytics for Decision Support:** • Description: Implement AI-driven analytics platforms that scale to analyse large datasets and provide actionable insights for academic and administrative decision-making. **Implementation Steps:** • Develop AI algorithms for predictive analytics that forecast enrolment trends, student performance, and resource allocation needs. • Scale data processing capabilities using distributed computing frameworks such as Apache Hadoop or Spark to handle increasing data volumes. • Integrate AI-powered dashboards and visualisations that enable staff to explore data insights and make informed decisions in real time. • Provide staff training and support on leveraging AI-driven analytics tools for strategic planning and operational optimisation.
Example 4	**AI-Assisted Administrative Processes:** • Description: Streamline administrative processes using AI-driven automation tools that scale to handle routine tasks efficiently across departments. **Implementation Steps:** • Deploy AI-powered chatbots or virtual assistants to handle staff inquiries regarding administrative procedures, HR policies, and IT support. • Implement natural language understanding (NLU) capabilities to enable chatbots to interpret and respond to a wide range of staff queries autonomously. • Scale automation capabilities to encompass diverse administrative functions such as scheduling, document processing, and inventory management. • Monitor performance metrics and user feedback to optimise AI-assisted processes and ensure scalability across the institution continuously.

In conclusion, the principles for staff to use AI ethically in HEIs highlight the importance of taking a responsible and principled approach to integrating AI into teaching and learning. These principles aim to ensure that AI enhances educational outcomes while protecting students' well-being, promoting fairness, and maintaining the integrity of the institution. Firstly, transparency and accountability are key. HEIs must communicate clearly with everyone involved about how AI is used, its benefits, and what it might mean for education. This openness builds trust among students, academics, and staff, making sure everyone understands and agrees with how AI is used in education. Protecting privacy is also crucial. HEIs must follow strict rules to keep student data safe when using AI systems. This means making sure data is anonymous, stored securely, and only used for educational purposes with students' permission. These steps help protect students' privacy and build confidence in how AI is used.

Dealing with bias and ensuring fairness is vital in AI. HEIs should regularly check AI systems to find and fix any biases that could unfairly affect groups of students. This commitment to fairness makes sure AI follows ethical standards and makes education more inclusive. Aligning AI with teaching methods is important too. AI should support academics rather than replace them, making teaching better and helping students learn in ways that suit them best. By adapting lessons to different learning styles and needs, academics can create fairer and more engaging learning environments that respect each student's individuality. Accessibility is essential for ensuring AI tools can be used by all students, including those with disabilities. HEIs should design AI applications based on Inclusive Design Learning principles. This means making sure AI tools can be used by everyone, helping to bridge gaps between different groups of students and making education more equal. Therefore, academics and staff need good training to use AI effectively. HEIs should invest in training that gives academics the skills and knowledge to use AI responsibly in teaching. This includes understanding ethics, being good with technology, and using the best methods to help students learn well.

Finally, HEIs should always check how well AI is working in education. They should regularly review AI systems to see how they help students learn, keep them interested, and make education better overall. By using data to see what works and what does not, HEIs can improve AI use in education, making sure it helps students succeed while keeping risks low. In short, by following these guiding principles—being clear and accountable, protecting privacy, ensuring fairness, matching AI with teaching methods, making AI accessible, training staff well, and checking how well AI works—HEIs can use AI in education in a responsible and ethical way. These principles not only improve how education works but also make sure AI helps students do their best.

EMPLOYABILITY GUIDING PRINCIPLE FOR USING GENERATIVE AI IN STUDENT SKILL DEVELOPMENT AND QUALIFICATION

Preamble

In today's world of rapid technological growth and the widespread use of artificial intelligence (AI), HEIs need to prepare students for a complex and ever-changing job market. The 'Employability Guiding Principle for Using Generative AI in Student Skill Development and Qualification' outlines guidance to integrate AI technologies into education to enhance student skills, encourage innovation, and improve job readiness.

GenAI, which includes technologies that can create new content and solutions, has great potential to change education. Using GenAI, academics can provide personalised learning experiences, mimic real-world problem-solving, and help develop essential skills that employers value. This principle recognises that while traditional academic achievements are still important, being able to adapt, innovate, and apply knowledge in real-life situations is crucial for students' success in today's workforce. The principle highlights the need for a balanced approach that combines expertise in specific subjects with transferable skills like critical thinking, creativity, communication, and adaptability. GenAI tools can support this comprehensive development by offering interactive and adaptive learning experiences tailored to individual student needs and industry requirements. Additionally, incorporating AI into education promotes a collaborative learning environment where students can participate in project-based learning, interdisciplinary studies, and hands-on learning opportunities.

This guiding principle also stresses the importance of ethical considerations and social-emotional skills for responsible AI use. It calls for including ethical AI practices, data privacy, and digital literacy in the curriculum, ensuring that students become skilled in using AI technologies and understand their broader impact on society. The 'Employability Guiding Principle for Using Generative AI in Student Skill Development and Qualification' provides a strategic plan for educational institutions. It aims to equip students with the skills, knowledge, and ethical foundation needed to succeed in a technologically advanced and constantly changing professional environment, promoting lifelong learning and adaptability.

P1: Simulated Work Environments

Enhance student employability by leveraging generative AI to simulate real-world work environments and tasks.

Rationale:

- Utilising advanced AI algorithms to replicate real-world environments and scenarios will provide students with a more engaging and effective learning experience, making it easier to grasp complex concepts and practical skills.
- Designing simulations that reflect actual job responsibilities and workflows will help students understand what to expect in their future careers, reducing the learning curve when they enter the workforce.
- Integrating classroom learning with hands-on practice in simulated environments will ensure students can apply what they have learned in real-world situations, enhancing their overall competence and confidence.
- Creating scenarios where errors are part of the learning process will foster a growth mindset and resilience, as students can learn from failures without negative repercussions.
- Providing virtual platforms where students can practice without the fear of real-world consequences will enable them to take risks and experiment, leading to better learning outcomes and skill mastery.
- Providing hands-on experience with tools and technologies they will encounter in their careers will make them more prepared and adaptable to the evolving technological landscape of modern workplaces.

Incorporate:

1. Virtual Simulations of Professional Settings
    - **Industry-Specific Simulations:** Utilising AI to develop simulations tailored to different industries such as healthcare, finance, engineering, or marketing. For instance, students pursuing healthcare can engage in virtual patient care simulations, while finance students can practice trading in virtual stock markets.

- **Interactive Platforms:** Use platforms like VR (Virtual Reality) or AR (Augmented Reality) to create immersive environments where students can navigate and interact as they would in real job roles.

2. Scenario-Based Learning:

- **Real-Life Challenges:** Design scenarios that replicate the challenges and tasks professionals face in their fields. For example, engineering students might solve complex design problems, while management students might handle crisis situations in a virtual company.
- **Problem-Solving and Decision-Making:** Encourage students to make decisions and solve problems in these simulations, fostering critical thinking and adaptability. AI can provide immediate feedback on their decisions, helping them learn from mistakes in a risk-free environment.

Exposure to Career-Specific Scenarios:

1. Career Path Exploration:

- **Diverse Roles and Responsibilities:** Students are exposed to various roles within their chosen fields through AI-driven simulations. This helps them understand the different career paths and the required skills.
- **Professional Skills Development:** Tailor simulations to focus on developing specific skills such as project management, teamwork, communication, and technical expertise.

2. Customised Learning Experiences:

- **Adaptive Learning Paths:** Use AI to analyse student performance and adapt the complexity and type of simulations accordingly. This personalised approach ensures that each student can progress at their own pace and focus on areas where they need improvement.
- **Skill Assessment and Enhancement:** AI can track student performance over time, providing detailed analytics on their strengths and areas for growth. This data can be used to guide further learning and development.

Integration into Curriculum:

1. Collaborative Projects:

- **Team-Based Simulations:** Incorporate group simulations where students must work together to achieve common goals, mirroring workplace collaboration. This promotes teamwork and interpersonal skills.
- **Cross-Disciplinary Projects:** Design projects that require students from different fields to collaborate, reflecting the interdisciplinary nature of many real-world jobs.

2. Continuous Feedback and Assessment:
   - **AI Feedback Mechanisms:** Implement AI tools that provide continuous, real-time feedback on student performance. This helps students understand their progress and areas needing improvement.
   - **Assessment Tools:** Use AI to create assessments that accurately measure student learning and skill acquisition through these simulations, ensuring they meet industry standards.

Preparing for the Workforce:

1. Networking and Professionalism:
   - **Simulated Networking Events:** Create virtual networking events where students can practice interacting with professionals, learn how to present themselves, and build professional relationships.
   - **Soft Skills Training:** Incorporate simulations that focus on developing soft skills such as communication, negotiation, and leadership.
2. Real-World Integration:
   - **Internship Simulations:** Develop simulations that mimic internships, providing students with a preview of what to expect in actual internship roles.
   - **Employer Partnerships:** Collaborate with industry partners to ensure the simulations are aligned with current industry practices and needs, increasing the relevance and applicability of the skills learned.

Example 1	• Develop a virtual courtroom where law students can participate in mock trials and experience the roles of defence barristers, prosecutors, and judges. • Provides a hands-on understanding of courtroom procedures and the dynamics of trial practice, essential for aspiring barristers
Example 2	• Simulate a legal firm's office environment where students can work on drafting contracts, preparing case files, and conducting client consultations. • Helps students get accustomed to the daily tasks and responsibilities of legal professionals, bridging the gap between academic knowledge and practical skills.
Example 3	• Use AI to provide feedback on legal writing and argumentation, allowing students to improve their skills through trial and error. • Fosters a learning environment where students can improve by understanding and correcting their mistakes.
Example 4	• Create a simulated newsroom for journalism students where they can experience the fast-paced environment of a real news organisation, taking on roles such as reporters, editors, and photojournalists. • Offers practical experience in news production, enhances understanding of media ethics, and develops critical skills in research, writing, and editing, which are crucial for a career in journalism.

Example 5	• Develop a simulated corporate office for business management students where they can engage in activities such as strategic planning, project management, and team leadership. • Provides practical experience in managing business operations, enhances understanding of organisational dynamics, and develops essential skills in decision-making, leadership, and problem-solving, which are crucial for a successful career in business management.

P2: Align AI Integration with Curriculum Goals to Enhance Employability

Rationale:

- Aligning AI integration with curriculum goals ensures that students acquire skills and competencies that are directly applicable to the demands of the contemporary job market.
- Higher education institutions (HEIs) that integrate AI technology into their curriculum gain a competitive edge by producing graduates who are proficient in both traditional academic subjects and emerging technologies.
- By incorporating AI-driven simulations, HEIs can better address the evolving needs of various industries, preparing students to meet the demands of future workplaces.
- AI-driven simulations provide immersive, hands-on experiences that enhance student engagement and facilitate deeper learning, leading to improved academic performance and employability.
- AI tools can analyse individual student performance and provide personalised feedback and learning pathways, ensuring that each student's educational experience is tailored to their needs and strengths.
- Integrating AI into the curriculum equips students with essential digital literacy skills and prepares them for the increasing automation and digitalisation of the workforce.

Incorporation:

- Ensure that AI integration aligns with the overall learning objectives of the curriculum, focusing on developing key employability skills such as critical thinking, problem-solving, communication, and technical proficiency.
- Foster interdisciplinary collaboration to integrate AI technology across various academic disciplines, allowing students to apply AI concepts and tools in diverse contexts.
- Integrate discussions on ethical considerations and responsible use of AI technology into the curriculum, ensuring that students understand the societal implications of AI and are equipped to navigate ethical dilemmas in their future careers.

- Forge partnerships with industry stakeholders to co-design curriculum components that reflect current industry practices and trends in AI integration, ensuring that students are prepared for the demands of the workforce.
- Provide professional development opportunities for faculty to enhance their proficiency in integrating AI technology into teaching and learning, fostering a culture of innovation and lifelong learning within the institution.

Example 1	• Integrate AI tools and techniques into laboratory experiments and research projects for science degree programmes. Students will learn to use AI algorithms for data analysis, predictive modelling, and experimental design, aligning with curriculum goals of developing analytical skills and scientific inquiry. This integration enhances employability by equipping students with cutting-edge skills sought after in fields such as biotechnology, environmental science, and pharmaceutical research.
Example 2	• Incorporate AI-driven legal research platforms into the curriculum of law degree programmes. By teaching students to utilise these tools effectively, they develop proficiency in leveraging technology for case analysis, precedent identification, and legal writing. This alignment with curriculum goals enhances employability by preparing graduates with the advanced research skills required in modern legal practice, making them more competitive in roles such as legal associates, paralegals, and legal analysts.
Example 3	• Integrate AI algorithms and machine learning techniques into the mathematics degree programme curriculum. Students will apply AI to solve complex mathematical problems, analyse large data sets, and develop predictive models, aligning with curriculum goals of enhancing analytical and problem-solving skills. This integration enhances employability by equipping students with advanced computational skills and experience in AI, which are highly valued in industries such as finance, technology, and data science.

P3: Focus on Skill Development

Rationale:

- AI helps students develop crucial skills such as problem-solving, critical thinking, adaptability, and technical proficiency. These abilities are fundamental for employability and success in various professional fields.
- AI can help students develop essential soft skills such as problem-solving, critical thinking, creativity, and communication through simulated environments and interactive learning platforms.
- AI provides valuable analytics on student performance, helping universities identify strengths and areas for improvement. Optimising the teaching and learning process enables targeted skill development, ensuring students reach their full potential.
- By learning AI skills, students are better prepared to adapt to future technological advancements. This ensures long-term career sustainability and success in a rapidly

evolving job market, making them resilient to changes and advancements in their industries.

- Exposure to AI technology encourages students to think creatively and innovatively. This preparation equips them to contribute to advancements in their respective fields and fosters an entrepreneurial mindset, which is crucial for driving future innovations.

Incorporation:

- Develop language learning certifications that utilise AI-powered language processing tools. Incorporate features such as personalised learning paths, real-time feedback on pronunciation, and adaptive exercises based on individual proficiency levels. By mastering a new language with the aid of AI, learners can improve their global employability and access job opportunities in diverse linguistic environments.
- Integrate AI tools and methodologies into project management certification courses. Teach aspiring project managers how to leverage AI for task automation, resource optimisation, and risk prediction. By demonstrating proficiency in AI-driven project management techniques, individuals can enhance their competitiveness in industries where efficient project execution is paramount.
- Integrate AI-driven data analytics tools and techniques into a certification programme for business professionals. Include modules on using AI algorithms for data interpretation, predictive analytics, and decision-making. This would equip individuals with the skills needed to extract valuable insights from large datasets, a crucial competency in various industries such as finance, marketing, and healthcare.
- Develop a certification programme focusing on AI applications in digital marketing. Cover topics such as AI-driven customer segmentation, personalised marketing automation, and predictive customer behaviour analysis. By mastering these AI-powered marketing techniques, professionals can enhance their employability in the rapidly evolving digital marketing landscape.

Example 1	• Integrating AI-driven healthcare management systems into coursework allows medical students to analyse patient data, optimise resource allocation, and develop predictive models for patient outcomes. This aligns with employability objectives of enhancing data analysis and decision-making skills, preparing graduates for roles in healthcare administration where AI integration is increasingly valuable.
Example 2	• Incorporate AI-powered analytics tools into digital marketing modules, enabling marketing students to analyse consumer behaviour, optimise ad campaigns, and personalise marketing strategies. By gaining hands-on experience with AI in marketing contexts, students develop critical skills in data-driven decision-making and campaign optimisation, enhancing their employability in digital marketing roles.

Example 3	• Introduce AI-driven supply chain optimisation software in supply chain management courses, allowing students to model demand forecasts, optimise inventory levels, and streamline logistics operations. This aligns with the employability goals of developing analytical and strategic planning skills and preparing graduates for roles in supply chain management, where AI integration is revolutionising efficiency and decision-making processes.
Example 4	• Offer programming courses that incorporate AI development frameworks and libraries. For example, a Python programming certification could include modules on machine learning and natural language processing libraries like TensorFlow and NLTK. This would enable aspiring software developers to build traditional applications and AI-powered solutions, enhancing their attractiveness to employers seeking AI proficiency.

P4: Personalised Learning Paths

Rationale:

- Use AI to create personalised learning paths based on individual students' strengths, weaknesses, career goals, and interests.
- Implement adaptive learning systems that adjust content difficulty and type based on student performance and engagement.

Incorporation:

- Utilise AI to analyse the collected data and identify patterns and insights about each student's learning needs.
- Develop a curriculum that aligns with each student's career goals and interests, incorporating relevant skills and knowledge areas.
- Create Personalised Learning Plans (PLPs) that outline specific courses, projects, and extracurricular activities tailored to each student.
- Integrate adaptive learning systems that adjust the complexity of the material in real time according to student progress.
- Establish regular feedback mechanisms where students can receive personalised insights into their performance and improvement areas.
- Use AI to recommend additional resources, such as videos, articles, and interactive exercises, that cater to individual learning styles and paces.
- Collaborate with industry partners to understand the skills and competencies required in the job market and use AI to integrate these into the curriculum.

Example 1	• At the beginning of the LLB course, law students should take diagnostic tests on various areas of law (e.g., constitutional, criminal, corporate law) and complete surveys about their career aspirations (e.g., litigation, corporate law, public policy), interests (e.g., environmental law, human rights), and preferred learning styles. • Conduct individual career counselling sessions to understand students' long-term career goals and areas of interest. • Use AI to analyse the results of diagnostic tests and surveys to identify each student's strengths, weaknesses, and career goals. • Use the AI system to generate a detailed profile for each student, highlighting their current competencies, learning preferences, and career aspirations. • Based on the AI analysis, the system can create a personalised learning path for each student. ***For example:*** • *Student A (interested in corporate law but weak in contract law): The AI recommends a curriculum focusing on advanced contract law, business law courses, and internships with corporate law firms.* • *Student B (interested in human rights law with strong legal research skills but weak in public speaking): The AI suggests courses on international human rights law, moot court participation, and public speaking workshops.* • Law schools may use an adaptive learning platform that adjusts content difficulty based on student performance and engagement. • ***Example:*** *As Student A progresses through contract law modules, the platform monitors their performance. It provides additional resources and practice problems if they struggle with certain concepts. If they excel, it introduces more complex case studies and legal drafting exercises.* • Incorporate projects that simulate real-world legal scenarios tailored to students' career goals. ***For example,*** *Student A might work on a mock merger and acquisition deal, while Student B could prepare briefs for a simulated human rights case.* • Partner with law firms, NGOs, and government agencies to provide practical experiences and internships aligned with students' personalised learning paths. • Offer workshops and simulations to develop essential soft skills. For instance, mock trials, negotiation exercises, and client counselling simulations can help improve communication, negotiation, and advocacy skills. • Provide lecturers with dashboards to track each student's progress and engagement. ***Example:*** *If Student B shows low engagement in public speaking exercises, the lecturer arranges additional practice sessions and provides personalised feedback to boost confidence and skills.* • Conduct periodic reviews of students' learning paths and adjust them based on evolving interests, feedback, and performance. ***For example:*** *If Student A develops an interest in international corporate law, additional relevant courses and internships can be incorporated.* • Use AI to match students with internships and externships that align with their career goals and learning paths. ***Example:*** *Student A, aiming for corporate law, is matched with an internship at a top corporate law firm, while Student B is placed with an international human rights organisation.* • Offer AI-recommended workshops on topics like legal technology, data privacy, and emerging areas of law to ensure students stay current with industry trends.

Example 2	• At the start of the course, art and humanity students take diagnostic tests on core subjects (e.g., literature, history, philosophy, art history) and complete surveys detailing their career aspirations (e.g., writer, curator, public relations, academic), interests (e.g., contemporary art, medieval history, cultural studies), and preferred learning styles. • Conduct one-on-one career counselling sessions to understand students' long-term career goals and specific areas of interest. • Then use AI algorithms to analyse the results from diagnostic tests and surveys to identify each student's strengths, weaknesses, and career goals. • Develop an AI system that creates a detailed profile for each student, highlighting their current competencies, learning preferences, and career aspirations. • Based on the AI analysis, the system generates a personalised learning path for each student. ***For example***, *Student A (an aspiring curator with a strong art history background but weak digital skills): The AI recommends courses on digital curation, museum studies, and internships at local museums. Student B (interested in writing with strong literary analysis skills but weak in practical writing): The AI suggests creative writing workshops, internships at publishing houses, and courses on contemporary literature and editing.* • Universities may use an adaptive learning platform that adjusts content difficulty based on student performance and engagement. ***For example***, *as Student A progresses through digital curation modules, the platform monitors their performance. If they struggle with digital tools, it provides additional tutorials and hands-on projects. If they excel, it introduces more advanced topics and practical applications.* • Incorporate projects that simulate real-world scenarios relevant to students' career goals. ***For example***, *Student A might work on a virtual exhibition project, while Student B could develop a writing portfolio that includes various genres and formats.* • Partner with cultural institutions, publishing houses, media companies, and NGOs to provide practical experiences and internships aligned with students' personalised learning paths. Workshops and simulations should also be offered to develop essential soft skills. For instance, public speaking, project management, and teamwork exercises can help improve communication, organisational, and collaborative skills. • Universities may provide lecturers with dashboards to track each student's progress and engagement. ***Example***: *If Student B shows low engagement in creative writing exercises, the instructor arranges additional practice sessions and provides personalised feedback to enhance their skills and confidence. Universities should also conduct periodic reviews of students' learning paths and adjust them based on evolving interests, feedback, and performance. If Student A develops an interest in digital archives, additional relevant courses and internships can be incorporated.* • Universities may use AI to match students with internships and externships that align with their career goals and learning paths. ***For example, Student A, who aims*** *to become a curator, is matched with an internship at a renowned museum, while Student B is placed with a well-known literary magazine.* • Offer AI-recommended workshops on topics like digital humanities, grant writing, and cultural management to ensure students stay current with industry trends.

P5: Soft Skills and Behavioural Training

Rationale:

- Universities should incorporate AI-driven tools like chatbots and virtual collaboration platforms to enhance students' communication and teamwork skills. In today's globalised and digitally interconnected job market, communicating effectively and working collaboratively across diverse teams is crucial. AI-driven chatbots can simulate real-world communication scenarios, providing students with a safe and controlled environment to practice and refine their communication skills. These chatbots can offer immediate feedback, helping students to adjust their communication strategies in real-time.

- Virtual collaboration platforms can mimic the dynamics of remote working environments, which are increasingly common in many industries. By engaging with these platforms, students can develop essential teamwork skills such as coordination, project management, and digital collaboration. These tools can facilitate group projects and cross-disciplinary collaborations, preparing students for the collaborative nature of modern workplaces. Ultimately, by incorporating these AI-driven tools, universities can ensure that their graduates are well-equipped with the communication and teamwork skills that employers highly value.
- Emotional intelligence (EI) is a critical component of employability, encompassing the ability to understand and manage one's emotions and to interact effectively with others. Universities should incorporate AI systems that help students develop emotional intelligence through virtual role-playing scenarios. These AI systems can create immersive, interactive simulations where students practice empathy, conflict resolution, and other EI-related skills.
- For example, an AI-driven role-playing scenario might involve a student navigating a challenging workplace conflict. The AI can provide real-time feedback and suggest alternative approaches, helping the student to understand the emotional dynamics at play and to develop more effective interpersonal strategies. This experiential learning process is invaluable for building the soft skills that are increasingly recognised as essential for career success.

Incorporation:

- Incorporate group projects that require students to work collaboratively, simulating real-world business environments.
- Use case studies and business simulations to provide practical scenarios where students can apply soft skills.
- Conduct workshops focusing on improving verbal and non-verbal communication, public speaking, and presentation skills.
- Offer training sessions on emotional intelligence to help students understand and manage their own emotions and those of others.
- Encourage students to maintain reflective journals where they document their experiences, challenges, and growth in soft skills and behaviours.

Example 1	• At the start of the course, students complete AI-driven self-assessments that evaluate their current soft skills (e.g., communication, teamwork, leadership) and behavioural traits (e.g., adaptability, resilience, emotional intelligence). These assessments can use natural language processing (NLP) to analyse written responses and interaction data. • Utilise AI tools to gather feedback from peers, lecturers, and mentors, providing a comprehensive view of each student's strengths and areas for improvement.
Example 2	• Using AI to create a personalised learning path for each student, recommending courses, workshops, and activities that focus on developing necessary soft skills and behaviours. • ***For example:*** *Student A (strong in creative thinking but needs to improve teamwork): The AI recommends group projects and team-based workshops.* • *Student B (excellent written communication skills but weak in public speaking): The AI suggests public speaking courses and presentation practice sessions.*
Example 3	• Incorporate AI tools to facilitate and monitor group projects, ensuring balanced participation and collaboration. • *Example: Students use AI collaboration platforms (e.g., Microsoft Teams with AI features) to work on a virtual art exhibition, with the AI providing insights on group dynamics and individual contributions.*
Example 4	• Use AI simulations to create realistic scenarios where students can practice soft skills. • ***Example:*** *An AI-driven negotiation simulation where students must navigate a cultural heritage dispute, receiving real-time feedback on their negotiation and conflict resolution skills.*
Example 5	• Offer training sessions on emotional intelligence with the help of AI coaches that provide personalised feedback and suggestions. • ***Example:*** *Students interact with an AI coach like Replika, which helps them practice empathy and active listening in simulated conversations.*

P6: Career Readiness Programmes

Rationale:

- AI tools can analyse a student's resume and provide real-time, personalised feedback to improve content and format. This ensures that each resume is tailored to meet the specific requirements of different job postings.
- AI-driven platforms for interview practice can simulate real interview scenarios, offering instant feedback on performance, body language, and responses. This helps students to identify and improve upon their weaknesses.
- Job application tracking tools powered by AI can help students keep track of their applications, deadlines, and follow-ups, ensuring a systematic and organised job search process.
- AI tools can provide insights into hiring trends and the skills in demand across various industries by analysing vast amounts of data from job postings and market analytics. This allows students to align their resumes and interview preparations with current market needs

- AI tools are accessible 24/7, allowing students to work on their resumes, practice interviews, and track job applications at their convenience. This is particularly beneficial for students with tight schedules or those who need to balance work and study.
- These tools can be scaled to accommodate a large number of students, ensuring that all students have access to high-quality career preparation resources, regardless of the size of the university
- AI-driven career coaching systems can analyse individual student profiles, including their academic performance, interests, and career goals, to provide personalised advice on career planning. This helps students to identify suitable career paths and necessary steps to achieve their goals.
- These systems can also recommend specific job searching strategies and professional development opportunities based on real-time labour market information, ensuring that the advice is current and relevant.
- AI-driven career coaching can offer continuous support throughout a student's academic journey and beyond. By tracking a student's progress and updating recommendations accordingly, these systems ensure ongoing professional development and readiness for the job market.
- They can also help students to set and achieve long-term career goals by providing a structured plan and regular check-ins, ensuring that students stay motivated and focused on their career aspirations.
- By providing targeted career coaching and employability skills training, AI tools can help to bridge the gap between academic learning and practical job market requirements. This ensures that students are not only academically proficient but also job-ready.
- AI-driven career services can facilitate connections with potential employers, provide insights into company cultures, and help students to tailor their applications to fit specific organisational needs, increasing their chances of securing employment.

Incorporation:

- Universities can partner with AI-driven resume platforms like Resume Zety or Jobscan. These tools use machine learning algorithms to analyse resume content and structure, providing instant feedback on improvements needed to match job descriptions effectively. Integrate these platforms into the university's career services portal to provide seamless access for students.
- Tools like InterviewStream or Big Interview provide AI-powered mock interviews where students can practice and receive feedback on their performance, including body language, speech patterns, and response content. Conduct workshops to train students on how to use these tools effectively.

- Utilise platforms like Handshake or Symplicity that offer AI-powered job matching, application tracking, and alerts for deadlines and follow-ups. Develop a personalised dashboard for students where they can track their job applications, interview schedules, and follow-up actions.
- Tools like MyCareerShines or CareerExplorer use AI to create personalised career pathways based on students' skills, interests, and academic backgrounds. Implement AI chatbots that provide 24/7 career advice, job search strategies, and professional development tips.
- Platforms like Burning Glass Technologies or EMSI provide data on labour market trends, helping students to align their skills and resumes with in-demand roles. Career services can host regular workshops and updates on emerging job market trends, utilising the insights provided by these AI tools.

Example 1	• Universities can integrate AI-driven legal research tools such as LexisNexis, Westlaw Edge, or ROSS Intelligence into their curriculum. These platforms use AI to streamline the research process, providing comprehensive and efficient access to legal information and case law. Offer workshops and training sessions to help students proficiently use these tools for legal research and case preparation.
Example 3	• Use AI tools like VMock or Resume Worded that provide tailored feedback on legal resumes and cover letters, ensuring they meet industry standards. These tools can be integrated with the law school's career services portal, allowing students to receive continuous feedback as they apply for internships and jobs.
Example 4	• Implement AI-driven platforms like InterviewStream or Big Interview, which offer tailored mock interviews for legal positions and provide feedback on performance. Integrate these tools into the career services offered by the law school, ensuring students can practice and refine their interview skills specifically for legal careers.
Example 5	• Utilise AI-driven job search and application tracking platforms like Handshake, tailored for legal job markets. Create personalised dashboards for law students to manage their job applications, track deadlines, and receive reminders. • Use AI career coaching systems like MyCareerShines or CareerExplorer to provide personalised career advice based on individual profiles, interests, and career goals. Implement AI chatbots that offer career planning advice, job search strategies, and professional development tips tailored to legal careers.

P7: Inclusive Access

Rationale:

- As AI technology becomes increasingly prevalent in various industries, there is a growing demand for workers who are proficient in AI-related skills. By incorporating AI Inclusive Access into their curricula, universities can ensure that students are equipped with the necessary knowledge and competencies to thrive in the evolving job market.

- AI Inclusive Access provides students with opportunities to engage with AI tools and platforms, thereby enhancing their digital literacy skills. In today's digital age, proficiency in AI technology is a valuable asset for professionals across different sectors. By familiarising students with AI early in their academic journey, universities can help them develop the digital skills needed to succeed in the workforce.
- AI Inclusive Access encourages students to critically evaluate AI algorithms, data sets, and ethical considerations. This fosters the development of critical thinking and problem-solving skills, which employers highly value. Through hands-on experience with AI technology, students learn to analyse complex problems, identify solutions, and make informed decisions—skills essential for workplace success.
- AI technology intersects with various disciplines, including computer science, engineering, social sciences, and humanities. Universities can foster interdisciplinary collaboration and knowledge exchange among students and faculty by integrating AI Inclusive Access across different academic departments. This collaborative approach mirrors real-world working environments, where professionals from diverse backgrounds often collaborate on AI-related projects.

Incorporation:

- Universities should integrate AI-related content into existing courses across various disciplines. This can involve creating new modules or updating existing ones to include topics such as AI fundamentals, data analysis, machine learning, and ethical AI practices. By embedding AI education into the curriculum, students from diverse academic backgrounds can develop foundational knowledge and skills in AI.
- Invite guest speakers from industry to deliver lectures or workshops on AI-related topics. Collaborate with industry partners to provide students with access to real-world AI projects, internships, or work placements. Industry involvement exposes students to current trends, best practices, and career opportunities in the AI field, enhancing their employability skills.
- Offer professional development opportunities, such as AI-focused seminars, conferences, and certification programmes. Provide access to online resources, webinars, and AI communities where students can continue to learn and stay updated on the latest advancements in AI technology. Encourage students to participate in competitions and collaborative projects to develop their AI skills further and expand their professional networks.

Example 1	• **Master of Laws (LLM) programmes:** Introduce students to the basics of AI technology, including machine learning, natural language processing, and predictive analytics. Discuss the principles behind AI algorithms and their applications in legal research, contract analysis, and case prediction.

Example 2	• **Case Studies on AI in Legal Practice:** Analyse real-world examples of AI tools and platforms used in law firms, corporate legal departments, and government agencies. Explore how AI technologies are transforming legal processes, such as document review, due diligence, and litigation support.
Example 3	• Engage students in discussions on the ethical implications of AI in law, including issues related to bias, fairness, transparency, and accountability. Examine regulatory frameworks governing AI use in legal contexts and consider the role of legal professionals in ensuring responsible AI development and deployment.
Example 4	• Provide hands-on experience with AI tools and platforms commonly used in legal practice. For example, students could use AI-powered legal research platforms to analyse case law, draft legal documents, and identify relevant precedents. • Invite guest speakers from legal tech companies, AI research institutes, and law firms to share their insights and experiences with AI in law. Provide students with opportunities to learn from professionals at the forefront of AI innovation in the legal industry.
Example 5	**Assessment Methods:** • **Research Paper:** Students could write a research paper exploring a specific aspect of AI in law, such as the impact of AI on access to justice or the ethical challenges of using AI in legal decision-making. • **Case Study Analysis:** Students could analyse case studies of AI implementation in legal practice, critically evaluating the benefits, limitations, and ethical implications of AI technologies. • **Practical Project:** Students could undertake a practical project using AI tools to solve a legal problem or improve legal processes, such as developing a chatbot for legal assistance or creating an AI-powered contract review system.

P8: Authentic Assessment and Employability

Rationale:

- The integration of AI reflects the increasing use of technology in various industries. By incorporating AI into qualifications, universities ensure that students are equipped with the skills and knowledge needed to navigate the rapidly evolving digital landscape of the modern workplace.

- AI is a key driver of innovation across sectors such as finance, healthcare, manufacturing, and marketing. By engaging with AI technologies through authentic assessment tasks, students gain practical experience that prepares them for the demands of AI-driven industries and positions them as valuable assets to prospective employers.

- Through the integration of AI and authentic assessment, students develop a range of transferable skills highly valued by employers, such as critical thinking, problem-solving, collaboration, communication, and adaptability. These skills are essential for success in today's competitive job market and position students for long-term career growth and advancement.

- Authentic assessment tasks are designed to reflect the challenges and expectations of real-world professional environments. By engaging with authentic assessments, students gain insight into industry practices and expectations, allowing them to better understand and meet the requirements of potential employers.

- Authentic assessment tasks provide students with opportunities to demonstrate their applied knowledge and skills in practical contexts. This demonstration of competency goes beyond traditional assessments and provides employers with tangible evidence of students' capabilities, enhancing their employability prospects.
- Authentic assessment tasks require students to apply their knowledge and skills to real-world scenarios, fostering critical thinking, problem-solving, and decision-making abilities. By grappling with authentic challenges, students develop a deeper understanding of course concepts and enhance their ability to adapt and innovate in diverse professional contexts.
- Many authentic assessment tasks involve collaborative projects or presentations, which encourage students to work effectively in teams and communicate their ideas clearly and persuasively. These collaborative experiences mirror the teamwork and communication skills required in today's workplaces, enhancing students' employability and readiness for collaborative work environments.

Incorporation:

- Incorporate AI technologies into research projects across various disciplines. For example, in a biology course, students could use machine learning algorithms to analyse genomic data and identify patterns related to genetic diseases. This authentic assessment task not only enhances students' understanding of AI concepts but also develops their research skills and critical thinking abilities.
- Develop authentic case studies that incorporate AI technologies into real-world scenarios relevant to students' chosen fields. For instance, in a business management course, students could analyse data from a fictitious company using AI-powered analytics tools to make strategic decisions. This assessment task requires students to apply their knowledge of business principles and AI concepts in a practical context, fostering critical thinking and problem-solving skills.
- Create simulation exercises that simulate real-world situations using AI algorithms. For example, in a cybersecurity course, students could participate in a simulated cyberattack scenario where they must detect and respond to threats using AI-driven security tools. This hands-on experience with AI technologies enhances students' technical skills and prepares them for careers in cybersecurity.
- Assign collaborative projects that involve the development of AI applications or solutions. For instance, in a computer science course, students could work in teams to design and implement a chatbot using natural language processing techniques. This project-based assessment task promotes teamwork, communication, and problem-solving skills while also providing students with practical experience in AI development.

- Partner with industry organisations to offer AI challenges that allow students to solve real-world problems faced by industry stakeholders. For instance, in an engineering course, students could participate in a competition to develop AI-driven solutions for optimising energy consumption in buildings. This experiential learning opportunity exposes students to industry practices and enhances their problem-solving and innovation skills.
- Require students to complete a capstone project that integrates AI technologies into a comprehensive final project. For example, in a data science course, students could undertake a capstone project where they analyse large datasets using AI algorithms to derive actionable insights for a real-world client. This authentic assessment task allows students to showcase their AI skills and demonstrate their readiness for the workforce.
- Organise debates and discussions on ethical issues related to AI technology. For example, in an ethics course, students could debate the ethical implications of using AI algorithms for automated decision-making in healthcare. This authentic assessment task encourages students to critically evaluate ethical dilemmas and articulate their viewpoints, fostering ethical reasoning and communication skills.

Example 1	• Integrate AI technologies into digital arts projects, such as interactive installations, virtual reality experiences, or generative art. For example, students could use machine learning algorithms to create AI-generated artworks that respond to user input or environmental stimuli. This authentic assessment task not only enhances students' understanding of AI concepts but also allows them to explore the creative possibilities of AI in art.
Example 2	• Incorporate AI-driven textual analysis tools into literature courses to analyse and interpret literary texts. For instance, students could use natural language processing algorithms to analyse themes, characters, and stylistic elements in literary works. This authentic assessment task enhances students' critical reading and analytical skills while also introducing them to AI technologies relevant to the field of humanities.
Example 3	• Engage students in music composition projects that leverage AI technologies. For example, students could use machine learning algorithms to generate musical compositions based on input from a user or a set of predefined parameters. This authentic assessment task allows students to explore the intersection of AI and music composition while also developing their creativity and technical skills.
Example 4	• Assign storytelling projects that incorporate AI technologies into narrative creation. For example, students could use natural language generation algorithms to develop interactive storytelling experiences or chatbot characters. This authentic assessment task allows students to experiment with innovative storytelling techniques while also gaining hands-on experience with AI technologies.
Example 5	• Collaborate with other departments or external partners to organise AI art exhibitions or showcases. For instance, students from art and computer science departments could work together to curate an exhibition featuring AI-generated artworks or interactive installations. This collaborative project promotes interdisciplinary collaboration and provides students with opportunities to showcase their creative and technical skills to a wider audience.

Example 6	• Engage students in projects that use AI technologies to preserve and promote cultural heritage. For example, students could develop AI-powered tools for digitising and analysing historical artefacts or reconstructing ancient monuments. This authentic assessment task allows students to contribute to the preservation of cultural heritage while also gaining practical experience with AI technologies relevant to the field of humanities.

Embedding the Employability Guiding Principle for using GenAI in student skill development is essential for HEIs to stay relevant in today's job market. Recognising the many benefits of GenAI in skill development is the first step. GenAI can create real-world simulations and offer personalised learning experiences that adapt to individual student needs. For example, AI-driven platforms can provide interactive simulations in fields like engineering, healthcare, and business, allowing students to practise and improve their skills in a realistic, controlled environment. This hands-on experience is invaluable as it bridges the gap between theoretical knowledge and practical application.

GenAI can also boost critical thinking and problem-solving skills, which employers highly value. Through AI-assisted learning tools, students can tackle complex problems and receive instant feedback, promoting a deeper understanding of the subject matter and enhancing analytical skills. This ongoing learning process, supported by AI, helps students develop a resilient approach to problem-solving, preparing them for future professional challenges. Another significant benefit of embedding the Employability Guiding Principle is the ability to personalise education pathways. GenAI can analyse student performance data to identify strengths and weaknesses, tailoring learning experiences to meet individual needs. This personalised approach ensures that students can achieve expertise in their areas of interest, aligning their skills with specific career goals. For instance, a student interested in data science can use AI tools to master machine learning algorithms, while another focused on digital marketing can explore AI-driven analytics and consumer behaviour models.

GenAI also supports continuous skill assessment and development. Traditional evaluation methods, like exams and assignments, often fail to provide real-time feedback and can be limited in scope. In contrast, AI-driven assessments can continuously monitor student progress, offering immediate insights and suggesting areas for improvement. This real-time feedback loop is crucial for developing a strong skill set that evolves with industry standards and technological advancements. Therefore, embedding the Employability Guiding Principle also means promoting digital literacy and AI competency among students. As GenAI becomes more common in various sectors, understanding how to use these technologies is vital. HEIs should ensure that students are not only users of AI but also understand its principles and ethical implications. This comprehensive approach to AI education equips students with the knowledge to use AI responsibly and creatively in their future careers.

Moreover, the Employability Guiding Principle highlights the importance of collaboration between HEIs and industry. HEIs can align their curricula with current industry demands and trends by partnering with businesses and organisations. Such collaborations can include internship programmes, guest lectures from industry experts, and collaborative research projects. These initiatives give students exposure to real-world applications of AI and help them develop relevant skills that are directly transferable to the workplace. In addition to technical skills, GenAI can support the development of soft skills like communication, teamwork, and adaptability. AI-driven platforms can facilitate virtual team projects, enabling students to collaborate with peers from diverse backgrounds and geographies. These experiences are vital in preparing students for the increasingly global and interconnected workforce.

Hence, embedding the Employability Guiding Principle for using GenAI in student skill development and qualification is essential for HEIs to remain effective in today's rapidly evolving job market. By harnessing the power of GenAI, HEIs can provide students with a well-rounded education that combines theoretical knowledge with practical skills, personalised learning experiences, and continuous skill development. This approach enhances employability and prepares students to be adaptable, innovative, and responsible professionals in an AI-driven world.

CONCLUSION

In summary, using GenAI in higher education offers many benefits but also comes with challenges. The guiding principles in this chapter help manage these challenges, ensuring GenAI is used ethically and effectively. Research has shown that GenAI can personalise learning, improve teaching methods, and simplify administrative tasks. GenAI can customise learning to fit individual student needs, provide quick and personalised feedback, and allow academics to engage more with students. These benefits align with the broader move towards digital and automated systems, helping educational institutions stay competitive and relevant in today's tech-driven world.

However, using GenAI carefully is important, as well as keeping ethical and practical issues in mind. Concerns about data privacy, bias in AI, fair access, and potential cheating highlight the need for strong policies. Studies have pointed out that there is a lack of specific policies for using GenAI in higher education, making it urgent for HEIs and policymakers to take action. The principles suggested in this chapter offer a flexible framework for using GenAI responsibly. They are not strict rules but guidelines that can be adjusted to fit different institutions. Key suggestions include creating ethical oversight committees, training academics on GenAI, and encouraging collaboration among academics, technologists, and ethicists to share ideas and best practices.

The main goal of these guiding principles is to ensure that GenAI improves education while maintaining fairness and integrity. By following these guidelines, educational institutions can balance the benefits of GenAI with its risks. This approach will enhance the quality of education and prepare students and academics for a future with advanced technology. As GenAI evolves, it will be important to keep discussing, researching, and updating policies. Educational institutions must stay alert and adaptable, regularly reviewing and improving their strategies to keep up with technological changes. By doing this, they can ensure that GenAI is a positive force in education, fostering innovation, fairness, and excellence in teaching and learning.

CHAPTER 3

Conclusion

The discourse surrounding GenAI is not solely confined to the realms of technicality and engineering. The profound implications of GenAI extend well beyond these domains, touching on societal, ethical, and future-oriented considerations. This book has sought to illuminate the critical importance of integrating ethics and guiding principles into the discussion and development of GenAI, arguing that such integration can fundamentally reshape societal perceptions and applications of this technology.

At the heart of this argument is the recognition that ethics serve as a moral compass, guiding us in considering the far-reaching impacts of GenAI. Ethical considerations compel us to look beyond mere functionality and efficiency, urging us to reflect on the broader consequences of deploying GenAI in various sectors. Ethics help us address questions of right and wrong, fairness, justice, and the well-being of individuals and communities. By embedding ethical considerations into the development and deployment of GenAI, we can align technological advancements with societal values and norms, ensuring that the evolution of AI is in harmony with what society deems morally acceptable.

Guiding principles provide a practical framework for navigating the complex ethical dilemmas posed by GenAI. These principles act as actionable rules that help HEIs, academics, students, and practitioners make informed and responsible decisions. They bridge the gap between abstract ethical theories and concrete actions, offering a roadmap for handling the challenges that GenAI presents in HEIs and societal structures. By adhering to guiding principles, developers and users of GenAI can make intelligent choices that balance innovation with ethical responsibility, thereby fostering an environment where technology serves the greater good.

This book advocates for a more expansive view of GenAI, one that encompasses not only technical and ethical dimensions but also the broader societal impacts. It is essential to consider how GenAI affects various aspects of society, including employment, privacy, security, and social interactions. A holistic approach to discussing GenAI involves evaluating its potential benefits and risks from multiple perspectives, ensuring that the technology is developed and used in a manner that is socially beneficial and minimises harm.

DOI: 10.1201/9781003561507-4

One of the critical outcomes of integrating ethics and guiding principles into GenAI is the ability to effectively address ethical issues. By proactively considering potential ethical concerns, developers can anticipate and mitigate negative consequences, ensuring that GenAI applications are designed and implemented responsibly. This proactive approach helps build trust with users and stakeholders, as transparency and accountability become central to the development process.

Trust is a cornerstone of the successful adoption and utilisation of GenAI. When users and the public trust that GenAI technologies are developed with ethical considerations at the forefront, they are more likely to embrace and engage with these technologies. Transparency in the development and deployment processes, coupled with adherence to ethical standards, fosters confidence in the safety, reliability, and fairness of GenAI applications. The guiding principles also play a crucial role in reducing the risks associated with GenAI in HEIs and other organisations. These risks include issues such as bias, discrimination, privacy violations, and unintended harmful consequences. By systematically applying ethical principles, developers can identify and address potential risks early in the development cycle, creating safeguards that protect individuals and communities from harm.

Ensuring fairness is another vital aspect of ethical GenAI. Fairness involves creating technologies that do not disproportionately disadvantage any group or individual. This requires careful consideration of how GenAI systems are designed, trained, and deployed, with a focus on eliminating biases and promoting equitable outcomes. Fairness in GenAI not only aligns with ethical standards but also enhances the social acceptability and legitimacy of AI technologies.

The societal impact of GenAI is a central theme of this book. GenAI has the potential to transform various sectors, including healthcare, education, entertainment, and beyond. However, these transformations come with significant responsibilities. It is crucial to assess how GenAI affects social structures, cultural norms, and human relationships. By examining these broader impacts, we can ensure that GenAI contributes positively to societal progress and well-being. These ethical considerations help us navigate the complexities of these societal impacts. For example, in healthcare, GenAI can improve diagnostics and treatment plans, but it also raises questions about patient privacy and the ethical use of medical data. In education, GenAI can personalise learning experiences, but it must be done in a way that respects students' autonomy and does not reinforce existing inequalities. By applying ethical principles, we can harness the benefits of GenAI while addressing its challenges.

This book highlights the importance of fostering an environment where ethical GenAI development is the norm. This involves creating policies, frameworks, and institutions that support ethical practices. Governments, academic institutions, industry leaders, and civil society organisations all have a role to play in promoting ethical standards and ensuring that GenAI development aligns with societal values. Collaboration and dialogue among these stakeholders are essential. By working together, we can develop comprehensive strategies that address the ethical, technical, and societal dimensions of GenAI. This collaborative approach ensures that diverse perspectives are considered, leading to more inclusive and robust solutions.

In conclusion, the integration of ethics and guiding principles into the discourse and development of GenAI is not merely an adjunct to technical innovation but a fundamental necessity. By prioritising ethical considerations, we can navigate the complexities and challenges posed by GenAI, ensuring that this powerful technology is developed and used in ways that are fair, just, and beneficial for all members of society. The guiding principles outlined in this book provide a practical roadmap for addressing ethical dilemmas and making informed decisions. Ultimately, the goal is to create a future where GenAI contributes to human flourishing, enhances societal well-being, and upholds the values that are important to us as a global community. By embracing ethics and guiding principles, we can shape a positive trajectory for GenAI, fostering trust, reducing risks, and ensuring that the benefits of this transformative technology are realised in a fair and equitable manner.

Bibliography

Abelson, R. P., 1988. Conviction. *American Psychologist*, 43(4), pp. 267–275.

Abelson, R. P. and Miller, J. C., 1967. Effects of success and failure on pinion certainty: An attempt to resolve a theoretical ambiguity. In: R. Abelson, E. Aronson, W. J. McGuire, T. M. Newcomb, M. J. Rosenberg, and P. H. Tannenbaum (Eds.), *Theories of Cognitive Consistency: A Sourcebook* (pp. 53–71). Rand McNally.

Ajzen, I., 2012. The theory of planned behavior. In: P. A. M. Van Lange, A. W. Kruglanski, and E. T. Higgins (Eds.), *Handbook of Theories of Social Psychology* (pp. 438–459). SAGE Publications Ltd.

Aksoy, D. A. and Kursun, E., 2024. Behind the scenes: A critical perspective on genAI and open educational practices. *Open Praxis*, 16(3), pp. 457–470.

Albarracín, D., Johnson, B. T. and Zanna, M. P., 2005. *The Handbook of Attitudes*. Routledge.

Albarracin, D., Johnson, B. T. and Zanna, M. P. (Eds.), 2005. *The Handbook of Attitudes*. Lawrence Erlbaum Associates Publishers.

Albarracin, D. and Vargas, P. T., 2010. *Attitudes and Persuasion: From Biology to Social Responses to Health*. Psychology Press.

Albarracín, D. and Vargas, P. T., 2010. The influence of attitudes on affective responses. In: D. Albarracin, B. T. Johnson and M. P. Zanna, eds. *Handbook of Affect and Social Cognition* (pp. 253–273). Lawrence Erlbaum Associates Publishers.

Almars, A. M., Gad, I. and Atlam, E. S., 2022. Applications of AI and IoT in COVID-19 vaccine and its impact on social life. *Medical Informatics and Bioimaging Using Artificial Intelligence: Challenges, Issues, Innovations and Recent Developments*, pp. 115–127.

American Economic Association, Royal Economic Society and Simon, H.A., 1966. *Theories of Decision-Making in Economics and Behavioural Science* (pp. 1–28). Palgrave Macmillan UK.

Anctil, D., 2023. Higher education in the era of generative AI. *Pédagogie collégiale vol. 36, no 3, spring-summer 2023.*

Anderson, M. M., 2024. AI as philosophical ideology: A critical look back at John McCarthy's program. *Philosophy & Technology*, 37(2), p. 44.

Anderson, J. R. and Pelletier, R., 1988. A developmental theory of learning. *The American Psychologist*, 43(11), pp. 879–886.

Annas, J., 1993. Virtue as the use of other goods. *Apeiron*, 26(3–4), pp. 53–66.

Araujo, T., Helberger, N., Kruikemeier, S. and De Vreese, C. H., 2020. In AI we trust? Perceptions about automated decision-making by artificial intelligence. *AI & Society*, 35(3), pp. 611–623.

Asad, M. M. and Ajaz, A., 2024. Impact of ChatGPT and generative AI on lifelong learning and upskilling learners in higher education: unveiling the challenges and opportunities globally. *The International Journal of Information and Learning Technology.*

Atlas, S., 2023. ChatGPT for higher education and professional development: A guide to conversational AI.

Awad, E., Dsouza, S., Kim, R., Schulz, J., Henrich, J., Shariff, A., Bonnefon, J. F. and Rahwan, I., 2018. The moral machine experiment. *Nature*, 563(7729), pp. 59–64.

Baidoo-Anu, D. and Ansah, L. O., 2023. Education in the era of generative artificial intelligence (AI):a Understanding the potential benefits of ChatGPT in promoting teaching and learning. *Journal of AI*, 7(1), pp. 52–62.

Barakat, M., Salim, N. A. and Sallam, M., 2024. Perspectives of university educators regarding ChatGPT: A validation study based on the technology acceptance model. Available at: https://www.researchsquare.com/article/rs-3919524/v1 [Accessed 01 November 2024].

Bar-Cohen, Y. and Hanson, D., 2009. *The Coming Robot Revolution: Expectations and Fears About Emerging Intelligent, Humanlike Machines*. Springer Science & Business Media.

Bassili, J. N., 1996. Meta-judgmental versus operative indexes of psychological attributes: The case of measures of attitude strength. *Journal of Personality and Social Psychology*, 71(4), pp. 637–653.

Bassili, J. N., 2008. Attitude extremity. In: W. Donsbach (Ed.), *The International Encyclopedia of Communication* (pp. 225–227). Wiley-Blackwell.

Bengio, Y., Ducharme, R. and Vincent, P., 2000. A neural probabilistic language model. *Advances in Neural Information Processing Systems*, 13.

Bentley, P. J., 2020. *Artificial Intelligence and Robotics: Ten Short Lessons*. Johns Hopkins University Press.

Berkeley, E. C., 2023. *Giant Brains; or, Machines That Think*. Good Press.

Berners-Lee, T., 1999. *Weaving the Web: The Original Design and Ultimate Destiny of the World Wide Web by Its Inventor*. Harper San Francisco.

Bernhardt, C., 2019. *Quantum Computing for Everyone*. MIT Press.

Berthelot, A., Caron, E., Jay, M. and Lefèvre, L., 2023. *Estimating the Environmental Impact of Generative-AI Services Using An LCA-based Methodology*. CIRP LCE.

Berthelot, A., Caron, E., Jay, M. and Lefèvre, L., 2024. Estimating the environmental impact of Generative-AI services using an LCA-based methodology. *Procedia CIRP*, 122, pp. 707–712.

Biggs, J., 2014. Constructive alignment in university teaching. *HERDSA Review of Higher Education*, 1, pp. 5–22. Published by Peter Kandlbinder. Available at: https://www.herdsa.org.au/herdsa-review-higher-education-vol-1/5-22 [Accessed 23 Dec. 2024].

Biggs, J. and Tang, C., 2014. Constructive alignment: An outcomes-based approach to teaching anatomy. In *Teaching Anatomy: A Practical Guide* (pp. 31–38). Cham: Springer International Publishing.

Binhammad, M. H. Y., Othman, A., Abuljadayel, L., Al Mheiri, H., Alkaabi, M. and Almarri, M., 2024. Investigating how generative AI can create personalized learning materials tailored to individual student needs. *Creative Education*, 15(7), pp. 1499–1523.

Binz, M. and Schulz, E., 2023. Using cognitive psychology to understand GPT-3. *Proceedings of the National Academy of Sciences*, 120(6), p. e2218523120.

Birley, A. R., 2003. The Historia Augusta and pagan historiography. In: *Greek and Roman Historiography in Late Antiquity* (pp. 127–149). Brill.

Bloom, B. S., 1984. The 2 sigma problem: The search for methods of group instruction as effective as one-to-one tutoring. *Educational Researcher*, 13(6), pp. 4–16.

Bochniarz, K. T., Czerwiński, S. K., Sawicki, A. and Atroszko, P. A., 2022. Attitudes to AI among high school students: Understanding distrust towards humans will not help us understand distrust towards AI. *Personality and Individual Differences*, 185, p. 111299.

Bockting, C. L., Van Dis, E. A., Van Rooij, R., Zuidema, W. and Bollen, J., 2023. Living guidelines for generative AI—why scientists must oversee its use. *Nature*, 622(7984), pp. 693–696.

Bommarito II, M. and Katz, D. M., 2022. GPT takes the bar exam. *arXiv preprint arXiv:2212.14402*.

Bradley, M. M., Codispoti, M., Cuthbert, B. N. and Lang, P. J., 2001. Emotion and motivation I: Defensive and appetitive reactions in picture processing. *Emotion*, 1(3), pp. 276–298.

Bradley, M. M. and Lang, P. J., 2007. The International Affective Picture System (IAPS) in the study of emotion and attention. In: J. A. Coan and J. J. B. Allen (Eds.), *Handbook of Emotion Elicitation and Assessment* (pp. 29–46). Oxford University Press.

Brandt, R. B., 1992. *Morality, Utilitarianism, and Rights*. Cambridge University Press.
Brauer, M., Judd, C. M. and Gliner, M. D., 1995. The effects of repeated expressions on attitude polarization during group discussions. *Journal of Personality and Social Psychology*, 68(6), p. 1014.
Brauner, P., Dalibor, M., Jarke, M., Kunze, I., Koren, I., Lakemeyer, G., Liebenberg, M., Michael, J., Pennekamp, J., Quix, C. and Rumpe, B., 2022. A computer science perspective on digital transformation in production. *ACM Transactions on Internet of Things*, 3(2), pp. 1–32.
Burget, M., Bardone, E. and Pedaste, M., 2017. Definitions and conceptual dimensions of responsible research and innovation: A literature review. *Science and Engineering Ethics*, 23, pp. 1–19.
Burn, J. M. and Loch, K. D., 2003. The societal impact of the World Wide Web—key challenges for the 21st century. In *Advanced Topics in Information Resources Management*, Volume 2 (pp. 32–51). IGI Global.
Butt, M. A., Qayyum, A., Ali, H., Al-Fuqaha, A. and Qadir, J., 2023. Towards secure private and trustworthy human-centric embedded machine learning: An emotion-aware facial recognition case study. *Computers & Security*, 125, p. 103058.
Cacioppo, J. T., Berntson, G. G. and Crites, S. L., 1996. *Social Neuroscience: Principles of Psychophysiological Methods*. Cambridge University Press.
Cambridge Dictionary, 2022. Cambridge dictionary. *Artificial Intelligence*. [online] Available at: https://dictionary.cambridge.org/dictionary/english/artificial-intelligence [Accessed 26 March 2024].
Cambridge University Press. 2023. Integrating AI in Higher Education: Insights from Cambridge.
Campbell-Kelly, M., 2018. *Computer, Student Economy Edition: A History of the Information Machine*. Routledge.
Carbonell, J. R., 1970a. *AI in CAI: An Artificial-intelligence Approach to computer-assisted instruction*. IEEE.
Carbonell, J. R., 1970b. AI in CAI: An artificial-intelligence approach to computer-assisted instruction. *IEEE Transactions on Man-machine Systems*, 11(4), pp. 190–202.
Carbonell, J. R., 1970c. *Computer-assisted Instruction: A Synthesis of Theory, Practice, and Technology*. Academic Press.
Carter, M., 2007. *Minds and Computers: An Introduction to the Philosophy of Artificial Intelligence*. Edinburgh University Press.
Castells, M., 2001. *The Internet Galaxy: Reflections on the Internet, Business, and Society*. Oxford: Oxford University Press.
Chaiken, S., 1987. The heuristic model of persuasion. In: M. P. Zanna, J. M. Olson, and C. P. Herman (Eds.), *Social Influence: The Ontario Symposium* (Vol. 5, pp. 3–39). Lawrence Erlbaum Associates.
Chan, C. K. Y., 2023. A comprehensive AI policy education framework for university teaching and learning. *International Journal of Educational Technology in Higher Education*, 20(1), p. 38.
Chan, C. K. Y. and Colloton, T., 2024. *Generative AI in Higher Education: The ChatGPT Effect* (p. 287). Taylor & Francis.
Chan, C. K. Y. and Hu, W., 2023. Students' voices on generative AI: Perceptions, benefits, and challenges in higher education. *International Journal of Educational Technology in Higher Education*, 20(1), p. 43.
Chan, C. K. Y. and Tsi, L.H.Y., 2023. The AI revolution in education: Will AI replace or assist teachers in higher education? *arXiv e-prints*. Cornell University. Available at: https://arxiv.org/abs/2305.01185 [Accessed false23 December 2024]. DOI: 10.48550/arXiv.2305.01185
Chan, C. K. Y. and Zhou, W., 2023. Deconstructing student perceptions of generative AI (GenAI) through an expectancy value theory (EVT)-based instrument.
Chatila, R., Firth-Butterflied, K., Havens, J. C. and Karachalios, K., 2017. The IEEE global initiative for ethical considerations in artificial intelligence and autonomous systems. *IEEE Robotics and Automation Magazine*, 24(1), p. 110.
Chen, H., 2024. The ethical challenges of educational artificial intelligence and coping measures: A discussion in the context of the 2024 World Digital Education Conference. *Science Insights Education Frontiers*, 20(2), pp. 3263–3281.

Chen, X., Xie, H., Zou, D. and Hwang, G. J., 2020. Application and theory gaps during the rise of artificial intelligence in education. *Computers and Education: Artificial Intelligence*, 1, p. 100002.

Chergarova, V., Tomeo, M., Provost, L., De la Peña, G., Ulloa, A. and Miranda, D., 2023. Case study: exploring the role of current and potential usage of generative artificial intelligence tools in higher education. *Issues in Information Systems*, 24(2).

Chiu, T. K., 2024. Future research recommendations for transforming higher education with generative AI. *Computers and Education: Artificial Intelligence*, 6, p. 100197.

Cingillioglu, I., 2023. Detecting AI-generated essays: the ChatGPT challenge. *The International Journal of Information and Learning Technology*, 40(3), pp. 259–268.

Cismariu, L. and Gherheş, V., 2019. Artificial intelligence, between opportunity and challenge. *BRAIN. Broad Research in Artificial Intelligence and Neuroscience*, 10(4), pp. 40–55.

Clegg, B., 2010. *Armageddon Science: The Science of Mass Destruction*. St. Martin's Press.

Clore, G. L. and Schnall, S., 2005. The influence of affect on attitude. In: D. Albarracin, B. T. Johnson and M. P. Zanna, eds. *The Handbook of Attitudes* (pp. 437–489). Lawrence Erlbaum Associates Publishers.

Coccia, M., 2018. Disruptive firms and industrial change. *Journal of Economic and Social Thought*, 4(4), pp. 437–450.

Collingridge, D., 1980. *The Social Control of Technology*. New York: St. Martin's Press.

Confalonieri, R., Coba, L., Wagner, B. and Besold, T. R., 2021. A historical perspective of explainable Artificial Intelligence. *Wiley Interdisciplinary Reviews: Data Mining and Knowledge Discovery*, 11(1), p.e1391.

Cooper, S. B. and Van Leeuwen, J. eds., 2013. *Alan Turing: His Work and Impact*. Elsevier.

Cordeschi, R., 2002. *The Discovery of the Artificial: Behavior, mind and Machines Before and Beyond Cybernetics* (Vol. 28). Springer Science & Business Media.

Corea, F., 2019. *Applied Artificial Intelligence: Where AI Can Be Used in Business* (Vol. 1). Cham: Springer International Publishing.

Cornacchia, G., Anelli, V. W., Biancofiore, G. M., Narducci, F., Pomo, C., Ragone, A. and Di Sciascio, E., 2023. Auditing fairness under unawareness through counterfactual reasoning. *Information Processing & Management*, 60(2), p. 103224.

Cornacchia, G., Anelli, V. W., Narducci, F., Ragone, A. and Sciascio, E. D., 2023. Counterfactual fair opportunity: Measuring decision model fairness with counterfactual reasoning. *arXiv e-prints*, Available at: https://arxiv.org/abs/2302.08204 [Accessed 23 Dec. 2024]. DOI: 10.48550/arXiv.2302.08204.

Cotton, D. R., Cotton, P. A. and Shipway, J. R., 2024. Chatting and cheating: Ensuring academic integrity in the era of ChatGPT. *Innovations in Education and Teaching International*, 61(2), pp. 228–239.

Cranny-Francis, A., 2016. Robots, androids, aliens, and others: The erotics and politics of science fiction film. In: S. Redmond and L. Marvell, eds. *Endangering science fiction film* (pp. 220–242). New York and London: Routledge.

Crompton, H. and Burke, D., 2023. Artificial intelligence in higher education: The state of the field. *International Journal of Educational Technology in Higher Education*, 20(1), p. 22.

Cuthbert, B. N., Schupp, H. T., Bradley, M. M., Birbaumer, N. and Lang, P. J., 2000. Brain potentials in affective picture processing: Covariation with autonomic arousal and affective report. *Biological Psychology*, 52(2), pp. 95–111.

Dai, W., Lin, J., Jin, H., Li, T., Tsai, Y. S., Gašević, D. and Chen, G., 2023, July. Can large language models provide feedback to students? A case study on ChatGPT. In *2023 IEEE International Conference on Advanced Learning Technologies (ICALT)* (pp. 323–325). IEEE.

Davis, F. D., 1989. Technology acceptance model: TAM. *Al-Suqri, MN, Al-Aufi, AS: Information Seeking Behavior and Technology Adoption*, 205, p.219.

De Dreu, C. K. W. and van Knippenberg, D., 2005. Ego-defensive bias in conflict escalation: The automatic role of party-identity confirmation and the moderating role of expertise. *Journal of Personality and Social Psychology*, 89(4), pp. 589–601.

de Vicente-Yagüe-Jara, M. I., López-Martínez, O., Navarro-Navarro, V. and Cuéllar-Santiago, F., 2023. Writing, creativity, and Artificial Intelligence: ChatGPT in the university context. *Comunicar: Media Education Research Journal*, 31(77), pp. 45–54.

Dehouche, N. and Dehouche, K., 2023. What's in a text-to-image prompt? The potential of stable diffusion in visual arts education. *Heliyon*, 9(6).

Dempere, J., Modugu, K., Hesham, A. and Ramasamy, L. K., 2023, September. The impact of ChatGPT on higher education. In: *Frontiers in Education* (Vol. 8, p. 1206936). Frontiers Media SA.

Diéguez, A. and García-Barranquero, P., 2024. The Singularity, superintelligent machines, and mind uploading: The technological future? In *Ethics of Artificial Intelligence* (pp. 237–255). Cham: Springer Nature Switzerland.

Dwivedi, Y. K., Kshetri, N., Hughes, L., Slade, E. L., Jeyaraj, A., Kar, A. K., Baabdullah, A. M., Koohang, A., Raghavan, V., Ahuja, M. and Albanna, H., 2023. "So what if ChatGPT wrote it?" Multidisciplinary perspectives on opportunities, challenges and implications of generative conversational AI for research, practice and policy. *International Journal of Information Management*, 71, p. 102642.

Eagly, A. H. and Chaiken, S., 1993. *The Psychology of Attitudes*. Harcourt Brace Jovanovich College Publishers.

Edworthy, S. M., 1999. World Wide Web: Opportunities, challenges, and threats. *Lupus*, 8(8), pp. 596–605.

Fabrigar, L. R., MacDonald, T. K. and Wegener, D. T., 2005. The structure of attitudes. In: D. Albarracin, B. T. Johnson, and M. P. Zanna (Eds.), *The Handbook of Attitudes* (pp. 79–124). Lawrence Erlbaum Associates Publishers.

Fan, J., Fang, L., Wu, J., Guo, Y. and Dai, Q., 2020. From brain science to artificial intelligence. *Engineering*, 6(3), pp. 248–252.

Farazouli, A., Cerratto-Pargman, T., Bolander-Laksov, K. and McGrath, C., 2024. Hello GPT! Goodbye home examination? An exploratory study of AI chatbots impact on university teachers' assessment practices. *Assessment & Evaluation in Higher Education*, 49(3), pp. 363–375.

Fazio, R. H., 1995. Attitudes as object-evaluation associations: Determinants, consequences, and correlates of attitude accessibility. In: R. E. Petty and J. A. Krosnick (Eds.), *Attitude Strength: Antecedents and Consequences* (pp. 247–282). Lawrence Erlbaum Associates, Inc.

Fazio, R. H., Sanbonmatsu, D. M., Powell, M. C. and Kardes, F. R., 1986. On the automatic activation of attitudes. *Journal of Personality and Social Psychology*, 50(2), pp. 229–238. Available at: https://doi.org/10.1037/0022-3514.50.2.229

Festinger, L., 1957. *A Theory of Cognitive Dissonance*. Stanford University Press.

Flasiński, M., 2016. History of artificial intelligence. In: *Introduction to Artificial Intelligence* (pp. 3–13). Springer International Publishing .

Foot, P., 1967. *The Problem of Abortion and the Doctrine of Double Effect* (Vol. 5, pp. 5–15). Oxford.

Ford, M., 2018. *Architects of Intelligence: The Truth About AI from the People Building It*. Packt Publishing Ltd.

Ford, M., 2021. *Rule of the Robots: How Artificial Intelligence Will Transform Everything*. Hachette UK.

Forester, T., 1987. *High-tech Society: The Story of the Information Technology Revolution*. MIT Press.

Fosso Wamba, S., Queiroz, M. M. and Braganza, A., 2022. Preface: artificial intelligence in operations management. *Annals of Operations Research*, pp. 1–6.

Foung, D., Lin, L. and Chen, J., 2024. Reinventing assessments with ChatGPT and other online tools: Opportunities for GenAI-empowered assessment practices. *Computers and Education: Artificial Intelligence*, p. 100250.

Fuchs, C., 2014. *Social Media: A Critical Introduction*. Sage.

Galloway, M., 2021. *All Things to All Men: Ethos in Cicero's Post-Ides Correspondence* (Doctoral dissertation, Open Access Te Herenga Waka-Victoria University of Wellington).

Gao, C. A., Howard, F. M., Markov, N. S., Dyer, E. C., Ramesh, S., Luo, Y. and Pearson, A. T., 2022. Comparing scientific abstracts generated by ChatGPT to original abstracts using an artificial intelligence output detector, plagiarism detector, and blinded human reviewers. *BioRxiv*, pp. 2022–12.

García-Peñalvo, F. J., 2024. Generative Artificial Intelligence and education: An analysis from multiple perspectives. *Education in the Knowledge Society*, 25, p. e31942.

García-Peñalvo, F. J., Llorens Largo, F. and Vidal, J., 2023. The new reality of education in the face of advances in generative artificial intelligence.

Gardner, A., 2022. Responsibility, recourse, and redress: A focus on the three R's of AI ethics. *IEEE Technology and Society Magazine*, 41(2), pp. 84–89.

Gilson, A., Safranek, C., Huang, T., Socrates, V., Chi, L., Taylor, R. A. and Chartash, D., 2022. How does ChatGPT perform on the medical licensing exams? The implications of large language models for medical education and knowledge assessment. *MedRxiv*, pp. 2022–12.

Gimpel, H., Hall, K., Decker, S., Eymann, T., Lämmermann, L., Mädche, A., Röglinger, M., Ruiner, C., Schoch, M., Schoop, M. and Urbach, N., 2023. *Unlocking the power of generative AI models and systems such as GPT-4 and ChatGPT for higher education: A guide for students and lecturers* (No. 02-2023). Hohenheim Discussion Papers in Business, Economics and Social Sciences.

Glasman, L. R. and Albarracín, D., 2006. Forming attitudes that predict future behavior: A meta-analysis of the attitude-behavior relation. *Psychological Bulletin*, 132(5), pp. 778–822. doi: 10.1037/0033-2909.132.5.778

Gong, B. G., 2021. *Exploring Education Cyborg Space: Bibliographic and Metaphor Analysis of Educational Psychology and Artificial Intelligence Studies* (Doctoral dissertation, Arizona State University).

Goodfellow, I., Pouget-Abadie, J., Mirza, M., Xu, B., Warde-Farley, D., Ozair, S., Courville, A. and Bengio, Y., 2014. Generative adversarial nets. *Advances in Neural Information Processing Systems*, 27.

Grace, K., Salvatier, J., Dafoe, A., Zhang, B. and Evans, O., 2018. When will AI exceed human performance? Evidence from AI experts. *Journal of Artificial Intelligence Research*, 62, pp. 729–754.

Grübler, A., 2003. *Technology and Global Change*. Cambridge University Press.

Guan, C., Mou, J. and Jiang, Z., 2020. Artificial intelligence innovation in education: A twenty-year data-driven historical analysis. *International Journal of Innovation Studies*, 4(4), pp. 134–147.

Harari, Y. N., 2018. *Homo Deus: A Brief History of Tomorrow*. New York: HarperCollins Publishers.

Harari, Y. N., 2022. A review of Harari's "21 Lessons" On The coming technological challenges. *Social Science Asia*, 8(2), p.94.

Hart, W., Albarracín, D., Eagly, A. H., Brechan, I., Lindberg, M. J. and Merrill, L., 2009. Feeling validated versus being correct: A meta-analysis of selective exposure to information. *Psychological Bulletin*, 135(4), pp. 555–588.

Harvey, O. J., Hunt, D. E. and Schroder, H. M., 1961. *Conceptual Systems and Personality Organization*. Wiley.

Hatch, T., 2023. ChatGPT on ChatGPT in education: clear summaries and fake citations (The ChatGPT Six Month Anniversary Edition Part 1.

Heider, F., 1946. Attitudes and cognitive organization. *The Journal of Psychology*, 21(1), pp. 107–112.

Herring, S. C., 2000. Use of the world wide web in scholarly communication: A survey of psychologists. *International Journal of Human-Computer Studies*, 52(2), pp. 383–396.

Hick, A. and Ziefle, M., 2022. A qualitative approach to the public perception of AI. *International Journal on Cybernetics & Informatics (IJCI)*, 11(11), p. 1.

Hopfield, J. J., 1982. Neural networks and physical systems with emergent collective computational abilities. *Proceedings of the National Academy of Sciences*, 79(8), pp. 2554–2558.

Hopfield, J. J., 1984. Neurons with graded response have collective computational properties like those of two-state neurons. *Proceedings of the National Academy of Sciences*, 81(10), pp. 3088–3092.

Huang, S. and Fang, N., 2013. Predicting student academic performance in an engineering dynamics course: A comparison of four types of predictive mathematical models. *Computers & Education*, 61, pp. 133–145.

Imran, M. and Almusharraf, N., 2023. Analyzing the role of ChatGPT as a writing assistant at higher education level: A systematic review of the literature. *Contemporary Educational Technology*, 15(4), pp. 464.

Iskender, A., 2023. Holy or unholy? Interview with Open AI's ChatGPT. *European Journal of Tourism Research*, 34, pp. 3414–3414.

Islam, M. M., 2024. *Generative AI: Challenges and Opportunities in the Higher Education Sector in Cambodia*, in Lau, E., Paramita, W., Tee, K.-H. and Tan, L.M. (eds) *Economics and Finance Readings* (pp. 103–117). Singapore: Springer Nature Singapore.

Ivanov, S. and Soliman, M., 2023. Game of algorithms: ChatGPT implications for the future of tourism education and research. *Journal of Tourism Futures*, 9(2), pp. 214–221.

Jin, Y., Yan, L., Echeverria, V., Gašević, D. and Martinez-Maldonado, R., 2024. Generative AI in Higher Education: A Global Perspective of Institutional Adoption Policies and Guidelines.

Jisc, 2021. *Generative AI in Higher Education: Implications and Opportunities*. Jisc. Available at: https://www.jisc.ac.uk/reports/student-perceptions-of-generative-ai:contentReference [oaicite:0]{index=0}

Johnson, J. T. and Fujita, K., 2012. Is it good to be bad? Testing the hypothesis that people high in dark triad traits can facilitate collective goal attainment. *Personality and Individual Differences*, 52(1), pp. 113–118.

Johnson, B. T., Maio, G. R. and Smith-McLallen, A., 2005. Communication and attitude change: Causes, processes, and effects. In: D. Albarracin, B. T. Johnson, and M. P. Zanna (Eds.), *The Handbook of Attitudes* (pp. 617–669). Lawrence Erlbaum Associates Publishers.

Jovanovic, M. and Campbell, M., 2022. Generative artificial intelligence: Trends and prospects. *Computer*, 55(10), pp. 107–112.

Judd, C. M. and Brauer, M., 1995a. Correcting erroneous inferences in evaluations of social groups. In: R. E. Petty and J. A. Krosnick (Eds.), *Attitude Strength: Antecedents and Consequences* (pp. 127–154). Lawrence Erlbaum Associates, Inc.

Judd, C. M. and Brauer, M., 1995b. The polarising effect of group discussion. In: R. E. Petty and J. A. Krosnick (Eds.), *Attitude Strength: Antecedents and Consequences* (pp. 303–330). Psychology Press.

Katona, G., 1960. The Powerful Consumer.

Katona, G., 1975. *Psychological Economics*. Elsevier.

Katona, G., 1978. Behavioral economics. *Challenge*, 21(4), pp. 14–18.

Kepuska, V. and Bohouta, G., 2018, January. Next-generation of virtual personal assistants (Microsoft Cortana, Apple Siri, Amazon Alexa and Google Home). In: *2018 IEEE 8th Annual Computing and Communication Workshop and Conference (CCWC)* (pp. 99–103). IEEE.

Kim, J., Kim, J. H., Kim, C. and Park, J., 2023. Decisions with ChatGPT: Reexamining choice overload in ChatGPT recommendations. *Journal of Retailing and Consumer Services*, 75, p. 103494.

Kim, Y., Lee, J., Kim, S., Park, J. and Kim, J., 2024, March. Understanding users' dissatisfaction with chatgpt responses: Types, resolving tactics, and the effect of knowledge level. In *Proceedings of the 29th International Conference on Intelligent User Interfaces* (pp. 385–404).

Kitamura, F. C., 2023. ChatGPT is shaping the future of medical writing but still requires human judgment. *Radiology*, 307(2), p. e230171.

Kizilcec, R. F., Huber, E., Papanastasiou, E. C., Cram, A., Makridis, C. A., Smolansky, A., Zeivots, S. and Raduescu, C., 2024. Perceived impact of generative AI on assessments: Comparing educator and student perspectives in Australia, Cyprus, and the United States. *Computers and Education: Artificial Intelligence*, 7, p. 100269.

Klos, M., Escoredo, M., Joerin, A., Lemos, V., Rauws, M. and Bunge, E., 2021. Artificial intelligence-based chatbot for anxiety and depression in university students: Pilot randomized controlled trial. *JMIR Formative Research*, 5(8), p. e20678. Available at: https://formative.jmir.org/2021/8/e20678 [Accessed 23 Dec. 2024]. DOI: 10.2196/20678

Kohlberg, L., 1987. Developmental Moral Theory: The Psychology of Moral Development, *Ethics*, 97(2), pp. 441–456.

Kohnke, L., Moorhouse, B. L. and Zou, D., 2023. ChatGPT for language teaching and learning. *Relc Journal*, 54(2), pp. 537–550.

Kolasinska, A., Lauriola, I. and Quadrio, G., 2019. Do people believe in artificial intelligence? A cross-topic multicultural study. In: *Proceedings of the 5th International Conference on Smart Objects and Technologies for Social Good* (GoodTechs '19), 25–27 September, Valencia, Spain. New York: ACM, pp. 1–7.

Kosinski, M., Stillwell, D. and Graepel, T., 2013. Private traits and attributes are predictable from digital records of human behavior. *Proceedings of the National Academy of Sciences*, 110(15), pp. 5802–5805.

Krosnick, J. A., Boninger, D. S., Chuang, Y. C., Berent, M. K. and Carnot, C. G., 1993. Attitude strength: One construct or many related constructs? *Journal of Personality and Social Psychology*, 65(6), p. 1132.

Krosnick, J. A. and Smith, E. R., 1994. Attitude strength. In: R. E. Petty and J. A. Krosnick (Eds.), *Attitude Strength: Antecedents and Consequences* (pp. 4–25). Psychology Press.

Krueger, L., Clemenson, S., Johnson, E. and Schwarz, L., 2024. ChatGPT in higher education: Practical ideas for addressing artificial intelligence in nursing education. *Journal of Nursing Education*, pp. 1–4.

Kruglanski, A. W., 1980. *Lay Epistemics and Human Knowledge: Cognitive and Motivational Bases.* Springer.

Kublik, S. and Saboo, S., 2022. *GPT-3.* O'Reilly Media, Incorporated.

Kumar, D., Haque, A., Mishra, K., Islam, F., Mishra, B. K. and Ahmad, S., 2023. Exploring the transformative role of artificial intelligence and metaverse in education: A comprehensive review. *Metaverse Basic and Applied Research*, 2, pp. 55–55.

Kunda, Z., 1990. The case for motivated reasoning. *Psychological Bulletin*, 108(3), p. 480.

Kutty, S., Chugh, R., Perera, P., Neupane, A., Jha, M., Li, L., Gunathilake, W. and Perera, N. C., 2024. Generative AI in higher education: Perspectives of students, educators and administrators. *Journal of Applied Learning and Teaching*, 7(2).

Laird, J. E., 2019. *The Soar Cognitive Architecture.* MIT Press.

Laird, N., Lange, N. and Stram, D., 1987. Maximum likelihood computations with repeated measures: Application of the EM algorithm. *Journal of the American Statistical Association*, 82(397), pp. 97–105.

Landauer, T. K., 2003. Automatic essay assessment. *Assessment in Education: Principles, Policy & Practice*, 10(3), pp. 295–308.

Lang, P. J., Öhman, A. and Vaitl, D., 1988. *The International Affective Picture System [Photographic Slides].* Center for Research in Psychophysiology, University of Florida.

Lapierre, R. T., 1934. Attitudes vs. actions. *Social Forces*, 13(2), pp. 230–237. doi: 10.2307/2570339

Larson, A., Mattu, D. and Kirchner, L., 2016. Machine bias: There's software used across the country to predict future criminals. And it's biased against blacks. *ProPublica.*

Leavy, S., O'Sullivan, B. and Siapera, E., 2020. *Data, Power and Bias in Artificial Intelligence*, arXiv.org, 28 July. Available at: https://www.semanticscholar.org/reader/9c531b04d9833b0e47859478b818dd33f725fb66 (Accessed: 28 July 2020).

LeCun, Y., 2018. The power and limits of deep learning: In his IRI Medal address, Yann LeCun maps the development of machine learning techniques and suggests what the future may hold. *Research-Technology Management*, 61(6), pp. 22–27.

Lerner, M. J., Miller, D. T. and Holmes, J. G., 1976. Deserving and the emergence of forms of justice. In: L. Berkowitz and E. Walster (Eds.), *Advances in Experimental Social Psychology* (Vol. 9, pp. 133–162). Academic Press.

Li, H., Wang, Y., Luo, S. and Huang, C., 2024. The influence of GenAI on the effectiveness of argumentative writing in higher education: Evidence from a quasi-experimental study in China. *Journal of Asian Public Policy*, pp. 1–26.

Li, J. and Huang, J.-S., 2020. Dimensions of artificial intelligence anxiety based on the integrated fear acquisition theory. *Technology in Society*, 63(C).

Liebman, M., 2022. The role of artificial intelligence in drug discovery and development. *Chemistry International*, 44(1), pp. 16–19.

Lieto, A., 2021. *Cognitive Design for Artificial Minds*. Routledge.

Litjens, G., Kooi, T., Bejnordi, B. E., Setio, A. A. A., Ciompi, F., Ghafoorian, M., Van Der Laak, J. A., Van Ginneken, B. and Sánchez, C. I., 2017. A survey on deep learning in medical image analysis. *Medical Image Analysis*, 42, pp. 60–88.

Liu, M., Ren, Y., Nyagoga, L. M., Stonier, F., Wu, Z. and Yu, L., 2023. Future of education in the era of generative artificial intelligence: Consensus among Chinese scholars on applications of ChatGPT in schools. *Future in Educational Research*, 1(1), pp. 72–101.

Liu, K. and Tao, D., 2022. The roles of trust, personalization, loss of privacy, and anthropomorphism in public acceptance of smart healthcare services. *Computers in Human Behavior*, 127, p. 107026.

Lodge, J. M., Thompson, K. and Corrin, L., 2023. Mapping out a research agenda for generative artificial intelligence in tertiary education. *Australasian Journal of Educational Technology*, 39(1), pp. 1–8.

Long, A. A., 2006. *From Epicurus to Epictetus: Studies in Hellenistic and Roman Philosophy*. Clarendon Press.

Lubowitz, J. H., 2023. ChatGPT, an artificial intelligence chatbot, is impacting medical literature. *Arthroscopy*, 39(5), pp. 1121–1122.

Luger, G. F., 2021. Modern AI and how we got here. In: *Knowing our World: An Artificial Intelligence Perspective* (pp. 49–74). Springer International Publishing.

Malik, T., Hughes, L., Dwivedi, Y. K. and Dettmer, S., 2023. November. Exploring the transformative impact of generative AI on higher education. In *Conference on E-Business, E-Services and E-Society* (pp. 69–77). Cham: Springer Nature Switzerland.

Malinetsky, G. and Smolin, V., 2021. The artificial intelligence influence on real sociality. *Procedia Computer Science*, 186, pp. 344–351.

Marcus, G., 2018. Deep learning: A critical appraisal. *arXiv preprint arXiv:1801.00631*.

Marcus, G. and Davis, E., 2019. *Rebooting AI: Building Artificial Intelligence We Can Trust*. Vintage.

Marr, B., 2019. *Artificial Intelligence in Practice: How 50 Successful Companies Used AI and Machine Learning to Solve Problems*. John Wiley & Sons.

McArthur, D., 2009. Good ethics can sometimes mean better science: Research ethics and the Milgram experiments. *Science and Engineering Ethics*, 15(1), pp. 69–79.

McCarthy, J., Minsky, M. L., Rochester, N. and Shannon, C. E., 2006. A proposal for the Dartmouth summer research project on artificial intelligence, August 31, 1955. *AI Magazine*, 27(4), pp. 12–12.

McCrae, R. R. and Costa, P. T., 1987. Validation of the five-factor model of personality across instruments and observers. *Journal of Personality and Social Psychology*, 52(1), p. 81.

McCulloch, W. S. and Pitts, W., 1990. A logical calculus of the ideas immanent in nervous activity. *Bulletin of Mathematical Biology*, 52, pp. 99–115.

McGuire, W. J., 1960. A syllogistic analysis of cognitive relationships. In: E. E. Maccoby, T. M. Newcomb, and E. L. Hartley (Eds.), *Readings in Social Psychology* (3rd ed., pp. 83–94). Holt, Rinehart, & Winston.

Mezzoudj, F. and Benyettou, A., 2018. An empirical study of statistical language models: n-gram language models vs. neural network language models. *International Journal of Innovative Computing and Applications*, 9(4), pp. 189–202.

Michel-Villarreal, R., Vilalta-Perdomo, E., Salinas-Navarro, D. E., Thierry-Aguilera, R. and Gerardou, F. S., 2023. Challenges and opportunities of generative AI for higher education as explained by ChatGPT. *Education Sciences*, 13(9), p. 856.

Miller, C., 2014. *The Bloomsbury Companion to Ethics*. London: Bloomsbury Publishing.

Miller, N. and Peterson, C. R., 2004a. Extremity of attitudes as a function of the amount of information in the initial attitude position. In: A. Tesser, J. G. Campbell, and R. M. Fazio (Eds.), *The Role of Attitude Objects in Attitude Functions* (pp. 61–95). Psychology Press.

Miller, N. and Peterson, C. R., 2004b. Personality and the prediction of consequential outcomes. *Annual Review of Psychology*, 55(1), pp. 2–27.

Mitchell, I., 1998. Computing power into the 21st century: Moore's law and beyond. *Citeseer*. Available at: http://citeseer.ist.psu.edu/mitchell98computing.html (Accessed: 5 November 2024).

Mitchell, M., 2019. *Artificial Intelligence: A Guide for Thinking Humans*. Penguin UK.

Mizumoto, A. and Eguchi, M., 2023. Exploring the potential of using an AI language model for automated essay scoring. *Research Methods in Applied Linguistics*, 2(2), p. 100050.

Moore, B., 2014. *The Brain* (pp. 81–97). Springer International Publishing.

Moshayedi, A. J., Roy, A. S., Kolahdooz, A. and Shuxin, Y., 2022. Deep learning application pros and cons over algorithm deep learning application pros and cons over algorithm. *EAI Endorsed Transactions on AI and Robotics*, 1(1).

Muggleton, S., 2014. Alan Turing and the development of Artificial Intelligence. *AI Communications*, 27(1), pp. 3–10.

Munoko, I., Brown-Liburd, H. L. and Vasarhelyi, M., 2020. The ethical implications of using artificial intelligence in auditing. *Journal of Business Ethics*, 167(2), pp. 209–234.

Muthukrishnan, N., Maleki, F., Ovens, K., Reinhold, C., Forghani, B. and Forghani, R., 2020. Brief history of artificial intelligence. *Neuroimaging Clinics of North America*, 30(4), pp. 393–399.

Nakamura, Y. and Shibuya, M., 1996. Japan's technology policy: A case study of the R&D of the Fifth Generation computer systems. *International Journal of Technology Management*, 12(5–6), pp. 509–533.

Nartey, E. K., 2023. Neurological aspect of ethics and integrity: A fundamental compound element of law and tax compliance. *Athens Journal of Law*, 9, p. 245.

Nartey, E. K., 2024. Guiding principles of generative AI for employability and learning in UK universities. *Cogent Education*, 11(1), p. 2357898.

Natale, S., 2019. If software is narrative: Joseph Weizenbaum, artificial intelligence, and the biographies of ELIZA. *New Media & Society*, 21(3), pp. 712–728.

Nepal, S., Paris, C. and Bouguettaya, A., 2015. Trusting the social web: Issues and challenges. *World Wide Web*, 18(1), pp. 1–7.

Newell, A., 1982. Intellectual issues in the history of artificial intelligence. In: *Artificial Intelligence: Critical Concepts* (pp. 25–70). London: Routledge.

Newell, A., 1994. *Unified Theories of Cognition*. Harvard University Press.

Newell, A., Shaw, J. C. and Simon, H. A., 1959. Report on a general problem-solving program. In: *IFIP Congress*, vol. 256. Pittsburgh: Carnegie Institution of Technology, p. 64.

Nguyen, L., Abdalla, H. I. and Amer, A. A., 2024. 'Adversarial variational autoencoders to extend and improve generative model', *AI, Computer Science and Robotics Technology*, vol. 3. London: IntechOpen. doi:10.5772/acrt.20240003

Nguyen, H. and Nguyen, A., 2024. Reflective Practices and Self-Regulated Learning in Designing with Generative Artificial Intelligence: An Ordered Network Analysis. *Journal of Science Education and Technology*, pp. 1–15.

Norvig, P. and Russell, S. J., 2010. Intelligenza artificiale. *Un approccio moderno*.

Ntoutsi, E., Fafalios, P., Gadiraju, U., Iosifidis, V., Nejdl, W., Vidal, M. E., Ruggieri, S., Turini, F., Papadopoulos, S., Krasanakis, E. and Kompatsiaris, I., 2020. Bias in data-driven artificial intelligence systems—An introductory survey. *Wiley Interdisciplinary Reviews: Data Mining and Knowledge Discovery*, 10(3), p.e1356.

Nwana, H. S., 1990. Intelligent tutoring systems: an overview. *Artificial Intelligence Review*, 4(4), pp. 251–277.

Oksanen, A., Savela, N., Latikka, R. and Koivula, A., 2020. Trust toward robots and artificial intelligence: An experimental approach to human–technology interactions online. *Frontiers in Psychology*, 11, p. 568256.

Olari, V. and Romeike, R., 2021, October. Addressing ai and data literacy in teacher education: A review of existing educational frameworks. In *Proceedings of the 16th workshop in primary and secondary computing education* (pp. 1–2).

Oodfellow, I., Pouget-Abadie, J., Mirza, M., Xu, B., Warde-Farley, D., Ozair, S., Courville, A. and Bengio, Y., 2014. Generative adversarial nets. In: *Advances in Neural Information Processing Systems* (vol. 27). Montreal: Université de Montréal.

Ouyang, F., Zheng, L. and Jiao, P., 2022. Artificial intelligence in online higher education: A systematic review of empirical research from 2011 to 2020. *Education and Information Technologies*, 27(6), pp. 7893–7925.

Owen, R. and Pansera, M., 2019. *Responsible Innovation and Responsible Research and Innovation* (pp. 26–48). Edward Elgar Publishing.

Pavlacka, B., 2012. Artificial general intelligence and the future of the human race. *Berkeley Scientific Journal*, 16(2), pp. 22–25.

Peres, R., Schreier, M., Schweidel, D. and Sorescu, A., 2023. On ChatGPT and beyond: How generative artificial intelligence may affect research, teaching, and practice. *International Journal of Research in Marketing*, 40(2), pp. 269–275.

Perkins, M., Roe, J., Postma, D., McGaughran, J. and Hickerson, D., 2024. Detection of GPT-4 generated text in higher education: Combining academic judgement and software to identify generative AI tool misuse. *Journal of Academic Ethics*, 22(1), pp. 89–113.

Peterson, S. E. and Miller, J. A., 2004. Comparing the quality of students' experiences during cooperative learning and large-group instruction. *The Journal of Educational Research*, 97(3), pp. 123–134.

Petricini, T., Wu, C. and Zipf, S. T., 2023. Perceptions about generative AI and ChatGPT use by faculty and college students.

Petty, R. E., Tormala, Z. L. and Rucker, D. D., 2004. Resistance to persuasion: Resistance to persuasion and attitude persistence. In: J. P. Dillard and M. Pfau (Eds.), *The Persuasion Handbook: Developments in Theory and Practice* (pp. 213–232). SAGE Publications, Inc.

Philipsen, R., Brauner, P. M., Biermann, H. and Ziefle, M. C., 2022. *I Am What I Am-Roles for Artificial Intelligence from the Users' Perspective*. Universitätsbibliothek der RWTH Aachen.

Pinar Saygin, A., Cicekli, I. and Akman, V., 2000. Turing test: 50 years later. *Minds and Machines*, 10(4), pp. 463–518.

Placek, T., 1999. *Mathematical Intuitionism and Intersubjectivity: A Critical Exposition of Arguments for Intuitionism* (Vol. 279). Springer Science & Business Media.

Plata, S., De Guzman, M. A. and Quesada, A., 2023. Emerging research and policy themes on academic integrity in the age of chat GPT and generative AI. *Asian Journal of University Education*, 19(4), pp. 743–758.

Prescott, T., 2024. *The Psychology of Artificial Intelligence*. Taylor & Francis.

Pressey, S. L., 1926. A simple apparatus which gives tests and scores-and teaches. *School and Society*, 23, pp. 373–376.

Racine, E., Boehlen, W. and Sample, M., 2019, September. Healthcare uses of artificial intelligence: Challenges and opportunities for growth. In *Healthcare Management Forum* (Vol. 32, No. 5, pp. 272–275). SAGE Publications.

Rajaraman, V., 2014. John McCarthy—Father of artificial intelligence. *Resonance*, 19, pp. 198–207.

Rao, Q. and Frtunikj, J., 2018, May. Deep learning for self-driving cars: Chances and challenges. In *Proceedings of the 1st international workshop on software engineering for AI in autonomous systems* (pp. 35–38).

Rasul, T., Nair, S., Kalendra, D., Robin, M., de Oliveira Santini, F., Ladeira, W. J., Sun, M., Day, I., Rather, R. A. and Heathcote, L., 2023. The role of ChatGPT in higher education: Benefits, challenges, and future research directions. *Journal of Applied Learning and Teaching*, 6(1), pp. 41–56.

Rawlley, O., 2024. Leveraging Data Analytics for Promoting Environmentally Sustainable and Socially Artificial Intelligence-enabled City Infrastructure. *Authorea Preprints*.

Reid, M., 2016. Rethinking the Fourth Amendment in the age of supercomputers, artificial intelligence, and robots. *West Virginia Law Review*, 119, p. 863.

Reilly, K., 2011. From automata to automation: The birth of the robot in RUR (Rossum's Universal Robots). In *Automata and Mimesis on the Stage of Theatre History* (pp. 148–176). Palgrave Macmillan UK.

Reuters. 2023. Top French University bans use of ChatGPT to prevent plagiarism.v. https://www.reuters.com/technology/top-french-university-bans-use-chatgpt-prevent-plagiarism-2023-01-27/ (open in a new window).

Rist, J. M., 2002. *Real Ethics: Reconsidering the Foundations of Morality*. Cambridge University Press.

Ritzer, G. (Ed.), 2007. *The Blackwell Encyclopedia of Sociology* (Vol. 1479). Blackwell.

Rizer, A. and Watney, C., 2018. Artificial intelligence can make our jail system more efficient, equitable, and just. *Texas Review of Law & Politics*, 23, p. 181.

Rodriguez-Bustelo, C., Batista-Foguet, J. M. and Serlavós, R., 2020. Debating the future of work: The perception and reaction of the Spanish workforce to digitisation and automation technologies. *Frontiers in Psychology*, 11, p. 555877.

Roland, A. and Shiman, P., 2002. *Strategic Computing: DARPA and the Quest for Machine Intelligence, 1983–1993*. MIT Press.

Roney, C. J. and Sorrentino, R. M., 1995. Political cognition and social cognition. *Political Psychology*, 16(3), pp. 485–504.

Rosenblatt, F., 1957. *The Perceptron, A Perceiving and Recognizing Automaton Project PARA*. Cornell Aeronautical Laboratory.

Ross, D., 1956. Aristotle: The Nicomachean Ethics. *Philosophy*, 31(116), p. 77.

Ross, P., 1987. Intelligent tutoring systems. *Journal of Computer Assisted Learning*, 3(4), pp. 194–203.

Rothman, D., 2022. *Transformers for Natural Language Processing: Build, Train, and Fine-tune Deep Neural Network Architectures for NLP with Python, Hugging Face, and OpenAI's GPT-3, ChatGPT, and GPT-4*. Packt Publishing Ltd.

Rudebusch, G. and Turner, C., 2014. A philosophical solution to the problem of socrates. *Journal of Ancient Philosophy*, 8(2), pp. 1–39.

Rudolph, J., Tan, S. and Tan, S., 2023. ChatGPT: Bullshit spewer or the end of traditional assessments in higher education?. *Journal of Applied Learning and Teaching*, 6(1), pp. 342–363.

Rumelhart, D. E., Hinton, G. E. and Williams, R. J., 1986. Learning representations by back-propagating errors. *Nature*, 323(6088), pp. 533–536.

Russell, J. A., 2003. Core affect and the psychological construction of emotion. *Psychological Review*, 110(1), pp. 145–172.

Russell, S. J. and Norvig, P., 2016. *Artificial Intelligence: A Modern Approach*. Pearson.

Sajja, R., Sermet, Y., Cikmaz, M., Cwiertny, D. and Demir, I., 2024. Artificial intelligence-enabled intelligent assistant for personalized and adaptive learning in higher education. *Information*, 15(10), p. 596.

Samuel, A. L., 1959. Some studies in machine learning using the game of checkers. *IBM Journal of Research and Development*, 3(3), pp. 210–229.

Satterfield, D. and Abel, T. D., 2020. AI Is the New UX: Emerging Research Innovations in AI, User Experience, and Design as They Apply to Industry, Business, and Education, and Ethics. In: *Advances in the Human Side of Service Engineering: Proceedings of the AHFE 2020 Virtual Conference on The Human Side of Service Engineering, July 16-20, 2020*, USA (pp. 182–188). Springer International Publishing.

Schiff, D., 2022. Education for AI, not AI for education: The role of education and ethics in national AI policy strategies. *International Journal of Artificial Intelligence in Education*, 32(3), pp. 527–563.

Schimmack, U. and Crites, S. L., Jr., 2005. The structure of affect. In: L. F. Barrett, P. M. Niedenthal, and P. Winkielman (Eds.), *Emotion and Consciousness* (pp. 55–83). Guilford Press.

Seager, N., 2022. Jonathan Swift, Gulliver's Travels (1726). *In Handbook of the British Novel in the Long Eighteenth Century*, 16, p. 175.

Self, J. A., 1990a. Toward a cognitive theory of computer-assisted instruction. *Journal of Educational Computing Research*, 6(4), pp. 469–486.

Self, J. A., 1990b. Adaptive testing and the learning skills instruction program. *Educational Assessment*, 4(3), pp. 255–279.

Self, J., 1998. The defining characteristics of intelligent tutoring systems research: ITSs care, precisely. *International Journal of Artificial Intelligence in Education*, 10, pp. 350–364.

Shanklin, R., Samorani, M., Harris, S. and Santoro, M. A., 2022. Ethical redress of racial inequities in AI: Lessons from decoupling machine learning from optimization in medical appointment scheduling. *Philosophy & Technology*, 35(4), p. 96.

Shannon, C. E., 1993. Programming a computer for playing chess. In *Claude Elwood Shannon Collected Papers* (pp. 637–656). IEEE Press.

Shao, F. and Shen, Z., 2023. How can artificial neural networks approximate the brain?. *Frontiers in Psychology*, 13, p. 970214.

Sheikh, S. ed., 2020. *Understanding the Role of Artificial Intelligence and Its Future Social Impact*. IGI Global.

Shirky, C., 2008. *Interview with Clay Shirky*. Interviewed by Jon Lebkowsky on 19 July 2017. Available at: https://polycotassociates.com/blog/2008-interview-clay-shirky insert link here [Accessed 31 October 2024].

Silag, W., 1984. The invention of the electronic digital computer at Iowa State College, 1930–1942. *The Palimpsest*, 65(5), pp. 1–28.

Silverman, J. A., Ali, S. A., Rybak, A., van Goudoever, J. B. and Leleiko, N. S., 2023. Generative AI: Potential and pitfalls in academic publishing. *Journal of Pediatric Gastroenterology and Nutrition*, 77(5), pp. 573–574.

Simon, H. A., 1995. Artificial intelligence: an empirical science. *Artificial Intelligence*, 77(1), pp. 95–127.

Simon, H. A. and Newell, A., 1971. Human problem solving: The state of the theory in 1970. *American Psychologist*, 26(2), p. 145.

Sindermann, C., Sha, P., Zhou, M., Wernicke, J., Schmitt, H. S., Li, M., Sariyska, R., Stavrou, M., Becker, B. and Montag, C., 2021. Assessing the attitude towards artificial intelligence: Introduction of a short measure in German, Chinese, and English language. *KI-Künstliche Intelligenz*, 35(1), pp. 109–118.

Sleeman, D. and Brown, J. S., 1982. *Intelligent Tutoring Systems*. Academic Press.

Slimi, Z. and Carballido, B. V., 2023. Navigating the ethical challenges of artificial intelligence in higher education: An analysis of seven global AI ethics policies. *TEM Journal*, 12(2), pp. 590–602.

Smith, A. and Anderson, J., 2014. AI, robotics, and the future of jobs. *Pew Research Center*, 6.

Smith, C. A. and Ellsworth, P. C., 1985. Patterns of cognitive appraisal in emotion. *Journal of Personality and Social Psychology*, 48(4), pp. 813–838.

Smith, A., Hachen, S., Schleifer, R., Bhugra, D., Buadze, A. and Liebrenz, M., 2023. Old dog, new tricks? Exploring the potential functionalities of ChatGPT in supporting educational methods in social psychiatry. *International Journal of Social Psychiatry*, 69(8), pp. 1882–1889.

Smith, R. A., Smith, E. and Price, M. D., 2024. Utilizing emergent AI Chatbot technology to generate mathematical writing models for elementary students with learning disabilities. *Intervention in School and Clinic*, 59(5), pp. 339–346.

Smith, S., Smith, C., Taylor-Smith, E. and Fotheringham, J., 2019. Towards graduate employment: exploring student identity through a university-wide employability project. *Journal of Further and Higher Education*, 43(5), pp. 628–640.

Sottilare, R. A., Graesser, A. C., Hu, X. and Holden, H. K., 2018. *Design Recommendations for Intelligent Tutoring Systems: Volume 7-Training, Simulation, and Virtual Environments*. US Government Printing Office.

Stahl, B. C. and Wright, D., 2018. Ethics and privacy in AI and big data: Implementing responsible research and innovation. *IEEE Security & Privacy*, 16(3), pp. 26–33.

Striker, G., 1987. Greek ethics and moral theory. *The Tanner Lectures on Human Values*, 9, pp. 183–202.

Sullivan, M., Kelly, A. and McLaughlan, P., 2023. *ChatGPT in Higher Education: Considerations for Academic Integrity and Student Learning*. Singapore: Kaplan Higher Education Academy.

Sumari, A. D. W. and Ahmad, A. S., 2018. Cognitive artificial intelligence: concept and applications for humankind. *Intelligent System*, 23, p. 55.

Taherdoost, H., 2018. A review of technology acceptance and adoption models and theories. *Procedia Manufacturing*, 22, pp. 960–967.

Taylor, S. E., Fiske, S. T., 1978. Salience, attention, and attribution: Top of the head phenomena. In: L. Berkowitz (Ed.), *Advances in Experimental Social Psychology* (Vol. 11, pp. 249–288). Academic Press.

Tesser, A., Martin, L. L. and Mendolia, M., 1995. The impact of thought on attitude extremity and attitude-behavior consistency. In: R. E. Petty and J. A. Krosnick (Eds.), *Attitude Strength: Antecedents and Consequences* (pp. 91–126). Psychology Press.

The Guardian, 2023. *UK universities draw up guiding principles on generative AI.* This article is more than 1 year old. All 24 Russell Group universities have reviewed their academic conduct policies and guidance. Available at: https://www.theguardian.com/education/2023/may/15/uk-universities-draw-up-guiding-principles-on-generative-ai (Accessed: 4 November 2024)

The Tab, 2023. *These are the Russell group Unis that have banned students from using ChatGPT.* Available at: https://thetab.com/uk/2023/11/01/these-are-the-russell-group-unis-that-have-banned-students-from-using-chatgpt-358255 [Accessed 3 Nov. 2024].

Tindle, R., Pozzebon, K., Willis, R. and Moustafa, A. A., 2023. Academic misconduct and generative artificial intelligence: University students' intentions, usage, and perceptions. *PsyArXiv Preprints*, 13.

Topol, E., 2019. *Deep Medicine: How Artificial Intelligence Can Make Healthcare Human Again.* Hachette UK.

Turing, A. M., 1950. Computing machinery and intelligence. *Mind*, 49, pp. 433–460.

Turing, A. M., 2009. Computing machinery and intelligence. In *The Essential Turing: Seminal Writings in Computing, Logic, Philosophy, Artificial Intelligence, and Artificial Life, Plus The Secrets of Enigma* (pp. 23–65). Springer Netherlands.

Turnitin, 2020. *Challenges and Relationships of e-Learning Tools to Teaching and Learning.* Available at: https://www.turnitin.com

Tyson, P., 2015. *Returning to reality: Christian Platonism for our times*, (1) 1, pp. 1–228.

University of Cambridge, 2023a. *Guidelines for Generative AI Use in Communications.* Communications at Cambridge. Available at: https://www.communications.cam.ac.uk/generative-ai-tool-guidelines [Accessed 23 December 2024].

University of Cambridge, 2023b. *Generative AI in Coursework.* Cambridge International. Available at: https://www.cambridgeinternational.org/exam-administration/cambridge-exams-officers-guide/phase-3-coursework-and-moderation/generative-ai-in-coursework/ [Accessed 23 December 2024].

Urwin, R., 2016. *Artificial Intelligence: The Quest for the Ultimate Thinking Machine.* Arcturus Publishing.

Valdez, A. V., Amba, O., Jumalon Jr, R. A., Dimalna, H. D., Gomampong, A. M. and Manaol, N. B., 2023. Farmers perceptions on Artificial Insemination (AI): A mixed method design. *European Journal of Theoretical and Applied Sciences*, 1(3), pp. 299–323.

van Assen, M., Muscogiuri, E., Tessarin, G. and De Cecco, C. N., 2022. Artificial intelligence: A century-old story. In: *Artificial Intelligence in Cardiothoracic Imaging* (pp. 3–13). Cham: Springer International Publishing.

van den Berg, G. and du Plessis, E., 2023. ChatGPT and generative AI: Possibilities for its contribution to lesson planning, critical thinking and openness in teacher education. *Education Sciences*, 13(10), p. 998.

Visser, P. S., Krosnick, J. A. and Simmons, J. P., 2003. Attitude strength. In: J. P. Dillard and M. Pfau (Eds.), *The Persuasion Handbook: Developments in Theory and Practice* (pp. 229–250). SAGE Publications, Inc.

Vlaanderen, M. J., 1990. *Automated Knowledge Acquisition for Expert Systems: An Overview.* Rotterdam: Erasmus MC, University Medical Center.

Wang, J., 2021. Is artificial intelligence capable of understanding? An analysis based on philosophical hermeneutics. *Cultures of Science*, 4(3), pp. 135–146.

Wang, T., Lund, B. D., Marengo, A., Pagano, A., Mannuru, N. R., Teel, Z. A. and Pange, J., 2023. Exploring the potential impact of artificial intelligence (AI) on international students in higher education: Generative AI, chatbots, analytics, and international student success. *Applied Sciences*, 13(11), p. 6716.

Warschauer, M., Tseng, W., Yim, S., Webster, T., Jacob, S., Du, Q. and Tate, T., 2023. The affordances and contradictions of AI-generated text for writers of English as a second or foreign language. *Journal of Second Language Writing*, 62.

Watermeyer, R., Phipps, L., Lanclos, D. and Knight, C., 2024. Generative AI and the Automating of Academia. *Postdigital Science and Education*, 6(2), pp. 446–466.

Weizenbaum, J., 1966. ELIZA—a computer program for the study of natural language communication between man and machine. *Communications of the ACM*, 9(1), pp. 36–45.

White, N. P., 1979. The basis of Stoic ethics. *Harvard Studies in Classical Philology*, 83, pp. 143–178.

Wiener, N., 2019. *Cybernetics: Or Control and Communication in the Animal and the Machine.* MIT Press.

Williamson, B. and Eynon, R., 2020. Historical threads, missing links, and future directions in AI in education. *Learning, Media and Technology*, 45(3), pp. 223–235.

Wilson, J. B., 2019. *The Ghost in the Machine: Structural Metaphors in the 'Golden Age' of Artificial Intelligence Research, 1956–1976* (Doctoral dissertation, University of Toronto).

Wood, A. W., 2008. *Kantian Ethics.* Cambridge: Cambridge University Press.

Woodley, B., 2002. *The Impact of Transformative Technologies on Governance: Some Lessons from History.* Institute on Governance.

Yan, L., Sha, L., Zhao, L., Li, Y., Martinez-Maldonado, R., Chen, G., Li, X., Jin, Y. and Gašević, D., 2024. Practical and ethical challenges of large language models in education: A systematic scoping review. *British Journal of Educational Technology*, 55(1), pp. 90–112.

Yeralan, S. and Lee, L. A., 2023. Generative AI: Challenges to higher education. *Sustainable Engineering and Innovation*, 5(2), pp. 107–116.

Yoder-Himes, D. R., Asif, A., Kinney, K., Brandt, T. J., Cecil, R. E., Himes, P. R., Cashon, C., Hopp, R. M. and Ross, E., 2022, September. Racial, skin tone, and sex disparities in automated proctoring software. In: *Frontiers in Education* (Vol. 7, p. 881449). Frontiers.

Zhai, X., 2022. ChatGPT user experience: Implications for education. *Available at SSRN 4312418.*

Index

Kolibri 360 GmbH
Ferdinand-Jühlke-Straße 7
99095 Erfurt, Deutschland
produktsicherheit@kolibri360.de